The Creativity Advantage

Creativity is usually seen as a good thing, but why? *The Creativity Advantage* offers for the first time an overview of creativity studies with an emphasis on the little-discussed benefits of being creative. These include how creativity can lead to self-insight, help people heal, forge connections with others, inspire drive, and enable people to leave behind a meaningful legacy. Written in an engaging style and illustrated with interesting anecdotal material, this book offers a new perspective on creativity scholarship that can serve as an introduction to the field for newcomers or as a way to encourage new avenues for research.

Dr. James C. Kaufman is Professor of Educational Psychology at the Neag School of Education at the University of Connecticut, USA. He is the author/editor of more than fifty books, including *The Cambridge Handbook of Creativity* (2019). He is a past president of Division 10 (Society for the Psychology of Aesthetics, Creativity, & the Arts) of the American Psychological Association.

The Creativity Advantage

JAMES C. KAUFMAN
University of Connecticut

Shaftesbury Road, Cambridge CB2 8EA, United Kingdom

One Liberty Plaza, 20th Floor, New York, NY 10006, USA

477 Williamstown Road, Port Melbourne, VIC 3207, Australia

314–321, 3rd Floor, Plot 3, Splendor Forum, Jasola District Centre, New Delhi – 110025, India

103 Penang Road, #05–06/07, Visioncrest Commercial, Singapore 238467

Cambridge University Press is part of Cambridge University Press & Assessment, a department of the University of Cambridge.

We share the University's mission to contribute to society through the pursuit of education, learning and research at the highest international levels of excellence.

www.cambridge.org
Information on this title: www.cambridge.org/9781009244565

DOI: 10.1017/9781009244541

First published 2023

A catalogue record for this publication is available from the British Library.

Library of Congress Cataloging-in-Publication Data
Names: Kaufman, James C., author.
Title: The creativity advantage / James C. Kaufman, University of Connecticut.
Description: New York, NY : Cambridge University Press, [2023] | Includes bibliographical references and index.
Identifiers: LCCN 2022057065 (print) | LCCN 2022057066 (ebook) | ISBN 9781009244565 (hardback) | ISBN 9781009244558 (paperback) | ISBN 9781009244541 (epub)
Subjects: LCSH: Creative ability.
Classification: LCC BF408 .K3644 2023 (print) | LCC BF408 (ebook) | DDC 153.3/5–dc23/eng/20230322
LC record available at https://lccn.loc.gov/2022057065
LC ebook record available at https://lccn.loc.gov/2022057066

ISBN 978-1-009-24456-5 Hardback
ISBN 978-1-009-24455-8 Paperback

For my boys
Jacob Levi Kaufman
Asher Jonathan Kaufman
With all my love, forever

CONTENTS

PREFACE

I've written and edited a lot of books. There are many different reasons why I tackle a book, from inherent interest to wanting to work with desired collaborators, to curiosity, or to simply wanting such a book to exist. The reason why I'm writing this one runs a bit deeper.

There are times when it feels that these are the worst of times. In the sitcom *Community*, the character Abed grows to believe in a multiverse. He can connect with his alternate self living in the darkest timeline, where every character is living their worst life. I don't know about you, but sometimes it feels like we are living the darkest timeline right now. I'm writing this paragraph during yet another resurgence of the COVID-19 pandemic, after I thought we were rounding the corner (and the fact that this information doesn't particularly pin down the exact date is itself noteworthy). The world seems as divided as it ever has been. Climate change, systemic racism, threats of world war, poverty, rampant loss of civil rights, and so, so many other terrible issues dominate the news. My main comfort at times is reassuring myself that, although it may seem like all is doomed, we've *always* been doomed. The world has been a horrible place throughout the last century, throughout the millennium, and all the way back to the first group of protozoa that decided to hate the second group of protozoa.

Such thoughts may assuage panic but do not bring joy. I am often cynical and sarcastic, but I need to feel large-scale optimism. I want to hold on to hope and, to do so, I turn toward the lens through which I consider most things: creativity. Can creativity save the world? It has in the past. For example, engineering creativity helped solve the oil crisis of 1973 by finding new ways to access oil as well as by tackling how we might use less oil.[1] In the mid-1940s, as the Ku Klux Klan was on the rise, the Superman radio serials teamed up with the Anti-Defamation League to have Superman fight the Klan and, as legend has it, broadcast its secret passwords and lore on the air. It is hard to feel like a cool insider's club when your equivalent of secret

[1] Cropley, 2015a.

handshakes is being done by little kids everywhere.[2] The story of Oskar Schindler and his list of the Jews he saved during the Holocaust is well known,[3] but Raoul Wallenberg is more obscure. A Swedish diplomat to Budapest during World War II, Wallenberg came up with a creative (and courageous) plan to save Jews from the Nazis. He issued Swedish passports to Jews, saying that they were Swedish citizens who were planning to move back. He saved tens of thousands of Jews before disappearing mysteriously when the Russians liberated Hungary.[4]

So creativity has saved the world (or parts of it) and will continue to do so in the future. However, this book will focus on a different positive slice of creativity: how being creative can help you, the creator. We will explore the different types of benefits that can come from being creative. These comprise what I call "the creativity advantage."

Before I dive into this model, I cover some of the basics of creativity. I've covered this ground in the past,[5] but Part I in this book represents much more than an update. The recurring theme, to me, is that creativity is for everyone. The many myths of creativity have been discussed and studied extensively,[6] but I'll emphasize that creativity is not reserved for the genius, the artist, or the loner. Creativity manifests itself at different levels of accomplishment, including in small insights and everyday moments. I'll talk about the creative process, touch on creativity measurement, and end by examining how creativity stacks up against other constructs in predicting good outcomes. Then we'll take a little break with an aperitif and we'll cleanse our palate by acknowledging the dark and terrible side of creativity.

In Part II of the book, I'll talk about the different ways in which creativity helps the creator via my creativity advantage model: self-insight, healing, connection, drive, and legacy. I'll elaborate on what these entail, what the underlying research says, and under what circumstances creativity can enhance or boost them. I know that I run the risk of preaching to the converted, but I am hoping to give you specific ammunition when a supervisor, administrator, superintendent, or anyone else cautions against allotting too much time or too many resources to creativity. Unless, of course, the buzzkill is actually correct (that does happen), and then you can surprise them by taking

[2] Bowers, 2012. [3] Keneally, 1982. [4] Carlberg, 2016. [5] J. C. Kaufman, 2009, 2016.
[6] Benedek et al., 2021; Plucker et al., 2004.

their side. Most importantly, I am hoping that there is enough here that resonates with your own experiences, synthesizes different ideas together, or offers new fodder to help you ponder the positives of creativity – and, ideally, enjoy all these things yourself.

The first step, though, is to define the beast. So let's start by trying to define the undefinable.

ACKNOWLEDGMENTS

This book is my twentieth with Cambridge University Press (although my first solo authored book after nineteen edited ones). It has been a pleasure working with the terrific editors at the press over the years – from Phil Laughlin (now at MIT Press), who looked after my first book, to David Repetto, with whom I worked for several years, and to Stephen Acerra, with whom I'm currently working. Indeed, there are some more fun plans in store. My sincere thanks to everyone at Cambridge, including Rowan Groat, Joon Moon, Laura Simmons, Emily Watton, and my amazing copyeditor, Manuela Tecusan.

I went through a number of versions and even conceptions of this book before it reached its current form. Early input from Melissa Bray, Garo Green, David K. Hecht, Alan Kaufman, Allison Kaufman, Nadeen Kaufman, Jennie Kaufman Singer, and Robert Sternberg was invaluable. As it shifted form, I was stuck on a name for it for a long time. I discussed title ideas with many friends, colleagues, and students; it was ultimately an undergraduate in my Intro to Creativity class who suggested *The Creativity Advantage*. Thank you, Nia Samuels!

As I wrote this book, I had the luxury of being able to reach out to many of the world's experts on the topic, to make sure I was representing their work accurately and was not missing any key studies; and generally being allowed to annoy them with questions. Many, many thanks to John Baer, Baptiste Barbot, Roger Beaty, Ronald Beghetto, Bonnie Cramond, David Cropley, Jennifer Drake, Marie Forgeard, Vlad Glăveanu, Nicola Holt, Zorana Ivcevic, Hansika Kapoor, Maciej Karwowski, Todd Kashdan, Yoed Kenett, Alex McKay, Jonathan Plucker, Sally Reis, Fredricka Reisman, Roni Reiter-Palmon, Joseph Renzulli, Sandra Russ, Jeffrey Smith, Steve Stemler, Oshin Vartanian, Tom Ward, and Matthew Worwood for their encouragement, time, advice, stories, discussions, and ideas. I am also grateful to my graduate students Khalilah Arrington and Lihong Xie for their terrific suggestions. I would further like to thank three superstars in the arts: T. Coraghessan Boyle, for his mentorship and warm approval of my sharing my wonderful experiences with him; Robert Olen Butler, for his longtime friendship and advice; and Dana P. Rowe, for his continued collaboration and friendship.

Barbara Bengels, Molly Holinger, Alan Kaufman, Nadeen Kaufman, Kirill Miroshnik, Amanda Osmanlli, and Christa Taylor read through the entire book and gave invaluable input. My mom and my aunt Barbara (an English professor) caught countless typos, logical errors, and orphaned comments or thoughts. My dad focused on larger conceptual issues. Amanda, a McNair Scholar under my supervision, read through the whole book, making many different valuable suggestions. Finally, Molly, Kirill, and Christa, all rising stars in the field, went above and beyond the call of duty, providing thoughtful and detailed suggestions and insights about creativity scholarship.

Everyone mentioned above has helped to greatly improve the book you are reading. Much gratitude and love to all for their help, collegiality, and friendship.

PART I
THE BASICS OF CREATIVITY

1 TO DEFINE THE UNDEFINABLE

Creativity has played many roles in my life. The study of creativity is the driving force of my career, so at one level it is my livelihood. I study, think about, teach, and talk about creativity all the time. But my relationship with creativity is also deeply personal. My own creativity has helped me do many things across different dimensions of my life.

It's helped me connect with other people. Creativity is a common language that can bridge gaps. It's helped me recognize kindred spirits. It's enabled me to entertain people and show my love of friends and family. Creativity has improved the quality of my life. It lets me amuse myself when I'm bored and calm down when I'm panicking. It helps me figure out solutions and express my emotions. It gets me out of trouble (and sometimes gets me into trouble).

Applying my creativity to writing gave me my first true passion, one that exists to this day. Before I knew anything, I wanted to be a writer. I tried fiction, journalism, and the occasional poem before settling into playwriting. I've sat in the back of the theatre, in its blissful darkness, and seen my words come out of other people's mouths. I've felt intense gratitude and awe at the way a talented director and cast can take what I've done and make it so much better. I've experienced the numbness of repeated rejections (and, worse, seen acceptances and agreements fall through). I've bounced between intense pride and deep embarrassment as I've eavesdropped on audience members. It's broken my heart. It's given me a purpose.

Being able to use my creativity as a central part of my job helps me love what I do. I try to teach creatively (while teaching about creativity). I usually teach two Introduction to Creativity classes at the University of Connecticut (UConn) each semester. Before that, I taught a class on Intelligence and Creativity (and a Critical Thinking class that included creativity) at the California State University, San Bernardino (CSUSB). I've changed up and reorganized and played with the structure and content of these classes most semesters, to introduce often radical shifts that keep me from being complacent and getting bored. This constant shuffling softened the impact of the sudden transition to remote teaching that happened when the pandemic hit. The resulting chaos was manageable.

What has been consistent for many years is that the centerpiece of every class is a semester-long project where the primary requirement is simply to do something creative. This "something" can manifest itself in many different ways. I usually see roughly three categories of students. First there are the experienced creators. They are eager to try a new activity or return to an area of comfort and expertise. Then there are the rusty creators. These ones are trained to play the game of school and perform on cue.[1] They may hesitate for a few weeks, to make sure that it's not a trick, and then they tackle a forgotten passion or a back-burnered whim. Finally there are the skeptics. These are in the class because they've heard that it's fun (or that I'm an easy grader), but they don't think of themselves as creative. They need some coaxing and handholding. Some never fully commit. Others throw themselves into their creativity project. The results – for all students – vary wildly. They range from gems I still remember years later to smaller bursts of self-expression that nonetheless offered insight, amusement, or self-awareness.

It is possible to love something without making a life of studying it (indeed, I can't begin to tell you how they make Count Chocula, the cereal). But I have been lucky enough to get to do both. It can be hard to explain why a topic, a product, or an issue is so important to you. Sometimes you get a lot of practice, such as when you love a movie that is obscure, esoteric, or divisive (let's say, *I'm Thinking of Ending Things*, *The Quick and the Dead*, or *Under the Silver Lake*). But it can be even harder to explain your passion for a film that is generally accepted and even liked. If I'm asked to defend *The Godfather*,

[1] Beghetto, 2007.

Pulp Fiction, or *Citizen Kane*, it's a new experience. Most people either love these movies and respect them or hate them but know enough to keep quiet.

Even if someone, knowingly or not, is genuinely biased against creative people,[2] such a person is unlikely to break unspoken social norms and talk about it. Few people besides literal cartoon villains (like those in *Phineas and Ferb* and *The Simpsons*) will embark on a long rant against creativity. So it feels counterintuitive (frankly, the word I'm looking for is *weird*) to write a book that has the goal of highlighting many of the positive and meaningful outcomes that can flow from being creative. There aren't many books dedicated to why getting an unexpected salary increase is actually a good thing.

Creativity is popular when it is a vague concept or a buzzword. When it comes time to divvy up resources and priorities, though, usually creativity somehow ends up lagging behind.[3] Many of the people who publicly lead the call for creativity weave in misconceptions and misinformation. Perhaps most notably, the "why is creativity important?" aspect is often back-burnered – even by academics.[4] But before you can begin to tackle the "why" you need to take care of the "what."

I am well acquainted with the "what is creativity?" question. Between my time at UConn, my time at CSUSB, and my travels around the world, I've given the basic introductory creativity lecture to well over five thousand people (possibly more, but I wouldn't know – I'm a psychologist, not a mathematician). I've also given talks about the broader topic to many thousands of people.

How Do Real People Define Creativity?

I try to start with a basic definition of *creativity*. The word can be used with many different connotations, depending on the context. For example, it can be a true compliment:

> Dave, Wow! What a creative short story – good job.
> Alex, how creative to set your production of "West Side Story" in the Old West!
> Maria, it was very creative to build a working Jacuzzi out of papier-mâché.

[2] Mueller et al., 2012. [3] Runco & Abdulla, 2014. [4] Forgeard & Kaufman, 2016.

It can be a consolation prize:

I'm sorry you didn't win first place, Nate. But your entry was very creative.
Did I like it? Well, Avi, it was definitely creative.

Or it can be a backhanded aside:

The cake? Well, Christa, using toothpaste instead of frosting was... creative...
Dana, given that last month's deal fell through, I would say your salary demands are... creative...

I have found that most people have no particular opinion or inclination about how to use or define *creativity*. I am not surprised; I haven't spent time thinking about the larger definitional issues surrounding *collateral damage* or *will-o-the-wisp* or *schadenfreude*. The first Polish encyclopedia, under *horse*, told readers that a horse was a horse; anyone could just see what it is.[5] It's a horse. It's creativity. We all know what that is, right?

Well... it's complicated. Once you get people to take a moment, think, and discuss the question, you start to notice patterns. Whenever the question of how science might approach creativity comes up, people tend to assume that creativity is impossible to define. I am not talking only about students; I have read many academic papers that begin by stating, "No one knows how to define creativity." For a critical reader, this opening should raise a pretty big red flag right away.[6] It makes me cringe a little, much like when I read my tenth straight student paper that chooses the Oxford English Dictionary's definition of creativity as a starting point.

There have been some studies where researchers asked "average people" more pointed questions about creativity, such as whether different behaviors or characteristics are representative of a creative person. A study in the United States found that laypeople associated four different personal attributes with creativity dimensions: nonentrenchment (i.e., not seeing things as fixed or unchangeable), aesthetic taste, perspicacity (i.e., sharp insight), and inquisitiveness.[7] Comparable results were found in Korea.[8] Another study asked gifted adolescents (students) both about their own creativity and about

[5] Lynch, 2016. [6] E.g., D. Cropley, 2015b. [7] Sternberg, 1985.
[8] Lim & Plucker, 2001.

other people's creativity – how they saw it, for example. When participants were thinking about other people, the four factors were activity level (i.e., being active and energetic), artistic individualism, popularity, and questioning. These make sense, right? However, when the same people thought about themselves, they converged on four different dimensions: awkwardness, impulsiveness, intellect, and risk-taking.[9] It's a little funny and sad that a study about a totally different topic nonetheless captures the painful embarrassment and ennui of being a teenager.

A common thread I found both in conversations and in essays written by noncreativity researchers is the idea that no one can agree on a definition of creativity. I mean, in a very technical sense, you could argue that there is no universally agreed-upon meaning of the word *creativity*, much as there is no complete consensus on what constitutes "good literature." Do the *Harry Potter* books count? And, if *Harry Potter*, why not *The Hunger Games*, or *Twilight*? How about Stephen King? John Grisham? James Patterson? At what point do we wonder whether outstanding movies or television shows qualify as "good literature"? Or is the use of the term *literature* reserved for the written word? Is a play literature when it is written, but not when it is performed? What about audio books?

Plus, of course, there is never universal agreement on anything. One dentist out of ten (perhaps under the thumb of Big Sugar) may well recommend not brushing your teeth at all. Somewhere, right now, someone is insisting that llamas are simply female alpacas, that Homer wrote all of Shakespeare's plays, or that the "p" is pronounced in pterodactyl. Complete consensus is virtually impossible.

Nonetheless, within the small club of creativity researchers, we *absolutely* know how to define creativity. In fact there is an almost stunning level of agreement, which goes back more than seven decades.[10] I'm not saying that we have settled on a precise or helpful definition, but we have an established one. We are even slowly getting better at including an explicit definition of creativity in our studies. An excellent review of the field in 2004 noted that only 38 percent of papers offered an explicit definition outright;[11] a more recent study found that by 2016 the rate was up to 56 percent.[12] At least there is progress.

[9] Saunders Wickes & Ward, 2006. [10] Stein, 1953. [11] Plucker et al., 2004.
[12] Puryear & Lamb, 2020.

How Do Researchers Define Creativity?

Something is creative to the extent that it possesses two core components. The first is easy to guess: it needs to be original, new, novel, or different. If it's an exact copy of an existing object or idea, it's probably not creative. Think about a little kid getting a laugh with a funny line. With that positive reinforcement, their inclination will likely be to do it again. Exactly the same way. And then again, and again. The fourth identical punchline wouldn't be considered new or creative.

Similarly, imagine that you are eating at a burger joint and you think, "Hey, I bet a beef patty between two pieces of curved dough would taste great!" You are not being creative. You are holding a hamburger and eating it, so thinking of the existence of a hamburger is not new. It is possible that you are thinking only of a tiny, itty bitty new twist on a hamburger – and that would count. But it has to be at least the tiniest bit new. Remember, I don't necessarily mean groundbreaking or unique – just a little off the beaten path. As we will discuss, even your own version of an existing creative work can still qualify.

This first prong of being new is not enough. If your toilet clogs up and you decide to drop five boxes of instant pudding into the bowl to clear it out, that is certainly different. Few people have intentionally made this decision. Yet your toilet will still be stuffed up and it will now look disgusting (even if it may taste delicious). Deciding to try to swap out ingredients is great – but if your plan is to take out eggs from your recipe and substitute angry wasps, I would not call that creative (nor would I eat your omelettes).

If simple novelty were all that was required for creativity, then I could be incredibly creative right now, at will. I could write a brand-new sentence that would be a radical departure from what I've written before, maybe from anything ever written. I mean, if you think about it, then turtle pomegranate shark-infested waters with a ham on rye. I can see John Adams is eating fire ants while he juggles a puce unicorn or learns to hammer with pudding or makes Donny Osmond do handstands with bacon grease on the bottom of his feet. You could even argue that I'm still not being different enough – I'm using punctuation and some kind of word formation, in which case I 7JP-**~Kor5???

No, being new is not enough. The second requirement is that, to be creative, something must also be useful, task appropriate, or relevant.[13] At the most basic level, the creative work needs to do what it is supposed to do. A meal is useful if people eat it (enjoyment is preferred, but not required). A water filtration system is useful insofar as it successfully purifies your water; if the system actually adds particles of dirt or arsenic, it is not task appropriate. An abstract painting may be useful if viewers find it beautiful or if it inspires emotion, thought, or pleasure. A lawyer's closing argument should offer the defendant or plaintiff at least a reasonable chance of winning; if the lawyer looks at the jury and simply says "Kumquats" repeatedly for five minutes, the argument is not task appropriate.[14] A character in Tom Stoppard's *Artist Descending a Staircase* says, a bit bitingly, that "skill without imagination is craftsmanship and gives us many objects such as wickerwork picnic baskets. Imagination without skill gives us modern art."[15] With the caveat that I do not share the same disdain for modern art, there is a need for a happy balance between skill (or at least relevance) and imagination, to allow true creativity to emerge.

The importance of usefulness can vary according to how functional the creative work is supposed to be.[16] So, to paraphrase an example that my friend David Cropley uses, an architect may design a bridge that is so stirringly beautiful that it makes you weep. But if that bridge falls down, it's not useful, and therefore not creative. If the task-appropriate aspect of a functional creativity product fails, people can die. That's simply not true in the case of art (leaving aside the occasional death caused by some unfortunate accident, as when one of Christo's umbrella installations was torn from its steel base and killed a visitor).[17] I managed to see *Cats* in the movie theatre, in its original run (not to mention *Showgirls*, much earlier). The magnitude of its awfulness, which transcended camp, was so over the top that it almost inspired tenderness and pity rather than disdain. Yet, even as Rebel Wilson began eating the human-faced singing cockroaches, my kidneys continued to filter out impurities and excess liquids. My pancreas kept producing insulin. My larynx did not suddenly decide to leave my trachea unprotected. No matter how bad *Cats* was, I did not die from it.

It's also important to note that sometimes a use may not be obvious. Think about Matty Benedetto, an inventor with a self-styled "wall of unnecessary." He aims to solve nonexistent problems, which

[13] Hennessey & Amabile, 2010; Simonton, 2012. [14] Kaufman, 2016.
[15] Stoppard, 1988 , p. 7. [16] Cropley & Cropley, 2010. [17] Hall, 1991.

is usually not the best strategy for an entrepreneur. His inventions are numerous. They include the FurRoller, which adds fake dog hair to your clothing so you can pretend to have a dog, StubStoppers, small hats to protect one's toes, and a Chip-Xractor, designed to hoover out the last chip stuck in the packaging.[18] Obviously there was not a significant demand for these or any of his nearly 200 inventions. Yet, although his products are not useful in a traditional way, I would argue that inspiring amusement is a use. Further, he makes a living not by selling most of these items but by getting endorsements from big brands that like his idiosyncratic sense of humor and want to attract the type of people who would find Benedetto's work funny. At first glance, his inventions are not useful. If you look deeper, they do serve a purpose, even if not the one allegedly intended for them.

Although early pioneers such as J. P. Guilford[19] and Frank Barron[20] are often given credit (sometimes by me) for helping shape how we define creativity, the first scholar to actually articulate what is often considered the standard definition of creativity[21] was Moe Stein, who in 1953 wrote that a "creative work is a novel work that is accepted as tenable or useful by a group in some point in time."[22] Stein does not get enough credit; he was also a very early scholar to be interested in creativity and culture. When Paul Torrance, a legend we will soon discuss in more detail, passed away, I helped coedit a special issue of *Creativity Research Journal* in his honor.[23] I reached out to Stein, who was incredibly nice and gracious and agreed to contribute a piece. I was confused when, at some point in our communications, he stopped getting back to me, until I found out much later that he had passed. He is only one of many creativity greats with whom I had a small interaction before discovering the extent of their contributions. Stein's note about a specific group and a specific time period was also prescient in terms of the importance of context. What is considered creative in one particular situation (be that a culture, a time period, a scenario, or a population) may not be considered so in another.[24]

There are other proposed additions to this "new and useful" definition; some suggestions include the elements of surprise,[25] high

[18] Crockett, 2020. [19] Guilford, 1950. [20] Barron, 1955. [21] Runco & Jaeger, 2012.
[22] Stein, 1953, p. 311. [23] Kaufman & Baer, 2006. [24] Glăveanu et al., 2020.
[25] Boden, 2004; Simonton, 2012.

quality,[26] and authenticity.[27] It can be hard to articulate exactly how these necessarily differ; for example, can you easily imagine something that is not new yet is still surprising (not counting mediocre horror movies)? Relatedly, how do you know if a work is authentic? Would it bother you to know that its creator had disowned and criticized your favorite movie, book, or song? Perhaps – but would you consider it less creative for that reason, or of lower quality? These are all questions up for debate. However, if you stick with "new and appropriate," you cannot go too far wrong.

You may point out that this definition is quite open. So open, in fact, that it may not be terribly useful. What has been eliminated from creativity, other than pure repetition or total ignorance?[28] If you are trying to add 4 + 4 and someone says, "The answer is not 23 and it's not 59," that person's hint is of limited help.

In addition, as Kirill Miroshnik pointed out to me, there are even times when the standard definition doesn't seem to work perfectly, at least if we see creativity as confined to traditionally living things. A philosopher has noted that the Earth's natural movements can produce diamonds[29] – heck, Uranus' and Neptune's atmospheres may make it possible to rain diamonds.[30] Diamonds are certainly valuable, and most are, in their own way, unique (and thus novel). Using this same logic, Rudolf Arnheim argued that a tree behaves creatively as it seeks light and spreads out its branches.[31] Is the Earth creative? Other planets? Trees? I mean. . . maybe?

Why Bother?

Perhaps you are instead thinking about the futility of the whole endeavor. Who cares if researchers agree on a definition? Does it even matter? Certainly, some creativity researchers have already come to the conclusion that it does not.[32] Many other people who are not in the field might say the same – but for different reasons. What do I mean? Well, picture me at a cocktail party (or whatever you call it – the kind of event you attend once you are too old to drink regularly and not classy enough to be invited to nice affairs). I am likely standing awkwardly in a corner, debating the pros and cons of making another pass at the snacks or desserts, wherever they are set out. I may be glancing at my watch. Let us suppose that, right when

26 Sternberg, 1999. 27 Kharkhurin, 2014; Runco, 2018. 28 Simonton, 2016, 2018b.
29 Gaut, 2010 30 Ross, 1981 31 Arnheim, 2001. 32 Silvia, 2018.

I ponder making a quick dash for the door, someone stops me. For whatever reason, they recognize me and vaguely remember that I study creativity. They ask me what I do – what does it mean to be a creativity researcher?

If the person I am talking to is a scientist, they may interpret my study of creativity as being akin to saying, "I interpret the past lives of marshmallows." When I think of science, I think of things like galvanic skin responses, double-blind studies, hydrochloric acid, or centrifugal force. I understand that trying to examine some invisible, magical process may come across as a little silly or naïve.

If I am talking to a businessperson, whatever I say will likely sound random. If I say I study "innovation," they may be initially interested. Once they realize that I cannot guarantee any tangible outcome (such as increased product sales), they will probably lose interest. I sometimes count the minutes until the mild surge of boredom blends with the disappointment on their faces. As a species, we are not great at long-term thinking.

If I am talking to an artist, there may be a different problem. It sounds as though I am using a ruler to measure someone's dreams. I am less likely to encounter condescension and more likely to stir apprehension. Why would anyone want to study creativity? It may seem like watching a movie being made and then talking to the gaffer, or loving dogs yet feeling a compulsion to look at images of their spleens. Art is about doing, feeling, and caring. How can that be analyzed?

There are many potential issues to explore and questions to discuss. Can we measure creativity? How can creativity lead to specific (if often long-term) benefits? Can the study of creativity deliver practical advice on becoming more creative? Before we can really dive into these or any others, I feel compelled to tackle the deeper, underlying question: "why bother with any of these issues in the first place?" This is another way of referencing what I call the WGASA factor. It is named after a partially true urban legend about the San Diego Wild Animal Park.[33] For over thirty years, the zoo had a monorail that enabled visitors to see the entire park. It used to break down nearly as often as Lyle Lanley's monorails in *The Simpsons* and was replaced in 2007 by an open-air shuttle. When it debuted, however, it was a pretty big deal. The park asked staffers for input on the name, and a zoo

[33] Mikkelson, 2011.

designer named Chuck Faust scribbled down "WGASA" on a suggestion form. He meant it as an acronym for "who gives a shit anyway?" Indeed, what did the name of the monorail matter in the larger scheme of the world? Most of the board members were in the dark as to the acronym's meaning and felt that it sounded African and exotic. Thus the name was selected. For years, when guests asked, they were told that WGASA stood for "world's greatest animal show anywhere."[34]

So there are many WGASA factors to ponder. The larger WGASA is "why be creative" or "why value creativity," and answering these questions will be the main thrust of the book. But I'll start with a different one. Why does it matter how creativity is defined? Why can't we just crack open Webster's and use whatever it says? Why listen to all these almost scientists?

My answer lies in vegetables. First off, what constitutes a vegetable? You may vaguely remember from your grade school days that a tomato is actually a fruit and not a vegetable. You may not remember that avocados, cucumbers, eggplants, okra, olives, peas, peppers, string beans, and zucchini are also, technically, fruits.[35] Of course, they are all presumed more generally to be vegetables. Why does it matter? Am I arguing against my own argument (and is that possible)?

There have been times when the definition of a vegetable mattered a great deal. In the early 1980s, under the Reagan presidency, the United States Department of Agriculture (USDA) tried to relax the regulations around what constituted a vegetable. The proposal never actually suggested that ketchup was a vegetable – it used pickle relish as an example.[36] Yet the idea that ketchup could be considered a vegetable became a rallying cry for protests. A few decades later, similar ground was revisited when Congress did not allow the USDA to tighten regulations around what constituted a vegetable. As a result, a slice of pizza with the equivalent of two tablespoons of tomato paste continued to count as an actual serving of broccoli.

Playing fast and loose with definitions can have real-life consequences. Childhood obesity has continued to rise. School lunches that are given wide latitude over what counts as a vegetable are not the only reason, but they don't help. Similarly, having creativity

[34] Barrett & Dotinga, 2010. [35] Abadi, 2018. [36] Smith, 1996.

defined as the production of something original and task-appropriate does not magically change anything; but it does go a small way toward disentangling creativity from wild chaos.

From Definitions to Categories

This definition, as mentioned, does not rule out too much. We need to dip a little into theory to sort out some of the rest. Let's start by thinking about the word *love*. Make a mental list of whom or what you love (or, hell, write it in the margin; I won't be offended). When you have rooms filled with people who do this exercise, you get a wide variety of answers. Here are just a few of the ones I have heard from students over the years: myself, my mom, my girlfriend, my sorority sisters, ice cream, Beyoncé, America, UConn.

Now think about creativity. When I talk about creativity, I could intend many different meanings. Do I have in mind a creative genius of the past, such as William Shakespeare? Or maybe someone who is still active (and alive), such as Lin-Manuel Miranda? I could be thinking of an undergraduate in my class, who came up with an example I had never heard before; or else I could recall how my youngest son would make up jokes (when asked what type of cereal he was eating, he said "expired"). Am I thinking of the dynamic exchanges that take place in conversations with my colleagues or my graduate students? Do I picture an artist, a writer, a scientist, a chef, a businessperson, an engineer, or a whittler?

Perhaps I am thinking instead about how people create – that hesitant excitement when you believe you have an idea that no one has thought of before, or the blustering of different ideas that can pour out during brainstorming. It might be a company or an organization, perhaps Pixar or Apple, or at least my image of what their workspace must be like. It could be whatever I imagine a generic creative person might be like (smart? crazy? nice? doomed?). In short, it could be almost anything.

How can a single word have so many possible meanings? If your gut tells you to instantly remember the old story about Alaskan natives having multiple words for snow, I must tell you that the story is untrue. Most sources agree that they most likely have two words for snow.[37] Alas, there is no easy answer. One method by which we have

[37] Pullum, 1991.

approached this issue has been to develop many models and organizational systems.

If we want to sort out all the ways in which people think and talk about creativity, we have to go back a long way. Humans across civilizations have talked about these things for millennia. Ancient Greeks, for instance Plato[38] and Aristotle,[39] talked about muses, poetry, and genius. In modern times, the likes of Freud[40] and Einstein[41] weighed in on the matter. But very few actually studied creativity. One of the first was a woman named Laura Chassell. In 1914, at the age of twenty-one, she completed her master's thesis at Northwestern University in Illinois. She devised some possible measures of originality that she administered to students, along with already established tests of intelligence.[42] Chassell's creativity assessments were astoundingly prescient, predicting most of the ways in which we currently use them. She published her thesis two years later, before completing a PhD in educational psychology in 1920. Unfortunately Chassell's accomplishments could not overcome the sexism of the time. Ohio State University hired her husband as a professor, but it allowed her to teach just the occasional class – and even then, only until she became a mother. One of the most brilliant minds in creativity scholarship raised her kids while staying active in women's rights and helping faculty spouses from other countries. Chassell lived to be 101, still correcting spelling mistakes in her granddaughter's letters, but largely forgotten in the field.[43] I hope to give her at least a small measure of the credit she deserves.

Most other studies of creativity in the first half of the twentieth century are not shining examples of science. My personal favorite is a paper that helpfully notes that people who are given a lobotomy become less creative.[44] In 1950, however, there came a turning point at the annual American Psychological Association conference. The president, J. P. Guilford, devoted his spotlighted address to the topic of creativity. He argued there should be more research on creativity (particularly, one assumes, the type that does not require lobotomizing people). At that time, less than one in six hundred published papers involved creativity.[45] Indeed, one prominent scholar called the 1940s the "cry in the dark" stage of the research.[46] With

[38] Rothenberg & Hausman, 1976. [39] Becker, 2014. [40] Freud, 1908/1959.
[41] Calaprice, 2000. [42] Chassell, 1916. [43] Kaufman, 2019a.
[44] Hutton & Bassett, 1948. [45] Guilford, 1950. [46] Parnes, 1992.

Guilford's endorsement (and his research), studying creativity became less of an embarrassment.

Four Ps

In the decade that followed, many more studies of creativity were published. Although the basic definition of creativity as involving something new and task-appropriate had been proposed, the level of consensus that would eventually come was not there yet. An educator named Mel Rhodes decided to comb through the many books and articles on the topic (he used more than 300 reference cards, which reminds me again that I don't *actually* hate my computer). He didn't end up coming up with a new definition, but he suggested a model for how to approach the study of creativity: the four Ps.[47]

Rhodes proposed four main ways of thinking about, or categorizing, creativity:

Person: Who is creative?
Process: How (and why) are we creative?
Product: What is creative?
Press: In which environments are we creative?

You may wonder why Rhodes did not call "Press" by the simpler and more straightforward name "Environment"; but then you also have to admit that "the four Ps" sounds a lot cooler than "the three Ps and an E." The four Ps are useful in thinking about creativity. I'll certainly touch on all of them throughout the book. Although my main emphasis is on "Person," I'll spend a full chapter on "Process" and a decent portion of one specifically on "Product." In the latter half of the book, when I talk about positive outcomes, I'll highlight the interactions between "Person" and "Press."

The four Ps are still used by a lot of people today. It does strike me that even the people who study creativity rely a great deal on the tried-and-true. Our definitions go back seventy years; this sixty-year-old model is still dominant; and many of the core concepts we will touch on go back more than fifty years. Even in the world of creativity research there is the appeal of the status quo, existing work, and tradition. I am reminded of when a character in the movie *Hannah and Her Sisters* mocks a Holocaust documentary in which the usual

[47] Rhodes, 1961

talking heads discuss how such a tragedy could ever happen: "The reason they can never answer the question 'How could it possibly happen?' is that it's the wrong question," he says. "Given what people are, the question is 'Why doesn't it happen more often?'"[48]

It is easy to blame schools for not encouraging more creativity – indeed, apportioning this kind of blame has become a career for some – but it's important to emphasize that *creativity is hard*. Forging something new is difficult, even for creativity researchers. Expecting principals, bosses, funders, or any gatekeeper to take a leap of faith in creativity is asking a lot. I am more likely to marvel that creativity ever happens than to criticize those times when it is suppressed or not emphasized.

People have tried to build off the four Ps. For example, several possible additional Ps have been nominated (think of it as creativity's version of the fifth Beatle). These are Perception,[49] Persuasion,[50] Potential,[51] Phases,[52] Propulsion, and Public.[53] Yet the field tends to stick with the main four Ps, whether from inertia or because the perfect model just happened to have been developed in 1961. My favorite expansion on the four Ps, however, uses a different letter. It emphasizes that, although the four Ps take the perspective of the creator as an individual working alone, we often create collaboratively or in a social context.[54]

Five As

Much of the work in this area is by my dear friend Vlad Glăveanu, who has proposed the five As.[55] He recast the Person as "Actor," the Process as the "Action," and the Product as "Artifact." These new categories have similar meanings but incorporate the ideas of other people. An actor is observed, an action can be a joint effort, and an artifact implies that people will interact with it (it may help to imagine Indiana Jones hunting for the lost ark). Glăveanu split Press into two different categories that I will explain in a moment: "Affordances" and "Audience." All these five concepts are working together at the same time, blipping back and forth like a modem in the 1980s. They are less categories and more an intricate interaction.

[48] Allen, 1986. [49] Kharkhurin & Yagolkovskiy, 2019. [50] Simonton, 1990.
[51] Runco, 2003. [52] Cropley, 2015a. [53] Sternberg & Karami, 2022.
[54] Sawyer & DeZutter, 2009. [55] Glăveanu, 2013.

Affordances are anything you may need or use to be creative. They can vary widely – an affordance could be a Latin tutor, $500,000, a xylophone, a master's degree in engineering, or three pounds of custard. An affordance is whatever you have or can access that might give you a leg up on others in being creative. If you stop and think about all your possible affordances, you may already begin to get ideas for new projects. Indeed, it's one of the strategies I use when I am trying to help a student get an idea for a class project or a research study. What are the random resources that you have access to and most people don't?

Affordances tend to be material, whereas the audience tends to be social. The audience represents anyone who may interact with your creation. It can include mentors, collaborators, or people who read, watch, or try out an early draft of your creation. It can represent the folks you want to reach, too. You might be creating for your family or friends. Perhaps you are aiming to reach a local community, or the world, or even posterity. Your audience could consist of people who haven't been born yet.

Maybe you are doing something creative only for yourself. That's okay. That is still a perfectly good reason to create. I have found that much of what I have written over the course of my career, especially my theories, comes down to three words: *it all counts.* At this point, if I were delivering a lecture, someone would remind me about the basic repetition or copying, or the lawyer saying "kumquats" for his closing argument. And – okay: it doesn't all count. But that person is a pain in the ass.

As we are going to see and discuss, creativity is everywhere. It's found in accounting and data entry and toilet cleaning and anything you might assume is uncreative. Creativity percolates at all levels and through all the domains and types of contributions. It can be the littlest spontaneous bit of wordplay. Glăveanu used to teach at Aalborg University in Denmark. After presenting one day, someone came up to him and said, "You live in Aalborg starting with two As, and you want to add three more." That quip, that (very) minor witticism – *that* counts.

In the next chapter we'll find creativity in the smallest of the small, as I talk about another theory: the four Cs. It is a developmental trajectory that encompasses a wide variety of creators who aim for a wide variety of audiences – including those being creative just for themselves.

2 FROM TINY TO SMALL

I wanted to be a writer for as long as I can remember. I wanted to tell stories, create characters, make up plots, and carve out dialogue. I first tried writing fiction in first grade, eventually filling a big yellow binder. I still remember the first story I finished. It was about an elephant seeing an airplane lose its wheels as it attempted to land. The elephant knew that, without the wheels, there would be friction and the plane would crash, because. . . Science? He called for help and somehow the police, airport security, emergency medical technicians, and firefighters put aside any potential turf war to rescue the plane. The elephant was hailed as a hero (instead of being studied as a curiosity – because he would have needed opposable thumbs to place a phone call).

I kept writing. Stories, vignettes, essays, and one interminable play. I would consistently prepare outlandishly complicated outlines for novels on topics that ranged from time travel to the Holocaust. The actual book would inevitably putter out after five or six pages, as my own plot stumped me – but then I'd be starting another one within a week. I was always dreaming up new story ideas. I would go to sleep thinking about my characters.

Big and Little

Even as a kid, I was vaguely aware that there were two meanings of "writer." There were the great writers, such as the ones I read for school, and then everyone else. This very broad distinction was also true in creativity scholarship. There was everyday creativity, and there was genius. These categories are often called "Big-C" and "little-c."[1] They are almost instinctual. If I ask you to think of a creative writer, you may think of Shakespeare, Maya Angelou, Jane Austen, Gabriel García Marquez, Ernest Hemingway, Langston Hughes, or your favorite Brontë; in other words, legendary geniuses (Big-C). Or, instead, you might think of your nephew, or a friend, or that one guy you know – everyday people who are not that different from yourself (little-c).

Although I couldn't have come close to verbalizing it at the time, this dichotomy wasn't encompassing enough. As a kid, I loved some of the "great" children's literature (such as the Oz books), but I also devoured Choose Your Own Adventure books and the Three Investigators mystery series. I could also sense that there was a vast difference between the quality of the works in my school's middle school literary magazine and the stories written by older, more experienced students.

Years later, I would meet a fellow creativity researcher, Ronald Beghetto, at a conference. We hit it off and began many in-depth conversations about the nature of creativity. Beghetto and I talked about how little-c had to carry an awful lot of weight for a single category. Everyone who wasn't a genius would fall under little-c, which could theoretically include published writers. Indeed, I thought about when I was in elementary school and starting out and falling in love with language and storytelling. I would have been placed in the same category then as I would be later, when I was a college student, published multiple times – not to mention in the same category as much more accomplished people, with many years of experience.

Such comparisons are not only fundamentally unfair. They go beyond labels or semantics; there may be actual negative consequences. How? Well, creativity can be a fragile thing. Many people implicitly contrast themselves to others with more success, especially when they start out in a field. If they are thinking of coworkers or colleagues, upward comparisons can be beneficial to their creativity because they may motivate them to work harder to keep up with their peers.[2] But if they are using loftier and more abstract ideals, such as those of creators with much more experience or renown, there can be

[1] Csikszentmihalyi, 1998; see Simonton, 2013. [2] Paulus & Dzindolet, 2008.

a bit of a risk. We are often not mindful when evaluating how we creatively stack up against others, ignoring key variables such as the role of context.[3]

Beghetto and I built on existing work on personal[4] and developmental perspectives[5] on creativity, and we came to propose a new "c" designed to take its place alongside little-c and Big-C: mini-c[6]. We envisioned mini-c as a place for the kind of creativity that occurs when someone is learning, playing, or improvising. Mini-c was designed to represent those epiphanies or moments of insight that could be intensely meaningful to the creator but of notably less interest or value to other people. If creativity is traditionally defined as being new and task appropriate, then mini-c should be new and task appropriate for the creator, whereas others may consider an act of mini-c to be less original and to have less obvious relevance.

Although mini-c is typically associated with students or young people, it can (and does) happen to anyone. When I was preparing a very quick dinner with instant mashed potatoes, I decided to use soup instead of water. It added a bit of a kick and some more substance. Such a moment may not seem creative to anyone else, but it was an idea that struck me and held some type of value for me. Mini-c can also lead to greatness. One of the examples Beghetto and I like to give is George de Mestral's mini-c burst that led to the invention of Velcro.[7] The engineer was hunting with his dog when he noticed that a large amount of burr had stuck to the dog's fur. De Mestral's mini-c moment was to transform this observation into the idea that a similar setup could make for a good fastening system. As de Mestral kept working on almost Velcro, this project soon evolved beyond mini-c.

But mini-c that never advances is still valuable in its own right. Someone experiencing mini-c is engaged with an idea. Such passion can help that person learn and understand core concepts, which is particularly important in education.[8] The mini-c insight may well occur as you are creating in your mind a new metaphor or example about a new piece of information. Mini-c can also manifest itself in pretend play,[9] which is associated with a variety of benefits that range from better coping skills[10] to higher emotion regulation[11] and higher mathematics achievements.[12] Much work on this topic is

[3] Langer et al., 2010. [4] Runco, 1996. [5] Cohen, 1989.
[6] Beghetto & Kaufman, 2007. [7] Beghetto & Kaufman, 2009.
[8] Beghetto et al., 2014. [9] Hoffmann & Russ, 2012. [10] Fiorelli & Russ, 2012.
[11] Hoffmann & Russ, 2016. [12] Wallace & Russ, 2015.

by Sandra Russ, who has carried out several fascinating experimental studies that show that children who engage in a play facilitation module of approximately five sessions display higher imagination and divergent thinking than controls.[13] In addition, play can help children with autism learn specific, play-based skills and develop emotional understanding.[14] Another study found that the same type of play module helped patients with Prader-Willi syndrome improve their divergent thinking.[15] Promisingly, this last study was conducted over Zoom; Russ told me that she is actively doing more work with Anastasia Dimitropoulos on play interventions on Zoom.

Can Mini-c Be Overlooked?

Before we go up the model, let's look down for a moment (metaphorically; your shoes look fine). Is there a middle ground between acts that are clearly uncreative, such as a random and irrelevant response, and the self-recognized insight of mini-c? Glăveanu and I proposed the CASE model to account for what we call "shadow creativity."[16] We describe as shadow creativity those situations in which the world, the field, or even the creators themselves do not recognize an action or a product as being creative.

CASE is an acronym, and each of the four different components that these letters stand for could be lacking. C is for "capital," which refers to the tools of the trade – the jargon, knowledge, and status that help someone to be recognized in a field (or domain). I admit I'm guilty of judging creative works in this way; if I'm reviewing a paper that doesn't cite the relevant creativity research, it's hard for me to see past that and figure out whether the author has anything interesting to say. A is for "awareness." Many people just don't think of themselves as being creative (including many students in my classes, some of whom have produced terrific final projects). This may be a self-esteem issue, or may reflect a lack of understanding of exactly what constitutes creativity. It's the opposite of what we know about narcissists, who think that they are more creative than other people... Except that other people don't agree.[17]

S is for "spark," which is the initial inspiration. The person who has the original idea is often the only one recognized as the

[13] Hoffman & Russ, 2016; Moore & Russ, 2008. [14] Doernberg et al., 2021.
[15] Dimitropoulos et al., 2021. [16] Kaufman & Glăveanu, 2022a.
[17] Furnham et al., 2013; Goncalo et al., 2010.

creator, even for long-running works. Most people (at least those my age) know Rod Serling (*The Twilight Zone*), Gene Rodenberry (*Star Trek*), and Matt Groening (*The Simpsons*). They are much less likely to have heard of Charles Beaumont, Arthur Singer, or Cesar Mazariegos, the people who wrote the second-largest number of episodes in those shows. Finally, E is for "exceptionality." We have an image of creativity as being a special and rare event. But some people are creative as part of their daily routine or job. Being creative may become so habitual that they simply do not recognize it or label it as such.[18]

I remember when I was in graduate school, before I had even the smallest conception that I might study creativity, my class was assigned a paper by Mihaly Csikszentmihalyi. He was a legend in the field; his book *Creativity*[19] was the first book I ever read on the topic and a tremendous inspiration. Anyway, in the class reading, Csikszentmihalyi argued that creativity was a crucial, needed attribute. Many of my fellow students pushed back quite a bit. One person argued that creativity was a luxury and that the paper came across as elitist; how dare the author push for creativity when people went starving every day?

I remember that this struck me as a bit of a straw-man fallacy. Life is not some kind of zero-sum game, where people are being forced to choose between an apple and a paintbrush at regular intervals. I didn't particularly care either way at the time, but now I would go back and respond that creativity is *essential* for survival.[20] Think about the creativity needed in hard circumstances. It might be about finding out how to escape a dangerous or abusive situation, or figuring out how to scrounge food or shelter each day. We don't consider that "creativity" because it's not someone painting or reciting a sonnet. But that doesn't mean that creativity is elitist – it means that the person making that argument has a skewed (and ignorant) belief system about creativity.

Further, Csikszentmihalyi himself[21] noted that the first modern creativity tests came about during World War II, when the US Air Force asked our friend J. P. Guilford to design measures they could give pilots to see who could engage in creative problem-solving under extreme pressure. This is about as high an endorsement of the life-saving importance of creativity as you can get. It is also, incidentally, a nice mirror of how IQ tests underwent huge developments

[18] Glăveanu, 2012. [19] Csikszentmihalyi, 1996. [20] See Puccio, 2017.
[21] Csikszentmihalyi, 1996.

when the army commissioned a group of psychologists, including David Wechsler, to create (or adapt) tests to help select potential officers, identify malingerers, and figure out how to place immigrants who could not speak English.[22]

Mini-c to Little-c: Feedback

As we've hit this point, an important question arises. How exactly do you get from mini-c to little-c? There is no set way (if there were – and I knew it – I'd be touring the world giving private coaching lessons for obscene amounts of money). But two very important concepts are feedback and metacognition. Before I begin, I want to emphasize that mini-c is an absolutely wonderful end goal on its own. Advancing up the Cs is largely about becoming more creative *as perceived and consumed by other people*. It is perfectly fine to not care about what other people think, or to care only about what a small number of people think. Much of the second half of this book is devoted to the many benefits of creativity, and they are just as true for mini-c as they are for Big-C. There are so many reasons to be creative, and a vast number of them have nothing to do with anyone other than the creator.

I also want to note that the idea of different levels of creativity has a certain amount of subjectivity inseparably involved in it. When exactly does someone cross the border from mini-c to little-c? Well, it's not like a frog jumping from one lily pad to another. Like so many concepts in creativity, the path from mini-c to little-c is more akin to someone slowly turning a dimmer switch brighter and brighter in a dark room. At what point is the room officially light?

That said, receiving good feedback and then using it to improve is a pretty good strategy. I have been lucky enough to benefit from feedback on my writing throughout my life; one mentor who stands out is T. (Tom) Coraghessan Boyle. He taught the advanced creative writing classes at the University of Southern California, but when I entered as an eager first-year student I didn't want to wait until I was an advanced student. So I camped outside his office door and finally corralled him. I asked: "Do you need an assistant or helper?"

Boyle asked me if I knew anything about Kellogg (of cereal fame). By one of those rare and glorious coincidences, two weeks

22 A. S. Kaufman, 2009.

earlier I had read an *Uncle John's Bathroom Reader*[23] that contained a brief essay on the rivalry between Kellogg and Post. Without blinking, I was able to speak with some level of credibility on the topic. I became Boyle's research assistant for the next four years. As an aside, I should note that Boyle remains one of the coolest people I've ever known. He had a plume of striking red hair and a goatee, a silver ear clip, and a skull ring. He wore leather jackets and bright red tennis shoes. Boyle was like no one I had ever met; he was exactly what you would want a famous writer to be like.

His book on Kellogg would become *The Road to Wellville*,[24] which became a hit in the literary world. It was turned into a movie starring Anthony Hopkins, Matthew Broderick, and John Cusack that somehow missed all the book's charm and quirk. As his assistant, I tracked down quotations, historical details, and occasional gloriously random information (such as the direction you would be facing when you left the train station in Battle Creek, Michigan, in 1907).

Boyle's astounding generosity with his time became the most amazing perk of the position. I spent so much time in his office, absorbing advice and stories. He regularly turned away journalists; his office hours were devoted to his students. My favorite story was the one he told my parents when they came to visit me. He talked about a friend of his who spent his twenties living in his parents' basement doing three things: lifting weights, drinking milk, and trying to write. I can hear Boyle's pause and then his question: Do you know where he is now? My parents and I waited, entranced. Was this person a Pulitzer Prize winner now? No. His friend, Boyle said, was still living in his parents' basement – lifting weights, drinking milk, and trying to write.

He also read my work and gave feedback. I did not remember just how many of my stories he critiqued until a few years ago, when I stumbled across his notes on my work in a large cardboard box. His insights were incisive and brutally honest. I still remember his feedback on what would become my first published story: "Nope. Very skillfully done, but no dice. No, sir. Nope." I have many thoughts in looking over his comments; one is how spot-on he was. You might think that, because the story he critiqued here was published, he was wrong... but he wasn't. It's a terrible piece, accepted by a tiny literary magazine. I think if I made myself read it again today, I would spontaneously combust.

[23] The Bathroom Readers' Institute, 1989. [24] Boyle, 1993.

Boyle's comments represent great examples of how to give good feedback on creative work. It's important to note, first of all, that giving appropriate feedback is *hard*. The easiest thing is to offer bland platitudes or vague praise, neither of which helps in any palpable way.[25] Extremely harsh feedback, especially when it is directed at a product that is important to the creator, can actually cause feelings of shame. People can feel so mortified that they can lose their passion for creating[26]. Yet if a creator hears only undeserved compliments, any honest feedback eventually encountered can become devastating. There is a sweet spot that Beghetto and I called the Goldilocks Principle[27] and that exists between being too harsh and too soft. My student Amanda Osmanlli, upon reading a draft of this book and offering comments, reminded me of when she rehearsed her first research presentation to me. I apparently ended up shifting the conversation around to discussing a museum that specialized in terrible art.[28] I seem not to have mastered the Goldilocks Principle myself.

What else made Boyle's critiques of my work so helpful? His comments were always directed at the work, not at me. Feedback that focuses on you as a person tends to have less impact (good or bad).[29] Boyle's feedback was constructive and informational, which are hallmarks of what good comments should be. They should help someone feel competent even in the face of criticism.[30] One repeated theme I noticed, for example, is that I was able to write a short-short story (two or three pages), but I tended to run short. For one story, Boyle wrote, "A moment captured... But I think this could do with a little less brevity – especially in building up the final scene, just a bit, to locate us, and perhaps slowing down the earlier pages just a hair to give us a fuller picture of the characters. One more page?" Nearly thirty years later, I am still struggling with this core issue. I undershoot. If I am asked to write a 7,500-word chapter, I'll turn in 6,500 words. I know from first-hand experience that editors much prefer a piece that is too short rather than too long, but I wish I naturally struck a better balance with length and depth. In writing this very book, I had to revise and revise and revise; if I am not careful, I write in shorthand and jump over topics and concepts that are important and needed if one is to understand what follows.

[25] Hattie & Timberlay 2007. [26] Beghetto, 2014. [27] Kaufman & Beghetto, 2009.
[28] Frank & Sacco, 2008. [29] Holinger & Kaufman, 2018. [30] Ligon et al., 2012.

There are a number of factors that can make feedback more conducive to creativity (and, thus, can nudge one from mini-c to little-c). For one, feedback should be sought out and desired by the creator. Because I was eager to hear what Boyle thought, his suggestions may have had an even bigger effect. Boyle's comments were also open in how they let me respond. Again, this style was a boon; if someone feels as though they are being too closely monitored or controlled, even encouraging feedback can reduce creativity. However, there is no one perfect route; somebody who is rather shy and neurotic is likely to be less creative just by anticipating feedback.[31] All things considered, if a friend shows you their creative work and asks for honest advice, your best bet would be along the lines of "I really like this part. I think if you added this aspect or that thought it might be even better. Maybe check out this related thought about how this other idea might add to your stuff?"

As always, people are complicated. Some people have a strong need for order and structure. They want to know what someone thinks. Ambiguity and uncertainty drive them crazy. Heck, maybe I'm describing you right now. In these cases, the type of feedback does not matter as much. They just want feedback – any type of feedback.[32] I remember in high school I called up a girl, gathered all my courage, and asked her out. There was a long silence, and then she said that she didn't think her parents would let her go out. I stared at the corded yellow phone (now an antique) and, with the grace of a buffalo, persisted. What if her parents might let her go out? Then would she be interested? There was an even longer silence before I heard a soft but unmistakable "No." Sometimes uncertainty can be your friend.

Mini-c to Little-c: Metacognition

Quality feedback helps you increase your metacognition. Metacognition is, in essence, how you think about your own thinking.[33] Those who have strong metacognitive abilities are able to evaluate their own work, have insight into their learning process, and regulate their progress on an activity.[34] In a cruel or poetic twist, someone with high metacognition tends to also be a better performer. The smarter you are, the more likely you will be able to better predict

[31] Chamorro-Premuzic & Reichenbacher, 2008. [32] Slijkhuis et al., 2013.
[33] Flavell, 1979. [34] Everson & Tobias, 1998.

how well you do on a test of your knowledge.[35] Unfortunately, this tendency means that people who are not terribly good at an activity are also not aware that they are bad. Think of the people who go on talent shows with no discernible abilities. Once upon a time their silently mocking audiences would have been limited to a high school auditorium; now they risk the wrath of the world on live television. Perhaps even worse than sucking at something is not knowing that you suck.[36]

The concept of metacognition applies to creativity as well. Everyone has the ability at some level to understand what they can be creative in and what they would be better off avoiding,[37] assuming a minimal level of intelligence.[38] Understanding your personal creative strengths and weaknesses (both in general and your performance on a specific project) is one component of creative metacognition.[39] For example, I know I am a decent writer. When I collaborate on a research project with others, I often volunteer (or am coerced) to help draft the literature review or the discussion and interpretation of the results. I also know that, although I am better at psychological statistics than most random people, I am mediocre at best by comparison with others in my field. I try to team up with people who excel at making numbers sing. Assuming there's some validity to what I just said, that's a certain level of creative metacognition.

Consider, too, my approach to writing this book. I chose to use an "academic light" tone, aiming for a conversational style yet backing up what I say with unobtrusive references. I've used this approach before and enjoyed it.[40] Yet there are many other formats I could have tried. I debated trying a layperson's book or a more traditional monograph, but chose this middle ground. Hopefully I made a good decision. I can always turn to feedback from trusted colleagues and from my editor to either reinforce or challenge the creative decisions I have made in my writing approach and the content covered. Of course, if I have a true failure of creative metacognition, it might be all-encompassing. Maybe I'm so bad at judging my strengths and weaknesses that being a creativity scholar in the first place was a woefully misguided choice. Heck, perhaps I should have devoted my career instead to inventing a new color (like dark green but more joyful, and with a streak of pasta) or a new emotion

[35] Dunning et al., 2003; Kruger & Dunning, 1999. [36] Kaufman et al., 2010.
[37] J. C. Kaufman et al., 2016. [38] Karwowski et al., 2020.
[39] Kaufman & Beghetto, 2013. [40] I.e., J. C. Kaufman, 2009; 2016a.

(that feeling you get when you take two Tylenols but then realize an hour later that they were fiber pills).

There's a second component to creative metacognition: knowing when to be creative. As much as I am in favor of creativity, it's not always the best decision. If you're going to a doctor for a routine procedure – let's say, a colonoscopy – you don't want your doctor to decide to be creative. You've drunk that disgusting goop the night before, you are hopefully under some type of anesthesia or sedation, and all you want is to have it finished so you can go home. The last thing you want to hear is your doctor say, "These fiber optic cameras are so small! I bet I could fit five of them up there! I could get so many different angles and views as to make a collage of your colon and get some insights into the nature of polyps." Such a moment is not an opportunity for your doctor to be creative. However, if mid-procedure you start vomiting copious amounts of blood, you very much want your doctor to kick her creativity into high gear. You want someone who can think of many different possible reasons why you might be gushing blood and, ideally, fix it as quickly as possible.

If all creative people flung themselves chaotically into all projects like that ("Let's teach your kindergarteners how to vomit on cue!" "Why not land the plane upside down?"), then it would be quite understandable if being creative were an active stigma. Even in the real world, though, there are often hidden biases against creative people. Teachers will commonly say that they like creative students, but then will admit that they don't actually know what that means[41] or that they dislike specific behaviors associated with creativity.[42] Employees who are more creative (or who are simply thought to be more creative, regardless of whether they really are) are seen as being poor bets to be successful leaders.[43] One study looked at what is associated with company executives using words related to creativity and innovation during quarterly conference calls with investors. Their profits rose over the next three quarters, which sounds great – more creativity speak, more money! However, the immediate impact was negative. The firms performed worse in the market in the days after the call.[44]

I think that one reason for these negative feelings is the preponderance of people with low creative metacognition. It's not necessarily that we don't like creative people; we don't like folks who

[41] Aljughaiman & Mowrer-Reynolds, 2005. [42] Westby & Dawson, 1995.
[43] Mueller et al., 2011. [44] Haselhuhn et al., 2022.

think they are creative when they are not. We don't like those who insist on marching to their own beat – even when everyone is judged on synchronicity.

We're used to the idea that creativity should always be encouraged in everyone. It's easy to think that the best way to encourage creativity is by treating everyone like Batman. Bruce Wayne was an ordinary but rich guy who became a superhero with tools and help. He used technology and gadgets and other engineering wizardry to build himself up, just as many people need and can benefit from tricks and tips to become more creative. But we also have to realize that some people are more like Superman, who has naturally amazing superpowers. That's great; but in the real world it would be like that creative colonoscopy (or, you could say... a pain in the butt). Superman sneezes and blows you into the next town. He helps you move and accidentally crushes your favorite couch. He tries to impress you by taking you flying and drops you into Cleveland. The way in which Superman succeeded was by learning how to be Clark Kent. He can be the bumbling, achingly normal Clark – who functions just fine in everyday life – and then zap into Superman just in time to save the day. If you're someone who's lucky enough to have a creative prowess akin to Superman's, it may be just as important for you to learn how to harness, control, and even silence your active imagination as it would be for most people to learn how to be more creative.[45]

So, speaking of learning how to be more creative... This book isn't one of the helpful (but often deceptive) ones that offer you foolproof tips on becoming creative. But we do know a good bit about the creative process. Once you're plugging along at the little-c level, you are likely involved in some aspect of this process, even if you don't know it. As I move on to little-c in the next chapter, I'll also talk about the most important stages of this process.

[45] Kaufman & Beghetto, 2013.

3 HOW EVERYDAY MAGIC WORKS

As much as we associate creativity with genius (or at least with well-known creators), most of what we know about how we create is from the little-c schlubs. The people who are creative in an everyday way tend to be the ones whom we researchers ask to fill out our surveys, reflect on their creativity, solve our challenges and problems, answer our questions, and keep track of their creative activities.

There are several reasons for the dominance of the little-cs. To start with, there's a solid chance it doesn't matter. Some argue that the creative process in geniuses is quite similar to anyone else's process.[1] It is also reasonable to claim that it is preferable to study little-c, given that most people are going to be closer to little-c than to Big-C (although there just might be a fourth "c"... stay tuned). "Don't take advice from people like me, who have gotten very lucky," comedian Bo Burnham has said. "We're very biased. You know, Taylor Swift telling you to follow your dreams is like a lottery winner telling you, 'Liquidize your assets, buy Powerball tickets, it works!'"[2] Who knows if the thoughts and behaviors of geniuses or other extremely talented folks would extrapolate to us riff-raff?

Unsurprisingly, there are also dominating forces of reality that come into play. Let's consider the following genius-level writers: Shakespeare, Emily Dickinson, Agatha Christie, Mark Twain, Jane Austen, James Baldwin, Ernest Hemingway, Virginia Woolf, Pablo

[1] Weisberg, 2021. [2] Holub, 2016.

Neruda, Toni Morrison, and T. S. Eliot. This diverse group of writers spans eras, genres, and formats. Yet everyone in this group has one attribute in common: they won't be part of any of my experiments. I assume the reason is either that I have accidentally offended them, or else that they are dead. It is important to note that it is possible to study such geniuses in the historiometric way, as Dean Keith Simonton does, which is to gather information about their lives, careers, works, and writings.[3] However, unless you're analyzing old diary entries that happen to talk about how they create, process-related findings will be hard.

This is not just the whole "dead people offer few new thoughts" issue either. We can (and will) discuss which living people might qualify... but they usually have better things to do. As a creativity researcher, I've had the amazing benefit of getting to know a lot of artistic people who I'd argue are close to genius. I've enjoyed talking with writers, actors, composers, directors, and many others whose work I truly admire. But, although we chat about creativity informally, I'm not going to be springing any surveys on them. It would feel uncouth.

So most of what we know about how we create is from everyday creators (often college students). But if there's limited scope in who is studied, there is a lot of depth. There are many, many different theories and models of the creative process. I am not going to go over all of them, or even over most of them. But I will go over some key aspects; I will also tie them into some common measures of creativity.

Incubation and Insight

One of my hobbies is collecting older signatures, letters, and documents. Its roots are in my childhood, when I would write to various celebrities; in a world before eBay, many of them wrote back. I have several types of people I enjoy collecting, from signers of the Declaration of Independence to legends of musical theater. Scholars of creativity and intelligence form another such group. One of my favorites is a letter written by Graham Wallas, one of the cofounders (with George Bernard Shaw) of the London School of Economics. The letter's purpose, incidentally, was to introduce an investor to William

[3] Simonton, 2009, 2018c.

Filene (before his son would open up his basement to bargain hunters around the world). Wallas holds a special place in creativity scholarship. In 1926 he proposed the first model of the creative process that anyone still discusses in polite company.[4] For those keeping track, that's after Laura Chassell's pioneering work on creativity assessment and before J. P. Guilford's big APA speech.

Wallas' model had four main stages, but the first one was in essence "start working" and the last one was "go test it out." The two stages that are more interesting are the middle two, incubation and insight. Incubation happens after you've begun your problem-solving journey. You've done the needed reading, research, and resource gathering. You've started. At a certain point, though, you're going to get stuck or tired, or else you will simply need to focus on a different task. This period, during which you are not actively focused on your problem, is the incubation stage; when you get the idea you need, that is the moment of insight.

There is a very big difference between incubation as it might occur in real life and incubation as it is studied in the lab. I'll use my own writing of this section as an example. I was stuck a little at first, until I thought of my Wallas letter as a starting point. The words flowed reasonably well until I hit the concept of incubation (which I acknowledge means that I was actively writing for about a paragraph and a half). I then went back and read other stuff I'd written about Wallas' model. Then I looked up papers on PsycInfo and read through about six or seven. At this point, I could envision what I might write in the paragraphs that would follow. However, I couldn't see the part that would bridge the initial introduction of incubation and the actual getting into some of the nitty-gritty studies – especially since they seemed to be a little contradictory at times. I decided to try to find a book I'd written years ago where I thought I might have touched on some related studies, but I ended up instead finding a folder from a long-aborted project filled with interesting stories about psychology history. Thinking that I might find some relevant anecdote, I opened that document and began reading. One of the stories made me go to Wikipedia to check on a piece of information, which I then texted my dad about. We went back and forth a little bit, at which point my youngest son came into the room. I played on my phone for a while and decided to read through the

[4] Wallas, 1926.

original papers again. It struck me that the way they studied incubation was nothing like my own process, in part because, when I am creative, I am more likely to be writing, theorizing, or synthesizing; I'm not solving fun and quick puzzles. Well, I thought, what if I highlight the difference between my own creative process and how it is studied? And so we are here.

Most studies take place in the lab (or, more recently, online). People are given a creativity task that is usually very brief and artificial, and then an equally brief time to incubate. As incredibly minor as my own "a-ha!" moment from the last paragraph was, it nonetheless looms large over most of the experimental insights on offer. Perhaps the type that I favor least is that of visual insight problems, as they are called;[5] this type is exemplified by the nine-dot problem. A person is shown nine dots arranged in a square (three rows of three dots each), then asked to connect the dots without lifting the pencil off the paper. The correct answer is to draw "outside the box" and extend the lines beyond the assumed confines of the problem.[6] This problem is used so often that I genuinely wonder how many psychology undergraduates have taken it multiple times, ruining subsequent studies because they already know the answer. In the nine-dot problem there is one single correct answer, which certainly requires intelligence and critical thinking; the amount of creativity required is questionable.

I know it sounds like I'm criticizing these studies (let's not mince words: I am), but it doesn't mean that I have any better solution. I'd rather research be done than entire topics be ignored because they seem too difficult to study. At that rate, creativity may have remained a mystical and shadowy topic. All this being said, an interesting question in the research literature is whether it is better to incubate by doing a similar activity or a different one. So, if I get stuck writing this chapter, is it better for me to write something else, or should I go back to my sixth-grade shop days and try to carve and varnish a wooden candleholder? One study[7] suggest that it is better to do a different type of task, but all participants were forced to switch after a specific amount of time. A later study[8] gave participants a chance to choose whether they wanted to change what they were doing and reached opposite results: working on a task in the same domain increased creativity. I for one tend to keep writing but work

[5] Sio & Ormerod, 2009. [6] Kershaw & Ohlsson, 2004. [7] Gilhooly et al., 2013.
[8] Madjar et al., 2019.

on a different project when I am stuck. Another study, which used funny YouTube videos as a potential distraction, suggests that a moderate level of procrastination may boost incubation.[9] In that case I am going to go watch some videos of derpy animals before writing the next paragraph.

It is quite hard to study real-life *eureka* moments, which aren't guaranteed to come in a two-week span, let alone a ten-minute span. In discussing such moments of insight, people often talk about getting ideas in the shower or right before falling asleep. I sometimes get ideas in that netherworld before sleep; driving is also a good time for me (perhaps this is a reason why I felt so uncreative when telecommuting during the pandemic, although my bet is on a number of other factors). A retrospective study asked people to reflect on their insights, and eight types of situations emerged as most likely to yield an "a-ha!" The three I've mentioned – shower, bedtime, and transportation – were on the list. Work, home, and quiet moments seem a little too vague to be helpful; the other two were exercise and being around nature.[10] My other big time for creative insights is during faculty meetings. I'm sure this bit of information will come as a shock to my colleagues, who likely don't remember me attending such meetings at all.

Solving the Right Problem

Although Wallas' model is still used and studied, there are many others. You get more than five thousand results when you look up "creative process" in PsycInfo. If you try Google Scholar, you risk your laptop growing a hand so it can slap you in the face. That said, most models are in some way derived from parts of Guilford's structure of intellect theory.[11] There are four foundational stages that are common to many of these slightly different approaches (including design thinking,[12] which has developed a life of its own): problem finding, divergent thinking (DT), convergent thinking, and solution validation.[13]

Sometimes a label captures a concept pretty well. Problem finding is, well, finding the problem.[14] Problem finding may include searching for the relevant information,[15] identifying potential

[9] Shin & Grant, 2021. [10] Ovington et al., 2018. [11] Guilford, 1956.
[12] Brown, 2008. [13] Cropley, 2015a; Sawyer, 2012. [14] Abdulla et al., 2020.
[15] Harms et al., 2020.

limitations or constraints,[16] and specifically defining the problem.[17] At the most fundamental level, it is making sure that you are solving the right problem. We aren't taught this part too often.[18] Think about any mathematical word problems you were given in school; they always started by presenting you with a problem. "Chloe wants to calculate the area of a triangle but only has a toothpick and a block of cheese." "Bernard is traveling on a train to Cincinnati that is going 70 miles per hour and he wants to know the exact time his train will pass through Columbus." In real life, we don't always have problems handed to us; if we are not careful, it is easy to solve the wrong problem.

Here's an example. We have an African gray parrot named Eliza. Although one of the smarter animals out there, such birds can mimic nearly any sound. I am sure that, when we first decided to get an African gray parrot, the idea of a breathing tape recorder struck us as exciting. In reality, she is a creature who can conjure up the exact timbre of answering machine beeps, children's shrieks, barks, resigned groans, wheezed coughs, and loud, bleating farts. One day I tasked myself with getting Eliza to somehow stop imitating the sound of the carbon monoxide alarm. I waited in the room with her and each time she would blare out the shrill tones of the alarm, I would try to give her what animal trainers call a least reinforcing stimulus (LRS), which gives as little positive reinforcement as possible.[19] Yet, for all my efforts, I noticed that Eliza not only kept it up but also somehow began to throw her voice: the alarm sounds seemed to be coming from behind me. I suddenly realized that I was solving the wrong problem. I didn't need to teach Eliza to stop making an annoying sound; I needed to replace a dead carbon monoxide alarm.

Problem finding is part of our everyday lives even if we are not aware of it. When you try to balance your household budget, you engage in problem finding. Do you need to pick up more hours at work? Cut down on eating out? Look for a roommate? Stop using original Picassos as scratch paper? Before you add a second job, you need to make sure that someone isn't hacking into your bank account. Once you believe that you have found the right problem to solve, you dive into the guts of Guilford's contributions: divergent and convergent thinking.[20]

[16] Damadzic et al., 2022; Medeiros et al., 2014. [17] Reiter-Palmon & Robinson, 2009.
[18] Medeiros et al., 2018; Reiter-Palmon & Illies, 2004. [19] Ramirez, 2019.
[20] Guilford, 1956.

Divergent and Convergent Thinking

Guilford included creative abilities into his theory of intelligence as part of "divergent production." Problem solving was represented by "convergent production," although he acknowledged that the two may often overlap. I teach divergent and convergent thinking all the time and I typically give the quick summary that DT consists in coming up with many different possible ideas while convergent thinking consists in selecting the best idea to pursue. Guilford's original conception was a little different (which is a backhanded way of admitting that I've been teaching it a bit wrong for more than a decade). Convergent thinking most often has "one conclusion or answer that is regarded as unique, and thinking is channeled or controlled in the direction of that answer… In divergent thinking, on the other hand, there is much searching or going off in various directions. This is most clearly seen when there is no unique conclusion. The distinction is not so clear in some problem-solving tests, in which there must be and usually is some divergent thinking or search as well as ultimate convergence toward the solution. But the processes are logically and operationally separable, even in such activities."[21]

Although Guilford introduces convergent thinking first (in that paragraph and in the article itself), their role in creativity is typically portrayed in the opposite manner. The one–two punch of divergent and convergent thinking goes by other names, depending on the field or source. Some models of creative problem-solving call them "idea generation" and "idea evaluation,"[22] whereas some applied approaches use "idea finding" and "solution finding."[23] Whatever they are called, the two stages are typically at the heart of most theories of the creative process. The person solving a problem thinks of many different possible solutions (divergent), then selects the best solution to pursue (convergent). Both stages are important.[24]

In the real world, let's say that you've decided you want to eat better. How many different ideas might you generate? While you are engaged in DT, you might come up with anything from "eat more kale" to "eat less ice cream," "replace full-fat tasty ice cream with low-fat less tasty frozen yogurt," "snack less," and "skip dinner" (don't do that). Even when your problem is very specific – "I have a hole in my

[21] Ibid, p. 274. [22] E.g., Mumford et al., 1991. [23] Osborn, 1963. [24] Cropley, 2006.

bathroom wall" – there can be a wide array of solutions you could derive. Some might be very practical, if dull ("buy some spackle"), whereas others might be unique but silly ("collect my saliva for two weeks; shave my terrier; mix the hair and spit together and let it congeal; use that goop to fill the hole"). This part is similar to brainstorming.

When you think convergently, you go over all your suggestions and select the one that suits your purposes best. As you narrow in on the best idea, there may be many variables that go through your head. Maybe you want to choose the easiest answer, or the hardest, or the one that you think is the most creative, or else the one you think will be the cheapest. Our later ideas tend to be a little more creative,[25] so maybe you want to inch away from your first responses.

Many theories of the creative process have these two stages as their foundation. I'll describe some of the best known examples. The geneplore (generate and explore) model emerged out of the creative cognition approach.[26] Someone first generates different ideas, then explores them. In this model, the generative stage involves a person imagining, in his or her mind, a potential solution (this is called a "preinventive structure"). The person then considers constraints on the eventual desired outcome in order to determine the best option. A memory-focused framework (memory in creative ideation) begins with a person's searching through memory, then constructing different possible ideas. The final two stages consist in evaluating the potential ideas, first for novelty and then for effectiveness.[27] Finally, the blind variation and selective retention (BVSR) theory gives this concept an evolutionary spin.[28] Blind variation refers to idea generation over a vast period of time; the process includes random or spontaneous ideas. Those that are worthwhile or helpful are selectively retained over time. The core concept that a person needs to think both in a focused, analytical manner and in a defocused, associative manner recurs in creativity research.[29] This central notion is comparable to Daniel Kahneman's System 1 and System 2 thinking – one being quick and rather emotional, the other slower and rather logical.[30] Kahneman's work has had a wee bit more impact than that of creativity researchers, given the Nobel Prize aura and all that.

[25] Beaty & Silvia, 2012. [26] Finke et al., 1992. [27] Benedek et al., 2023.
[28] Simonton, 1999; 2011; 2022. [29] Pringle & Sowden, 2017; Vartanian, 2009.
[30] Kahneman, 2011.

The final stage of most creative problem-solving models, solution validation, is perhaps the most straightforward: you try to test out your idea. In other words, "do the thing and see if it works." If it does, you can bask in your accomplishment. If it is a spectacular failure, you go back to an earlier stage. You might have the wrong problem, or never thought of a good idea, or else perhaps you chose the wrong one.

People may also have preferences for distinct stages, although a lot more work is needed on this point. Some prefer to think of lots of different ideas; others like sorting through ideas and picking their favorite.[31] I have informally found that a lot of the people who like convergent thinking the most tend to think of themselves as less creative than the people who prefer DT. Indeed, DT is sometimes (incorrectly) conflated with creativity itself; most types of creativity-training exercises focus on this stage.[32] Perhaps for this reason, DT is the basis for the most common type of creativity measure (besides self-report).[33] Let us take a brief detour to unpack this type because, when I discuss research (particularly in the second half of this book), different findings will be associated with different tests at several points. Plus, it's fun.

Paul Torrance and Divergent Thinking Tests

Although several scholars developed early versions of DT tests,[34] the most well-known and complete one is the Torrance Tests of Creative Thinking (TTCT).[35] Its creator, Paul Torrance, is a legend in creativity research. I have many personal connections to him. As department chair, he hired my father at the University of Georgia the year I was born. When I began studying creativity in graduate school, my father encouraged me to reach out to Torrance. I thought it was absurd – why would he bother to respond to some kid? – but I received from him a warm, encouraging letter. We stayed in touch until his passing.

One thing I've learned in my life is that it doesn't matter whom you're talking about – there's always someone who will say something nasty behind their back. Think of the nicest person you've ever met – and there will be somebody somewhere saying what a jerk that person is. I have gotten to know and work with many of

[31] Reiter-Palmon & Kaufman, 2018. [32] Vernon et al., 2016.
[33] Callahan et al., 1995; Snyder et al., 2019.
[34] Getzels & Jackson, 1962; Wallach & Kogan, 1965. [35] Torrance, 1974, 2008.

Torrance's former students and with legions of people who knew him. I have never heard a bad comment. Two different former students told me (separately) that when they were in dire straits he paid their tuition for one semester out of his own pocket. I later found out from his longtime colleague Bonnie Cramond (who later became director of the Torrance Center for Creative Studies and Talent Development) that Torrance's benevolence went even further. Many students received "stipends" that actually came from him, and they did not find out until about it he was audited by the Internal Revenue Service years later.

Torrance spent much of his career in the deep South – especially during the 1960s, a time when many people were on the wrong side of history regarding civil rights. Indeed, many early programs of the "talented and gifted" (TAG) type were established to maintain segregation.[36] Torrance saw creativity tests as a way to enhance equity and pushed for their use in gifted programs. He was a man ahead of his time.[37] I may occasionally criticize his professional contributions, but he was unsurpassed as a human being.

Torrance's tests include both verbal and figural components. The verbal tests offer an open-ended task or question, then ask you to give as many different possible responses (e.g., by naming, asking, suggesting, or answering) in a specified amount of time (usually a couple of minutes or more). For example, one question could be: "What are all the different uses you can think of for a toothpick?" Let's imagine that someone wrote:

To pick your teeth
A crutch for a mouse
To stab a butterfly
To build a house
To build a hut
To build an apartment
To flap your biscuits

There are three different values for which this item would be scored. The first is fluency, which is reflected in the number of responses. In this case, the participant gave six responses that make sense and one that is completely random. The random one would be discarded – remember, creativity means being new and task-

[36] Ford, 2003. [37] Grantham, 2013.

appropriate – hence six would be the basis for your score. Fluency represents quantity, your creative horsepower. Some IQ tests include a less creative version of fluency, in which they ask you, let's say, to list as many items of a kind as you can: as many animals whose name starts with a C, or as many haberdasheries whose name starts with an I.[38]

The next score is for flexibility, which is reflected in how many different categories your responses span (or, sometimes, in how many times you switch to a different category).[39] Here you would have four categories represented, because a house, a hut, and an apartment are all in the same category. The last score would be for originality. The TTCT has a large database of responses, and you would receive credit for answers that are not commonly given. In this case, a crutch for a mouse would very likely be a quite rare response. Stabbing a butterfly might be; the rest are probably pretty common. The TTCT scores originality on the basis of statistical rarity; in order for a response to count as original, it needs to be given by less than a certain percentage of participants (which can vary from one percent to five or ten percent).[40] DT tests used in research studies sometimes use human raters[41] and, more recently, automated scoring by computer.[42]

The TTCT figural test has you modify shapes and expand on drawings. These tests are also scored for fluency and originality, but not flexibility. They, too, yield three additional scores. One is elaboration, which is about the amount of detail you use. Resistance to premature closure scores your capacity to keep a drawing incomplete; it is related to the ability to tolerate ambiguity,[43] which is a marker of creativity.[44] Finally, some of the items have you give a caption to your drawing; these can be scored for abstractness of titles. There is a difference between titling a picture "A lion with a thorn in his paw who is being assisted by a little mouse" and titling it "Future reciprocity." The figural TTCT also offers a checklist for thirteen creative strengths, such as humor and emotional expressiveness.

There are many critiques of the reliability or validity of the TTCT or similar measures,[45] although many studies certainly offer support,[46] I have mixed feelings about the TTCT or any other DT tests. Speaking broadly, the fact that it's been more than sixty years and

[38] Kaufman et al., 2011. [39] Acar & Runco, 2017. [40] Reiter-Palmon et al., 2019.
[41] Silvia et al., 2009; Silvia et al., 2008. [42] Acar et al., 2021; Cropley & Marrone, 2022.
[43] Liu, 2015. [44] Zenasni et al., 2008. [45] Baer, 2011a, 2011b. [46] Plucker, 1999b.

we're still primarily relying on the same basic type of measure feels stagnant, as if you were watching your neighbor standing outside and polishing a Ford Mustang, listening to the Grateful Dead, and dropping acid. But then again, most key assessments in psychology (such as IQ tests) are a bit too similar to measures from decades past.

DT tests are artificial and their connection to real-world creativity can be inconsistent. Relying exclusively on DT tests seems to ignore many different types of creativity (such as science and music). The decision to make existing knowledge as unimportant as possible in many DT studies is understandable, but it may limit generalizability to how people solve problems in the real world.[47] There have been domain-specific DT tests created for research purposes that focus for example on history,[48] mathematics,[49] or real-life problems.[50] I am curious about work on this topic and would like to see more of it. As it is, such explorations of DT in different domains have yet to gain popularity: they are nowhere near the classics on that score. In addition, they would bring new issues. For one, there would be the question of which domains should be chosen for testing (which I will discuss in more detail in the next chapter). For another, more realistic DT questions tend to yield responses that are more appropriate but less original.[51]

Beyond content, tight time limits (particularly when DT is measured in empirical studies) don't help. I understand why the TTCT, so often used in high-stakes situations, is specifically timed (indeed, so are IQ tests). In my view, it is even more frustrating when studies that aim to make larger statements about creativity choose to rely solely on a DT task in which people are allotted only two or three minutes. It is common for creativity researchers to talk about how we should use batteries of different types of measures, but much less common for us to actually do it.[52]

Being able to crank out lots of ideas in response to a hypothetical question, while being as original as possible, is a very specific dimension of creativity. It's not representative of the way we usually think. My friend Tom Ward and his colleagues[53] have a model they call "the path of least resistance." In essence, if I ask you to give me an example of something – a baseball player, a fruit, a color, a US city – then you're more likely to give an obvious, standard response. You're

[47] Yang et al., 2022. [48] Diakidoy & Spanoudis, 2002. [49] Meier et al., 2021.
[50] Okuda et al., 1991. [51] Runco et al., 2005. [52] Plucker, 2022.
[53] Ward, 1995; Ward et al., 2000; Ward & Kolomyts, 2010.

much more likely to say "Derek Jeter, apple, red, Chicago" than to say "John Balaz, durian, puce, Enid." John Balaz, by the way, was a coach at my high school who played major league baseball for two years with the Angels. That was – and still is – the coolest thing in the world.

If I ask you – as they did in a study – to imagine what animal life might look like on other planets, the odds are strong that you will stick to the same basic components that we see on our earthling animal friends. You'll picture alien animals with fairly normal-looking eyes, ears, and legs. It won't matter if I ask you to imagine an animal on a planet that is specifically different from our Earth.[54] Unsurprisingly, this response is not restricted to animals; we stick to what we know when we imagine a lot of stuff.[55] There are, in fairness, ways in which this tendency might be combatted; a different study found that, if students were shown an especially creative example before taking a DT test and drawing pictures, their creativity increased.[56]

Incidentally, there are reasons why we take this path of least resistance – beyond pure laziness. Our responses may be less original, but they are usually more practical.[57] And here lies the rub with the field's focus on DT. To be creative, as I've mentioned, we also need the metacognition involved in knowing when to be original and when to stick to the tried and true.[58] There are many, many other variables – including dimensions of creative thinking[59] – that are also crucial. Yet DT's intense focus on fluency has produced a ripple effect. Scholars overemphasize fluency at the expense of research on different components of creativity.

That said, DT tests, particularly the TTCT, absolutely measure something. They predict some degree of personal (if not professional) creative achievement across many years.[60] A recent meta-analysis that included nearly 15,000 people found that the TTCT and related DT tests are significantly (if weakly) connected to self-reported creative achievements.[61] If they are considered a measure of creative potential as opposed to creativity[62] (which Torrance always intended),[63] that mollifies me a bit. Also, a variety of advances are being made that I find exciting. For example, a computer game called Physics Playground[64] makes players create basic machines or draw objects

[54] Ward & Sifonis, 1997. [55] Ward et al., 2002. [56] Yi et al., 2015. [57] Ward, 2008.
[58] Kaufman & Beghetto, 2013. [59] Boldt, 2019. [60] Runco et al., 2010.
[61] Said-Metwaly et al., 2022. [62] Acar & Runco, 2019. [63] Cramond et al., 1999.
[64] Shute et al., 2019.

with the goal of propelling a ball into a balloon.[65] Fluency, flexibility, and originality are scored in real time via "stealth assessment."[66] Another twist on the classic concept is that a person, instead of being given one prompt and then generating many different responses, receives many rapid prompts and is allowed to make only one response. Fluency is measured not in quantity but in response time[67] (and yes, I am aware I was just criticizing the TTCT for being timed; I can shrug off cognitive dissonance as a snake sheds its skin).

Remote Associations

A last tidbit (which introduces a creativity measure I like even less): one way you might think of new ideas is by using associative thinking, which means being able to bounce from one concept or word to another.[68] So, if you are given the word "dog," you might jump to "bark," "hot" (hot dog), "cat," "pet," "wood" (dogwood), or "wolf." Maybe you have some personal associations; maybe your childhood dog's name was Bowser, or you have a poodle, or you live on Dog Lane Road. People who can make more remote associations are considered to be more creative. The Remote Associates Test (RAT) is a creativity assessment based on these ideas.[69] A person is given three words that are connected to a fourth, for example fish, mine, and rush, and asked to identify that fourth word. The correct answer here is gold – goldfish, gold mine, gold rush.[70] Other examples are Swiss, cake, and goat (cheese); shelf, worm, and end (book); and jack, dumb, and hole.

I am not a huge fan of the RAT for a number of reasons. It relies heavily on vocabulary and intelligence, to the point that scores on the RAT align more with intelligence than with creativity.[71] It can be argued that this connection is due to the fact that the RAT measures convergent thinking as opposed to DT,[72] but I for one disagree. The RAT is heavily dependent on culture and on being able to understand particular idioms; it also ages very quickly, as phrases such as "party line" or "soda pop" go out of fashion. However, there are new versions that are updated every so often.[73]

I love the idea of associative thinking, but reducing it to compound words makes it noticeably less interesting in its execution. There has been some work on a visual version of the RAT, which

[65] Shute et al., 2016; Shute & Rahimi, 2021. [66] Shute, 2011. [67] Barbot, 2018a, 2019.
[68] Mednick, 1962. [69] Mednick, 1968. [70] Bowden & Jung-Beeman, 2003.
[71] Lee & Therriault, 2013. [72] Lee et al., 2014. [73] Bowden & Jung-Beeman, 2003.

might show pictures of a glove, handle, and pen – the correct answer being a hand, which is used for all three of them.[74] I find it compelling, although it still has the same intelligence-versus-creativity issues as the original.

Why is the RAT still used reasonably often? It's quick to administer, free (if you Google enough, anyway), and quick to score. For fields such as neuroscience, in which every additional minute may cost a great deal of money on equipment use, I do understand why it continues to be chosen[75] (although even in those situations DT tests are more common).[76]

Onto Pro-c

We've moseyed around discussing little-c and the creative process. We've talked about incubation and insight; the fundamental creative stages of divergent and convergent thinking; problem finding; and how components of the creative process have been operationalized in DT tests and in the RAT. Everyday creativity is the marrow that holds everything together. It represents a place where mini-c can be shared with others. It is a perfectly good end goal by itself. It is also a way to continue advancing with your creativity. What happens after little-c? It sure does seem like a pretty big leap to go from little-c to Big-C. Given that the theory is called "the four Cs," you might surmise that Beghetto and I did propose a category between everyday creativity and genius. Indeed, we'll discuss Pro-c in the next chapter.

[74] Olteţeanu & Zunjani, 2020; Toivainen et al., 2019.

[75] Wu et al., 2020.

[76] Benedek et al., 2019.

4 STUMBLING TOWARD GENIUS

As much as we talk about genius, a good amount of what we actually spend our days doing is created by people who will probably end up falling just short (or way short) of that mark. I know I am more likely to read Tana French than William Shakespeare. I can appreciate prestige television, but I gravitate toward crime shows. I love classic movies, but I'll put on the latest mediocre Netflix time travel flick first.

The people who invented the ideas that enable me to write this book on a laptop and to look up papers on my Wi-Fi are undoubtedly Big-C. But the actual laptop and software I'm using are equally (if not even more) the work of many top-notch computer science professionals whose names I will never know. Where do all of these folks factor in on the creativity landscape?

Between Little and Big

These questions were firmly in our minds after Beghetto and I proposed mini-c. We knew there were still gaps to fill. We considered a few different possible Cs. I remember baby-c being floated around a bit, and I so wanted to come up with seven so we could talk about "sailing the seven Cs" (which was later used by someone else, for a different theory).[1] We ended up with just one more, but it held great meaning for me because of my one-time aspirations to be a creative writer. Still mentored by Boyle, I was taking a creative writing

[1] Lubart, 2017.

seminar in the first semester of my senior year. I remember it was one specific class in which everything crystallized. One of my stories was being workshopped, and the class was unimpressed. Meanwhile they were overpraising another student's story. There were no especially harsh comments. It was less of a sudden thunderbolt and more of a crystallization: I wasn't good enough to become the writer I wanted to be.

Herein lies the crux of the matter: I had implicitly accepted the little-c–Big-C dichotomy. There were the everyday writers, such as the other students in the class, and then there were the writers with a capital W, like Tom Boyle. Boyle is one of the greatest living literary novelists. He's won many awards; my parents' book club has chosen at least three of his works to discuss. People will be reading his novels and stories for many years to come. I was fine being a lowercase writer as long as I had the vague confidence that I might someday cross over to become a Writer. When I lost that belief, I could no longer see a future in which I pursued creative writing as a career.

For the first time, I wasn't sure what I wanted to do when I grew up. When I received the applications for Master of Fine Arts (MFA) creative writing programs, one of them came with a note that read: "Every year we award 20 MFAs in creative writing, and every year there are 25 jobs in the entire country for people with MFAs. If you can do anything but becoming a writer, *do that.*" When I reread the note that evening, I didn't feel inspired or resolute. Instead I thought: *I can do something else.*

As it turned out, I was lucky. I had a double major in psychology and creative writing. I applied in a scattershot manner to graduate schools, for a place in every imaginable discipline of psychology (note to any undergraduates: don't imitate me). I ended up getting into four great schools and went to Yale for a PhD in cognitive psychology under Robert Sternberg. Who knows what the path of trying to succeed in the arts would have taken? We only hear about the success stories; we don't usually hear about people like Boyle's friend, still drinking milk and lifting weights in his parents' basement.

That said... What if I had internalized the idea that there might be a career as a writer between little-c and Big-C? I would return to this issue many times in my life, and ultimately Beghetto and I would propose a fourth C: Pro-c.[2] We conceptualized this stage as

[2] Kaufman & Beghetto, 2009.

the type of expert-level creativity one reaches after years of deliberate practice.[3] If mini-c is a personal spark of imagination and little-c is creativity that others can share and appreciate (think of the food, crafts, and performances at a county fair), then Pro-c is a situation where a creator begins to have an impact on the domain. Pro-c happens when someone gets published, produced, recorded, distributed, or funded. Pro-c happens when your scientific paper, movie, restaurant, invention, or building design starts to influence (or provoke) other people.

Like all the Cs, Pro-c has gradations. I am not claiming that a recording artist who has an extended play album and four digital singles available on Spotify belongs in the same bucket as a musician with multiple top forty songs who has been releasing hit songs since the days of the cassette tape. I like to avoid the bucket concept altogether; I envision the four Cs more as four ascending conveyor belts.

Even within Pro-c, there are many types of creativity that can be overlooked or undervalued. So, for example, the propulsion theory of creative contributions[4] highlights eight different categories of creative works. They range from small incrementations to huge leaps forward. The category I'd like to emphasize, however, is the first one: replication. This type of contribution occurs when someone creates a new thing with the primary goal of reproducing a past work. There is typically some kind of slight spin or twist. Generic medicine is often incredibly similar to brand-name medicine, but cheaper. Robert Ludlum has mastered the art of continuing to write popular thrillers (including at least three in 2023) despite dying in 2001. The Ludlum books of the last two decades have, of course, been written by other people, who are trying their best to imitate the style and plotting of the original books. In psychological science, replication studies are designed to repeat a past study in order to ensure its accuracy and generalizability, while avoiding questionable research practices.[5]

Although replication is presented as the first (or "lowest") category in the model, I feel compelled to note that – as with mini-c – *it still counts*. Replications are still someone's own version of a creative work. A reproduction with no personal touch isn't creative – so if I xeroxed the Mona Lisa, I'm not being creative. But if I paint my own version, trying my best to capture the original, it is

[3] Ericsson et al., 2007; Simonton, 2014a. [4] Sternberg et al., 2001, 2002, 2019.
[5] Lilienfeld, 2017.

meaningful to me. If someone produces only replications, that person is nonetheless creative at some level.

How else might we keep thinking of creativity and expanding our conceptions of what it might include? Another way is by considering the wide variety of possible creative domains.

Categorizing Creativity: By Domain

In general, the higher up the C-ladder you go, the more domain-specific creativity becomes.[6] What do I mean? Don't worry. I will tell you (if this book were an audiobook, this is where I would burst into song, ideally dubbed by Josh Groban).

At the mini-c level, you can be creative in anything. Nuclear engineering? Constitutional law? Greek architecture? Simply learning a core concept and forming a new metaphor in your head counts. When you reach the little-c level, the question of domains starts to become an issue. When you hit Pro-c (let alone Big-C), the domain is a key component. It is part of a larger debate on whether creativity is domain-general or domain-specific.

The extreme position on domain generality would be that someone who is creative is simply creative. Someone who can creatively play the piano should also be predisposed to be creative at painting, conducting scientific experiments, or making soufflés. The extreme domain-specific perspective would hold that someone who is a creative mathematician would be no more likely to be creative at doing historical research or performing improv comedy than someone who is not creative at all in mathematics.[7]

Of course, the answer is somewhere in the middle. There are some traits, abilities, attitudes, and values that help people be creative regardless of the domain. At the most basic level, for example, people who greatly value tradition and security are less creative across several different domains.[8] Another broad predictor of creative performance is the belief that you are capable of being creative.[9]

There are also, however, some skills, bases of knowledge, and specific attributes that will matter very much for one domain but not for another. A detailed understanding of human anatomy is needed for someone to be creative in medicine, but is not (or much less) needed for someone to be creative in inventing a new iPhone case

[6] Kaufman, Beghetto et al., 2010. [7] Baer, 2015; Kaufman & Baer, 2002a.
[8] Kasof et al., 2007. [9] Farmer & Tierney, 2017.

or in knitting an afghan. A creative writer will likely need a better vocabulary than a creative painter.

The domain specificity versus domain generality issue used to be a source of much debate,[10] although there has been strong convergence over the last two decades. The way in which creativity is measured[11] and statistically analyzed[12] matters a great deal. Neuroimaging research suggests some degree of domain generality; drawing, music improvisation, and writing share common mechanisms (particularly writing and drawing) in the prefrontal cortex, which is associated with cognitive and motor control. However, there are also separate neural circuits for each, and this suggests an element of domain specificity.[13] Further, these were still three domains within the arts.

There are also theories that have tried to meet in the middle. One of them is the amusement park theory (APT), which I developed with John Baer.[14] We had begun meeting regularly for coffee, pastries, and conversation when I lived in New Jersey. I was fresh out of graduate school and was still getting used to that transition from reading the works of great creativity scholars to getting the chance to collaborate with them. Baer and I were wrapping up an edited book on creativity across domains,[15] and we'd written a coda but kept thinking and talking about the chapters. Each contributor wrote about a different domain, from music to psychology to business, and some attributes consistently popped up all over the book and others were less common.

As I was trying to fall asleep, the metaphor of Disney World kept popping into my head. The next day I fleshed it out with Baer. If you wanted to go to Disney World, you had many different theme parks in it to choose from – such as the Magic Kingdom, Epcot, and the Animal Kingdom. But within the parks there were additional choices: the Magic Kingdom had lands, Epcot had pavilions, the Animal Kingdom had areas, and so on. Even once you'd picked a land, pavilion, or area, there were more choices. Which attraction, ride, or show did you want to see? It was a series of nesting dolls. We saw domains in this way.

[10] Baer, 1998; Plucker, 1998. [11] Plucker, 1999a, 1999b, 2004.
[12] Qian & Plucker, 2018; Qian et al., 2019. [13] Chen et al., 2020.
[14] Baer & Kaufman, 2005, 2017; Kaufman & Baer, 2004a, 2005b, but see also Plucker & Beghetto, 2004.
[15] Kaufman & Baer, 2005a.

We quicky switched to a more generic amusement park metaphor, both to be more encompassing and out of sheer terror of lawyers with Mickey Mouse ears. The first step, we realized, was that there were some initial requirements if you wanted to go to any amusement park. You needed a ride, a ticket, and money; perhaps also a friend or two, sunscreen, or sandwiches – if you didn't want to buy a ten-dollar hot dog. Similarly, if you want to be creative – in anything, at any level, in any way – you need to have the desire to be creative (I'll eventually cover this broad topic later); you need a basic level of cognitive ability (by which I mean a bare minimum; creativity is in no way reserved for geniuses); and, finally, you need an environment that tolerates or allows creativity (even if it does not nurture it in any way). These were the initial requirements that we proposed; others have suggested different traits and abilities that are needed for any type of creativity. One study proposed three: divergent thinking and two others that I will dive into later: openness and creative self-efficacy.[16]

We then proposed a matryoshka nesting doll view of domains, as a parallel of the park–land–ride decision tree. The broadest level we called "general thematic areas." We saw these as the core areas of creativity. One natural split is between art and science, which are sometimes called "the two cultures."[17] Most divergent thinking tests use a different split, tapping into visual–graphic–artistic creativity versus verbal–writing creativity.[18] But there are many different ways to categorize creative domains.

One methodology for measuring creative performance is the Consensual Assessment Technique (CAT), developed by Teresa Amabile.[19] This method has people actually do something such as write a poem,[20] draw a picture,[21] compose a song[22] or a graphic design,[23] compose a mathematical equation,[24] or even cooking[25]. After the works have been completed, expert judges proceed to separately evaluate each product.[26] Traditionally the judges use their own implicit definition of and beliefs about creativity. They assign a rating to all products (usually in random order), do not discuss their scores among themselves, and compare the products with one another, not with an ideal.[27] These procedures are a bit of a pain, but such

[16] van Broekhoven et al., 2020. [17] Snow, 1959. [18] Barbot et al., 2016; Torrance, 1974. [19] Amabile, 1996. [20] Baer et al., 2004. [21] Hennessey et al., 2008. [22] Priest, 2006. [23] Jeffries, 2017. [24] Baer, 1994. [25] Horng & Lin, 2009. [26] Cseh & Jeffries, 2019. [27] Baer & Kaufman, 2019.

guidelines are there for a reason. Raters generally show a high level of agreement (the first project I ever did using the CAT methodology had such high reliability that it made me suspicious enough to ask our statistician to rerun the data); and high agreement offers some evidence of trustworthiness. Emphasizing the experience and context of the creators (as opposed to using some type of absolute scale) makes sure that a study of 200 kindergartners doesn't simply conclude that kids suck at art.

Judges should ideally be genuine experts, such that published authors would judge creative writing.[28] However, studies have shown that quasi-experts tend to agree with one another and with the experts; and these can include creativity researchers (we're good for something!),[29] teachers,[30] laypeople with demonstrated knowledge of and interest in the area,[31] and gifted novices.[32] Unfortunately for the budget-minded scholar, novices (such as college undergraduates) do not show solid agreement with the experts.[33] There are many possible reasons for this type of discrepancy; perhaps experts are more likely to recognize familiar tropes and clichés. A stream of research on how experts and novices evaluate art has revealed other possible reasons. For example, experts have been shown to like art more than novices,[34] especially art with a negative valence.[35] Novices are more likely than experts to rely on their personal feelings in evaluating art[36] and are not as well equipped to appreciate complex work.[37]

The idea that expert judgments on creativity are important makes a lot of sense, particularly for Pro-c. Movies are given awards (such as the Oscars) on the basis of evaluations made by expert-level peers or by critics – the other group that people ignore. One could perhaps argue that academic metrics such as h-indexes or citation counts are a version of expert consensus.

In the real world, such opinions likely carry substantial weight, for the present day and beyond. Classic creativity scholarship from the 1960s had professional architects take a number of creativity tests, which were then evaluated by peers, expert architects, and editorial board members of architecture journals.[38] In 2007, a major survey of both architects and laypeople was conducted to determine

[28] Kaufman & Baer, 2012. [29] Baer et al., 2009. [30] Kaufman et al., 2013.
[31] Plucker et al., 2009. [32] Kaufman et al., 2005.
[33] Kaufman et al., 2009; Kaufman et al., 2008.
[34] Leder et al., 2014; Van Paasschen et al., 2015. [35] Leder et al., 2012.
[36] Augustin & Leder, 2006. [37] Mullenix & Robinet, 2018.
[38] Hall & MacKinnon, 1969.

their favorite structure (I admit that my own favorite structure is probably just my house). A clever modern study linked the classic data to find out what features predicted whether an architect's work from the 1960s would be presented on the professional and laypeople's lists. Performance on divergent thinking tests – no matter how they were scored – predicted bupkes.[39] In contrast, the judgments of all three groups predicted an architect's presence on both lists.[40]

Because the CAT is quite resource-intensive, there are very few studies that use this technique on more than three or four domains. Hence most studies of creativity across many different domains use self-report measures. Such tests ask people to rate or indicate their skill, preference, or achievements across many areas.[41] This method is not ideal but, if the goal is to expand the scope beyond a core of two or three domains, self-assessments are already used in the largest array of studies.

Some of the more commonly used multi-domain assessments are the Creativity Achievement Questionnaire,[42] the Creative Behavior Inventory,[43] the Inventory of Creative Activities and Achievements,[44] and my own Kaufman Domains of Creativity (and earlier versions);[45] and many others.[46] As one surveys the domains that emerge across these instruments and studies, the basic arts–science dichotomy certainly surfaces. But science is usually a single domain that also encompasses mathematics, engineering, logic, and technology; only the occasional reanalysis[47] splits any of the latter off from the core "science" dimension. Scholarly or academic creativity occasionally pops up, sometimes as its own domain and sometimes as a subfactor of science.

The arts, in contrast, are nearly always split, often in multiple ways. The visual arts and the performing arts tend to form separate and distinct domains, and creative writing is also commonly on its own. Sometimes people distinguish visual arts from either arts and crafts[48] or design.[49] Music frequently breaks off from performance;

[39] Vartanian, 2017. [40] Vartanian et al., 2017. [41] Kaufman, 2019b.
[42] Carson et al., 2005. [43] Hocevar, 1976, 1979; Rodriguez et al., 2023.
[44] Diedrich et al., 2018.
[45] Kaufman, 2012; Kaufman & Baer, 2004b; Kaufman et al., 2009.
[46] E.g., Elisondo, 2021; Ivcevic & Mayer, 2009; Karwowski & Brzeski, 2017; Kerr & McKay, 2013.
[47] Kandemir & Kaufman, 2020. [48] I.e., Diedrich et al., 2018; Hocevar, 1979.
[49] I.e., Fürst & Grin, 2018.

dance and theater or film sometimes do as well. Sports is often associated with dance or performance, as in Howard Gardner's concept of bodily kinesthetic intelligence.[50] Architecture is also sometimes included.

The third large area, beyond arts and science, to be most commonly included in such assessments is general everyday creativity. The everyday can explicitly encompass interpersonal interactions (although social creativity is, rarely, its own factor) as well as related domains such as cooking, humor, or problem-solving. There often are also items that fall under the everyday because there's no other broad category that's appropriate. Being creative in teaching, for example, has many different components.[51] If it ever appears on these types of scales, it's usually as an item that reads something like "I am creative in teaching." As a result, it can get lumped under everyday (or interpersonal) creativity – because most of these measures are developed using college student data. A 19-year-old looking at that item would likely either think "no" or else extrapolate to tutoring or to explaining a concept to someone else. They're not going to think about lesson planning or curriculum design or classroom management, because why would they?

You can have a similar conundrum in business. Very few general creativity scales consider business (or, if they do, they only have one or two questions). Again, this gap can come down to usage. Organizations tend to not do research across multiple domains because, frankly, who cares if your human resources manager can make sculptures out of paper clips? When people in business study creativity, there tends to be a certain admirable practicality about it all.

So if I'm trying to make an argument about what the general thematic areas are "in real life," I have to do some extrapolating and guessing. My personal picks? The everyday, the visual arts, writing, performance, scholarly domains (e.g., the humanities), science, and business. There are several others that are currently ping-ponging around my brain, however. Music composition feels different from performance. Science feels like it encompasses too much, but I don't know where engineering, technology, and mathematics fit into the picture.

General thematic areas, no matter how many they are, break down into domains, fields, or disciplines. Science becomes chemistry,

[50] Gardner, 1999. [51] E.g., Gregerson et al., 2013.

physics, biology, and many more disciplines. Visual art becomes painting, sculpture, and photography. Performance becomes acting, dancing, and singing. Under each domain are many microdomains. Dancing has ballet, jazz, tap, and others. Biology yields botany, zoology, anatomy, entomology, paleontology, and other areas that I could Google if you want more examples.

As I'm writing this bit up, I realize that the non-arts disciplines have many more branches than the arts disciplines. "Science" is unfathomably broad, and its microdomains (e.g., botany) likely have their own set of micro-microdomains, or whatever term we want to use. In contrast, with writing I'm not sure where I'd go beyond its microdomains. Let's take poetry and assume that its microdomains include sonnets, haikus, free verse, cinquains, and many more. I don't know how much more specific you get than "writing sonnets." Writing sonnets without using the letter e? Writing sonnets about proper dental hygiene? In contrast, the microdomain of botany seems to be at the same level as the domain of poetry; college students can major in either, although they are more likely to major at the next level up – that is, in English, in creative writing, or in biology.

Botany and poetry are in no way equivalent in how they are treated in creativity self-report inventories. Most scales not only have a specific item about poetry but may even include items on haikus or sonnets. In contrast, I can't think of any creativity scale that mentions botany (I can't even think of a joke to make about botany and creativity). Why? One reason is that, when it comes to creativity, most people show an art bias, rating artistic professions as being more creative than non-artistic professions.[52] A recent large-scale study that asked people what they thought of when they heard the word "creativity" found that arts-related answers came second only to answers that associated creativity with novelty of thought.[53] Similarly, people tend to not associate their own scientific or mathematical creativity with their overall conception of their creativity, but they view their artistic creativity as being very closely related to it.[54] Nevertheless I think there is more to it than that.

I've been talking about areas and domains on the basis of content or what is pursued (e.g., dancing). Yet another way to look at domains is according to their format, or how they are pursued. In other words, are you being creative for your job or as a

[52] Glăveanu, 2014. [53] Novak-Leonard et al., 2022.
[54] Kaufman et al., 2009; Kaufman & Baer, 2004b.

hobby?[55] Content and format, I would argue, interact. Most artistic domains make straightforward hobbies. You can paint in your garage. You can write a novel on your laptop. Want to play the ukulele or try your hand at making a clay vase? There are start-up kits and cheap instruments that will get you ready to go. Most towns have a community theater and dance classes. YouTube has thousands of videos on how to start any imaginable artistic endeavor.

People can easily be mini-c and little-c creative in the arts. They can absolutely be creative in an everyday way at these levels. Many components of business creativity are also attainable at mini-c and little-c levels; most weeks there's a viral news story about kids who have started a small business or a non-profit venture and seen it succeed beyond their wildest dreams. It is certainly possible to be creative in the sciences at lower-c levels, but most examples would be school-related. You don't hear as many stories about people coming back from their nine-to-five job and diving into their molecular engineering lab in the garage, or spending their weekends calculating derivative functions for fun.

Where does Big-C come into play? Beghetto and I generally see Big-C as being determined after the creator's death.[56] What distinguishes Pro-c creativity and will keep it at that level, in contrast with the creativities that will become immortal? I'll briefly touch on these questions to round out the present chapter.

Creative Genius: The Resilience of Corkscrews

I remember one student wrote in an essay that they did not want to be Big-C because they did not want to die. There are many problematic concepts in that sentence that I will not attempt to unpack here, but I do want to reinforce a few thoughts. Although Big-C is reserved for people who have passed (and, usually, passed a while ago), there are certainly many living people whom I would call "very likely future Big-C." Such people range, as of early 2023, from Paul McCartney to Barack Obama, Bill Gates, Margaret Atwood, and many more. Further, death itself is not necessarily some morbid prerequisite as much as the ample time that is needed to see whether someone's creative ideas truly take root and stay remembered and even influential in the years to come. Finally, we're all going to die, Big-C or not.

[55] Reiter-Palmon et al., 2012.   [56] Kaufman & Beghetto, 2009.

What does it take to hit Big-C? Certainly, groundbreaking, paradigm-shifting contributions are more likely to be remembered. There's also how the creator's work interacts with the field and the domain.[57] As Mihaly Csikszentmihalyi proposes in the systems model, creators (specifically, their creative work) are the constant. Let's consider Stephen Sondheim, the musical theater composer and lyricist who I believe will be Big-C. (I should add that, when I first drafted this paragraph, both Csikszentmihalyi and Sondheim were alive; very sadly, both passed away within two months of each other in late 2021.)

Sondheim tinkered with his shows as new productions were mounted; the 2021 Broadway revival of *Company*, which opened shortly after his death, featured gender-flipped casting with his approval. However, the essence of his musicals, from *A Little Night Music* to *Sweeney Todd* and *Assassins*, remains largely the same. The field includes the gatekeepers – in Sondheim's case, these would be theater critics, producers, the societies and groups that bestow awards such as the Tonys, theater professors who determine which shows they teach to young artists, and many others. Gatekeepers can have a huge impact on who gets a big break, continues to get work, or is revived and kept in the public's mind. Although technological advances have allowed more creators to succeed with less impact from gatekeepers,[58] the latter still matter, even in an era in which creators can release their work independently on YouTube, Spotify, or CreateSpace.

The gatekeepers change over time – even across one's lifetime – although Sondheim's reviews have typically been positive even early in his career.[59] Given his proclivity for experimentation, he has received his share of mixed reviews (*Anyone Can Whistle* or *Pacific Overtures*) and outright pans (*Merrily We Roll Along*).[60] Today even his less famous shows are frequently revived and have produced many songs that are commonly sung by cabaret-style singers. The domain is the area of study itself (in this case, musical theater), including the standard practices and tools of the trade. Sondheim's impact on this domain is striking. He has directly mentored a wide variety of the top talents (including Lin-Manuel Miranda) and has influenced generations of young creators.

[57] Csikszentmihalyi, 1999. [58] Gangadharbatla, 2010. [59] Suskin, 1990.
[60] Suskin, 1997.

Is Sondheim Big-C? I mean, I clearly think so. But I can't say for certain. The gatekeepers will keep changing – and so will the domain. Broadway once catered primarily to locals, which meant a great deal of what has been called "tired-businessman theater."[61]

As prices have risen and risen, much of Broadway is geared more toward events that play well for tourists. Who can predict what the state of Broadway will be in twenty-five or fifty years? Will there be Broadway as we know it in a century or two? Or theater? Or life?

Certainly there are many ways in which a creator of Big-C caliber may hit a snag. In 1922, an editor expressed interest in seeing a work by the not-yet-legendary Ernest Hemingway. He had his wife pack up all his writing, put it in a suitcase, and bring it to him by train, from Paris to Switzerland. A moment of distraction and a never caught thief meant that all of Hemingway's early work (except for one submitted story) was gone – poof.[62] What if that suitcase had held *A Farewell to Arms* and *The Old Man and the Sea*?

In addition, some creative work is by its nature ephemeral; consider live (and unfilmed) performances, sand sculptures, or multi-colored sidewalk chalk drawings. Other creations are by their design rarely rewatched. Most television talk shows or newscasts are not revisited unless something particularly notable occurs. We also cannot forget times when the preserved format was poorly chosen. How many movies not only are impossible to find on any streaming service, but are available solely on Betamax or Laserdisc?

There are other factors, of course. Sometimes personal traits, professional circumstances, and simple luck can interact to produce devastating consequences. Let's turn to the case of Edwin B. Twitmyer. In a parallel universe, he is a legend whose work is taught in every Intro to Psych class. Twitmyer conducted his dissertation on the patellar reflex, which is when your doctor taps you on the knee with a rubber hammer and your knee goes boing. He paired a bell ringing with his hammer tap and found that people were soon kicking solely upon hearing the bell.

Well, you might say, who cares? Pavlov established classical conditioning years ago. Yes, but Twitmyer published his dissertation in 1902, a year before Pavlov. So why have we forgotten poor Twitmyer? Some reasons relate to his personal attributes. His big

[61] Murray, 2011. [62] Mumford, 2015.

chance came at the 1904 APA convention, when he presented his work to a room full of preeminent scholars, such as William James. His dissertation was printed privately; this decision meant that his work was not easily accessible. He was also apparently not a talented speaker or promoter; his audience was unimpressed. Upon not receiving positive (or any) feedback, he chose to move on. But there were also professional reasons. He studied people, not dogs; psychologists at that time were resistant to the idea that people could be manipulated that easily. Because it was very early in his career, he lacked the resources and respect that would have enabled him to take risks or devote more time to a less popular topic. Finally, there is luck. His talk was right before lunch, and James and the others were hungry, distracted, and eager to break.[63]

We like to focus on undiscovered genius that is eventually discovered. It is less comforting to consider greatness that might be lost to history. Thomasina Coverly, the teenage girl at the center of Tom Stoppard's *Arcadia*, asks her tutor, Septimus Hodge: "Can you bear it? All the lost plays of the Athenians! Two hundred at least by Aeschylus, Sophocles, Euripides – thousands of poems – Aristotle's own library!... How can we sleep for grief?"[64]

Yet such loss may be ameliorated by knowing that it is rare. Dean Keith Simonton's historiometric scholarship on opera indicates that the pieces most often performed in modern times were those that received public interest and critic support in their initial runs.[65] Indeed, the most prolific creators are also the ones more likely to produce the greatest and most creative work.[66] Sometimes the romantics are wrong. Further, as essential as creative genius is, there is often a zeitgeist or general discussions in the air that enable multiple discoveries, as when calculus was invented by both Newton and Leibniz.[67]

I will end this chapter with Septimus' response to Thomasina: "By counting our stock. Seven plays from Aeschylus, seven from Sophocles, nineteen from Euripides... The missing plays of Sophocles will turn up piece by piece, or be written again in another language. Ancient cures for diseases will reveal themselves once more. Mathematical discoveries glimpsed and lost to view will have their time again. You do not suppose that if all of Archimedes had

[63] Coon, 1982. [64] Stoppard, 1993, p. 42. [65] Simonton, 1998.
[66] Simonton, 1977, 1985. [67] Brannigan & Wanner, 1983.

been hiding in the great library of Alexandria, we would be at a loss for a corkscrew?"[68]

Such multiple discoveries, however, are rare; besides, they are not identical.[69] Leibniz's and Newton's calculus were different beasts.[70] So, when I explore in the next chapter how comfortably we can state that creativity is actually an important predictor of good outcomes, we will still start with Big-C. But what do we do with mini-c? Let's find out.

[68] Stoppard, 1993, p. 42. [69] Simonton, 2010. [70] Simonton, 2019.

5 AN OVERWHELMING QUESTION

I've spent four chapters trying to cover as many key points about creativity as I could, covering those particular topics (such as domains) or theories (such as the four Cs) that are interesting and dear to me. I've saved a few more core concepts to toss out when most relevant in the chapters to come. In no way do I claim this overview to be complete. I've already written and then revised an overview of the field[1] and made a very conscious choice to not do a third edition but instead tackle a new beast. This book is, rather, mostly designed to lead you, à la J. Alfred Prufrock,[2] to an overwhelming question: *Why creativity?* Or, to be specific, *why is creativity important and worth studying, promoting, and nurturing?*

In the past I've tried many different pathways to bring people to this question. Sometimes I focus on all the troubling, annoying, or costly aspects of creativity until it feels like I'm actually delivering an anticreativity manifesto before I pull the switcheroo. It probably flows more naturally this way. But it feels disingenuous. No one who's choosing to read a book about creativity is thinking it is a pointless endeavor.

My goal, instead, was to keep hitting the mantra that I actually subscribe to: *it all counts*. From mini-c to replications to random domains, virtually anybody can be creative in nearly any way. So, instead of having "why creativity?" emerge from someone who thinks "creativity sounds absolutely terrible; why would anyone

[1] J. C. Kaufman, 2009; 2016a. [2] Eliot, 1915.

want to be creative?," I'd rather approach the question from the perspective of "what great outcomes can emerge from this cool ability/trait/way of viewing the world that anyone can embrace?"

Here I'm going to tackle some of the most straightforward benefits of creativity, and then argue why I want to keep digging. I've been thinking about these ideas for a long time; they crystallized a bit when I was fortunate enough to write a target article[3] and response[4] for a special issue of my friend Maciej Karwowski's journal *Creativity: Theories–Research–Applications.*

My *mea culpa*

This direction represents a 180-degree turn from some of my earlier work, which emphasized creativity and mental illness.[5] It began in graduate school, largely by accident. I was trying to find a study I could do by myself. Given I had no external funding (which has largely remained consistent throughout my career), there was a limit on what I could do. I was in the Strand bookstore in New York City when I saw an enormous book on sale, *A Reader's Guide to Twentieth-Century Writers.*[6] It contained brief entries on more than 1,500 writers. I had maintained my love–hate relationship with creative writing and had also just discovered Simonton's historiometric method.[7] I realized I was looking at fodder for a possible solo project (or at least a long-burning fire, if circumstances became dire).

I began entering data for an exploratory look on creative writers. I included everything that seemed quantifiable and important, from birth and death dates to number of works to age at first publication to types of works written (such as novels versus plays). I also entered other information gleaned from the biographies in that book and in another volume,[8] for instance indications of personal tragedies, physical health issues, and mental health issues. As I've written on several occasions,[9] I uncovered a quirky little doodad of a finding: poets who were female were more likely than any other gender or writer-type group to show mental illness symptoms (as specified in the minibiographies). I did a second study using a volume on eminent women[10] and found a similar pattern.

[3] Kaufman, 2018a. [4] Kaufman, 2018c. [5] Kaufman, 2014b.
[6] Parker & Kermode, 1996. [7] Simonton, 1990.
[8] Webster's dictionary of American authors, 1996. [9] Kaufman, 2017a, 2017b, 2020.
[10] Webster's dictionary of American women, 1996.

I thought this was interesting and I presented the finding at a few conferences. One of my professors, Peter Salovey, suggested that I call it "the Sylvia Plath effect." It was a brilliant suggestion from a brilliant man (he is the cocreator of emotional intelligence and now the president of Yale). I was high on intellectual discovery and an early solo publication.[11] I was twenty-five years old. I couldn't fathom that anyone not within shouting distance would care.

I was an idiot.

I did a few follow-up studies and theory papers over the next couple of years, largely reinforcing the poetry–mental illness link (but without enough gender variation to actually test the Sylvia Plath effect).[12] I tried to see whether it held up cross-culturally, but it turned out that the number of biographies from Turkey[13] or China[14] that actually discussed the creator's mental health were too few to allow any type of analysis.

A confluence of a number of different factors conspired to give the Sylvia Plath effect a certain bit of renown. I had been at California State University, San Bernardino for a couple of years when the university hired a public relations firm to help draw attention to faculty research. I met with the people and excitedly mentioned many different studies and theories, but they zeroed in on the Sylvia Plath effect and on a similar recent paper I'd published, which showed that poets had a shorter lifespan than other writers.[15] Full disclosure: the main reason I'd written that paper was that I wanted to publish in a journal called *Death Studies*.

A month or two later, I got an e-mail from an Associated Press reporter asking a few questions. I answered a bit glibly. A couple of hours later, I checked CNN's website and saw a story about poets dying young and the Sylvia Plath effect was on the front page – what in my old newspaper days I would have called "above the fold."

The next few days were a bit crazy. I remember talking to the *New York Times* and answering call-waiting, to find the *Los Angeles Times* at the other end. I tried to convey that any Big-C finding wouldn't extrapolate to everyday folks, but I didn't choose my words carefully. The Sylvia Plath effect did not mean, I told the *New York Times*, that "an Introduction to Poetry class should carry a warning that poems may be hazardous to one's health."[16] It wasn't intentional, but I gave off a

[11] J. C. Kaufman, 2001b. [12] J. C. Kaufman, 2001a, 2005; Kaufman & Baer, 2002b.
[13] Oral et al., 2004. [14] Niu & Kaufman, 2005. [15] Kaufman, 2003.
[16] Lee, 2004, p. 4.

certain insensitive flippancy. That attitude permeated the coverage; one story included a drop head (that bit of text below the headline) that read, "This study found this/ Haiku holds the threat of death/ Write prose live longer."

Remember that 2004 was before Facebook meant anything outside Harvard. Social media had thankfully not yet reached the current behemoth status. But the story still went a bit viral. My favorite detail is that there were multiple indie rock songs with the title "The Sylvia Plath Effect" (one is actually quite good). What stuck with me, more than the nasty comments or complete misunderstanding of the work, were the blog posts from poets or those suffering with mental illness. Some were curious or relieved, but many more were concerned, sad, or upset.

Even more worrisome was the potential romanticization of mental illness. Consider the study that found that people enjoyed Van Gogh's paintings more if they were first reminded (or perhaps told for the first time) that he cut off his left ear.[17] Hell, Van Gogh's penchant for eating yellow paint became a rallying cry at one point on social media, young aspiring artists encouraging others to metaphorically eat their own yellow paint.[18] I am scared to find out whether people ever encouraged young poets to find their own gas ovens.

I learned at least two core lessons. I've mentioned the WGASA idea concept – scholarship should make some kind of difference or practical impact, or at least be able to answer the "who cares?" question. But I see the corollary as being that, just as the Hippocratic oath guarantees for medicine, research, too, should at least do no harm. Of course, such a principle is an ideal. We can't determine the impact, misuse, or unintended effects of our work.[19] The inventors of thalidomide were trying to make a benevolent drug to treat nausea; the subsequent birth defects were likely as horrifying to them as to the world. I am also not saying that this standard is any magical guideline; I have no particular objection to scientists and scholars taking unpopular positions or following a controversial passion. But it is a mantra I try to follow. The other lesson is that people care about this stuff. Creativity matters to a lot of people, especially on a topic like its relation to mental health. It isn't an abstract idea.

I've spent more than two decades studying creativity. Yet if I were to die tomorrow, the Sylvia Plath effect would be the headline

[17] Van Tilburg & Igou, 2014. [18] Drew, 2020. [19] E.g., Kapoor & Kaufman, 2021.

of any obituary (unless I were to die by eating a bucket of unpopped corn kernels, trip ping into a fire, and exploding popcorn all over Connecticut). I am under no illusion that my current work or this book will necessarily change that, but I remain doggedly optimistic.

Defending Pizza and Ice Cream

There are some foods that are an acquired taste, such as oysters, anchovies, kimchi, stinky cheeses, and olives. Other foods may be enjoyed by a very select few, such as durian fruit or haggis. Then there are the foods that are so beloved that those who do not like them may raise suspicion. What kind of person doesn't like pizza or ice cream? Of course, some people may dislike specific toppings (pineapple could work for both), or else generally be watching their weight. They may be lactose-intolerant, or (in the case of pizza) allergic to gluten. But pizza and ice cream sounds like a dinner that the whole family or group would agree on; even if it's nobody's top choice, everyone will likely come to a consensus.

Similarly, as I mentioned in the preface, creativity does not seem to need much defending. Surveys of educational administrators[20] and business VIPs[21] routinely show that creativity is a highly desired attribute in prospective students or employees. Creativity is traditionally considered one of the key twenty-first-century skills. The term "creativity" will pop up on employment websites from a wide range of positions encompassing nearly every imaginable industry.[22]

And yet... saying that you value something does not mean that you care about it enough to provide adequate resources, time, and personnel. Teachers[23] or employers[24] may say that they like creative students, but such assertions are not necessarily reflected in their attitudes or beliefs. I have consulted quite a bit, largely with schools. My experience has been that, when someone reaches out, there is one person there who "gets it." It is often a superintendent, a principal, or a vice principal. They are excited, full of ideas, and many times we have gotten initiatives off the ground. I love that part.

But it typically takes only a small hurdle (such as a budget crisis) or the leader's leaving for another job to have everything come

20 Lichtenberg et al., 2008; Walpole et al., 2002.
21 Adobe, 2016; IBM, 2010.
22 Kaufman et al., 2022.
23 Aljughaiman & Mowrer-Reynolds, 2005; Westby & Dawson, 1995.
24 Mueller et al., 2011.

crumbling down – even if other people seemed to be on board, even if we've been able to show solid results. So over the years I've been more and more determined to find specific and varied reasons why creativity is important. It feels like there should be thousands of studies to draw from, but there aren't. In a review of creativity scholarship I did with Marie Forgeard, we found that most studies focused on how different variables impacted creativity. This issue is important. "How can I be more creative?" is usually one of the first questions I am asked in my Introduction to Creativity class. But less than one fifth of papers looked at what creativity predicted (good or bad). More than 70 percent of papers made no or barely any mention of why we should bother studying creativity.[25]

In the musical *1776*, John Adams and Benjamin Franklin are trying to convince John Hancock (as a delaying tactic) that they need to have a written declaration stating the colonies' reasons for leaving England. When Hancock asks them why, they stammer until Thomas Jefferson answers for them: "To place before mankind the common sense of the subject, in terms so plain and firm to command their assent."[26] I am no Jefferson, but I am tilting at this windmill anyway.

Big-C and Pro-c and Straightforward Answers

When I wrote my target article about the need for more research on positive outcomes of creativity,[27] perhaps the most straightforward response came from Dean Keith Simonton.[28] As I have noted earlier, his focus is on creative genius. Who could possibly argue that creative genius is unimportant?[29] Take away Big-C and I'd be trying to write this book without my laptop, a word processing program, and the Internet. I'd also likely be dead, because there's no penicillin, corrective lenses, refrigeration, or waffles.

Genius is assumed to be such a good thing that most television shows with a brilliant and creative protagonist will often show that character as being a complete jerk (*House*, *Rick and Morty*, *Sherlock*), socially awkward (*Scorpion*, *The Big Bang Theory*), or at least eccentric (*Eureka*, *Numbers*). Or else the genius will have a past trauma (*Criminal Minds*, *The Pretender*, *The Queen's Gambit*), be on the autistic spectrum (*Bones*, *The Good Doctor*) or struggle with mental health issues (*Mr. Robot*, *Perception*). Such often troubling portrayals may well be a result of

[25] Forgeard & Kaufman, 2016. [26] Stone & Edwards, 1976, p. 55. [27] Kaufman, 2018a.
[28] Simonton, 2018a. [29] Simonton, 2018d.

simple jealousy,[30] or a sign that we value brilliance enough to overlook all other flaws. Hell, Hannibal Lecter comes off as much more of a hero than anyone but Clarice Starling in *Silence of the Lambs*.

Big-C creativity may not be possible for everyone, but it is also essential to note that it isn't *desirable* for everyone. There are many, many reasons why people who are Pro-c might not aspire to Big-C, including personal preference and desire for a better work–life balance.[31] I don't want to go off on a tangent (that would be a different book), but so much of the history of creativity research is, really, the history of White men's creativity.

There have always been huge obstacles in the paths of eminently creative women who might have been en route to a possible Big-C career – from lack of opportunities[32] to implicit and explicit sexist cultural values.[33] The hurdles my mother faced in getting her PhD (e.g., one mentor telling her that she was robbing a man of making a living) and in pursuing an academic career in the 1970s would not be surprising to anyone but the most naïve readers, really. Women have been and continue to be often forced to choose between advancing a creative career and having a family or a personal life, whereas men are not.[34] Even when women do have creative freedom, many make choices that do not advance them toward a traditional Big-C trajectory. They may become leaders or mentors, focusing on giving back or helping others,[35] even if they are aware that these choices come at a cost to their own creativity.[36] Choosing to nurture and engender creativity in other people tends, unfairly, to not "count" toward any Big-C tally.[37]

Having noted this point, I will continue to try hard to not fall down a rabbit hole (you're hearing from someone who gets stuck looking up the worst volcanic eruptions in recorded history during bouts of insomnia). It is therefore important to note that Pro-c creativity is also not hard to sell as a positive thing. Certainly organizations typically value on-the-job creativity or innovation (which refers not only to thinking creative ideas but also to implementing them in the real world).[38] Most companies would not care if an employee happened to be Pro-c in an area that wasn't work-related, as long as it wasn't embarrassing, a distraction, or too time-intensive.

[30] Schlesinger, 2020. [31] Sternberg, 2022. [32] Ochse, 1991. [33] Helson, 1990.
[34] Piirto, 1991. [35] Reis, 2002; Reis & Holinger, 2021. [36] Reis, 2020.
[37] Miller & Cohen, 2012. [38] West, 2002; West et al., 2004.

Richard Florida has written extensively about the creative class,[39] which encompasses skilled workers across a number of fields. These include people with careers in STEM (science, technology, engineering, and mathematics), the arts, business, and education (among other fields). Florida proposes that creativity is the twenty-first century's most important economic resource and that cities with higher percentages of creative workers are more likely to grow and thrive.[40]

As I've discussed earlier, there are absolute biases against creative people and negative associations or stereotypes. On the whole, however, I would argue that, even if we may not like Pro-c or (especially) Big-C creativity, we still recognize its importance. It's too easy to see how creative genius can actively help our lives. That said... as much as Pro-c is valued, its importance is not a foregone conclusion. Consumer resistance,[41] especially from older people,[42] is one reason why most creative products are still likely to fail.[43] Even when they succeed, the companies that have taken this initial risk may see competitors refine their innovations to make cheaper knock-offs.[44] Further, intelligence (or general mental ability) is regularly found to be the strongest predictor of job performance,[45] followed by conscientiousness.[46]

Even after all these warnings, we're still at the levels of creativity that intuitively strike people as valuable. What happens when we turn to the lower cs, where creativity may not even make any impact whatsoever? It is this core question that will dominate not only this chapter, but the rest of the book.

Academic Achievement, kinda?

Big-C changes the world, at least in a small way. Pro-c impacts a domain and contributes in some way to change. Such contributions are not inherently benevolent; I see creativity as inherently neutral, although Vlad Glăveanu and I have argued that the traits and abilities traditionally associated with a creator would lean on the good side.[47] It is important to note that most Big-C contributions are not simply the result of one genius. Such major works require the efforts of not

[39] Florida, 2019. [40] Florida, 2012. [41] Ram & Sheth, 1989.
[42] Laukkanen et al., 2007. [43] Heidenreich & Spieth, 2013.
[44] Martin-Rios & Parga-Dans, 2016. [45] Gonzalez-Mulé et al, 2014; Ree & Earles, 1992.
[46] Connelly et al., 2022. [47] Kaufman & Glăveanu, 2022a, 2022b, 2023.

only Pro-c people but often dozens if not hundreds of little-c and mini-c creators.[48]

We attribute the Declaration of Independence to Thomas Jefferson – as well we should – but there were four other people on the committee to draft the document. Two of them, John Adams and Benjamin Franklin, were also superstars. The other two, Roger Sherman and Robert Livingston, are less well remembered (although Sherman's house in New Haven is commemorated, it has also been turned into a restaurant). In addition, the other members of the congress made (occasionally helpful) suggestions and critiques. The text was then widely distributed and read out loud in major cities, meaning that a host of orators, printers, and other little-c types were part of the process.

One can make the argument that Big-C and Pro-c would not happen without mini-c and little-c. No one is instantly Pro-c (let alone Big-C), even if some people may ascend the trajectory faster than others. Yet the implication of such an argument is that encouraging, nurturing, or appreciating creativity in anyone who is not destined to be Pro-c or higher would be a waste of time.

The most logical place to start would seem to be creativity's role in academic achievement. As much as I talk about the discovery of Velcro (and about the feats of Angus MacGyver in the eponymous US series) as examples of mini-c, people still tend to visualize students. If creativity specifically helps a student get good grades and test scores, then that is likely enough to win over a lot of people, from principals to parents. Indeed, it's an angle that I have taken in the past, both in books[49] and in research studies.[50] Taking a quick look yields promising results.

Unsurprisingly, both intelligence and achievement test scores have been found to be significantly related to grade point average.[51] But if creativity can add more predictive power, that is still a plus. Many studies have found a significant positive relationship between creativity and both standardized test performance and grades. These studies encompass many ways of measuring creativity, from divergent thinking[52] through rated creativity[53] to self-reported creativity.[54] Indeed, a meta-analysis of 120 studies found similar results:

[48] Choi & Kaufman, 2021. [49] Beghetto et al., 2014. [50] J. C. Kaufman et al., 2021.
[51] Zwick, 2013; Strobel et al., 2019. [52] Gajda, 2016.
[53] Dollinger, 2011; Dollinger & Skaggs, 2011; Grigorenko et al., 2009.
[54] Powers & Kaufman, 2004; Pretz & Kaufman, 2017.

creativity was significantly correlated with markers of academic achievement.[55]

However, the relationship was $r = .22$ (higher associations were found for verbal tests, measures of performance as opposed to self-report, and test scores as opposed to grades). Creativity accounted for less than 5 percent of the variance, which. . . isn't that impressive, especially when meta-analyses of creativity and intelligence have shown relationships ranging from .16[56] and .17[57] to .30[58]. When studies add in other cognitive variables, such as short-term memory[59] or reasoning ability,[60] creativity tends to take a back seat. Further, standardized tests tend to be highly correlated with IQ;[61] often when intelligence was controlled, the significance of the creativity–grades or creativity–test relationship would simply disappear.[62]

It is even more damning, in my opinion, if other noncognitive factors are equally strong predictors of grade point average. A true exploration would take too much space, but let's just look at the personality factor of conscientiousness, which includes working hard, being disciplined and organized, and planning.[63] One meta-analysis found that creativity and conscientiousness showed a partial correlation (with intelligence controlled) of = .21.[64] That's pretty similar to creativity, so we can exhale a little bit, right?

Well. . . The issue is that using self-rated personality isn't the best practice for children because it takes a certain amount of cognitive development for their ratings to be particularly valid.[65] If we look at how academic achievement is related to conscientiousness in students when adults (such as parents or teachers) rate them, the relationship (depending on the measure and what is being controlled) varies from .33 to .50.[66]

I don't know about you, but writing that last page felt like adding a bunch of salt into my morning coffee. Regardless of the exact merits of creativity versus intelligence versus standardized tests versus conscientiousness, when it comes to predicting grades, I feel hard-pressed to put too many of my argument eggs in the academic achievement basket. I'm not saying that creativity is not related and potentially a key component. However, if someone's sole goal is to

55 Gajda et al., 2017. 56 Karwowski et al., 2021. 57 Kim, 2005.
58 Gerwig et al., 2021. 59 Vock et al., 2011. 60 Freund & Holling, 2008.
61 Frey & Detterman, 2004; Koenig et al., 2008.
62 Gralewski & Karwowski, 2012; McCabe, 1991. 63 DeYoung, 2015.
64 Poropat, 2009. 65 Measelle et al., 2005. 66 Poropat, 2014a, 2014b.

increase a student's academic achievement by any means necessary, I have a hard time making a strong case for why they should prioritize time and resources for nurturing and enhancing the kid's creativity.

So let's return to how we answer this overwhelming question of *why creativity*. Have I written all these chapters just to pull the rug out from under you, cackle madly that creativity has no value whatsoever at lower levels, and spend the next few chapters talking about musical theater and baseball? Although the Broadway musical *Damn Yankees* would beautifully fulfill both these parameters, the answer is, unsurprisingly, no. Let's try exploring it a bit more before descending into show tunes.

A Better World?

Many possible arguments for mini-c or little-c creativity end up feeling a little iffy. Does being creative make you happier? Not necessarily.[67] What about the idea that without mini-c or little-c there's no Pro-c or Big-C? It's true, but there's the unfortunate implication that the lower cs matter only insofar as someone can become an expert or a genius. What about all those people who may never reach Pro-c (let alone Big-C)? Does it simply not matter if they're creative? Such thoughts can lead to some existential angst. When you search for articles on creativity and positive benefits, one of the first papers to pop up is about craft beverage tourism.[68]

One way to advocate for everyday creativity is to focus on how it might improve the world. This perspective is consistent with many of the tenets of positive psychology, which considers creativity as one of its core character strengths.[69] In this context, creativity is valued to the degree to which it is benevolent and helps other people.[70] The outcome of creativity – the product – is key, as opposed to the process.[71]

Robert Sternberg has focused on this perspective recently, discussing how creativity,[72] along with giftedness[73] and intelligence,[74] can be considered transactional or transformational. Transactional creativity occurs, in essence, when someone has been identified, encouraged, and rewarded for being creative, and consequently is creative. Such creativity can be enjoyable and beneficial,

[67] Ceci & Kumar, 2016. [68] Gil Arroyo et al., 2021. [69] Peterson & Seligman, 2004.
[70] Seligman & Csikszentmihalyi, 2000. [71] Bacon, 2005. [72] Sternberg, 2021b.
[73] Sternberg, 2020, 2021a. [74] Sternberg, 2021d.

but its purpose is ultimately self-serving, or it implicitly fulfills the social contract. Helping others may be a happy side effect. In contrast, transformational creativity is aimed at making the world a better place. Transformational creators would still want to create for the purpose of helping the greater good, even if they had not benefited from the types of gifted programs, scholarships, and opportunities that may be proffered to those people who are obviously creative in a socially desirable way. Such transformational creativity would include a component of wisdom and, indeed, Sternberg's recent theoretical work has incorporated this view.[75] Many eastern conceptions of creativity, most notably Confucian perspectives, also have a focus on wisdom and benevolence.[76] A key next step would be to identify ways of nurturing, supporting, and measuring transformational creativity.[77] I broadly promote this work and am excited to see how Sternberg and others advance this topic. Yet, as much as I want to see this line of scholarship unfold and develop, it is ultimately not the argument I am taking for the rest of the book. Why?

The key question for me is: if creativity is a strength, what type of strength is it? One proposed distinction is that there are balance strengths and focus strengths.[78] Balance strengths aim to help you find harmony between yourself and others, with an emphasis on relationships; examples include wisdom, kindness, and fairness. Focus strengths strive for competence and personal achievement; career advancement is a priority, and interpersonal relationships may suffer. Examples include intelligence, leadership... and creativity. Positive psychology's emphasis on balance strengths may be one reason why creativity is not as emphasized.[79]

I'm more drawn to studying focus strengths, which tend to be associated with humanism (I will return to it in a few chapters). Why? Perhaps I am too cynical. I am not pessimistic to the point of believing that all people are evil in their hearts or anything like that, but I do think that people tend to be a bit self-focused. Most people are absolutely in favor of the world being a better place and are happy to help out in little ways, but I worry that steering the SS *Why Creativity* onto the better world navigation path would be more likely to end up in an iceberg than in a workable answer. Instead, I want to focus on and unpack what Sternberg[80] calls self-transformational creativity.

[75] Sternberg & Karami, 2022. [76] Dai & Niu, 2023; Pang & Plucker, 2022.
[77] Kaufman & Glăveanu, 2022b; Sternberg & Chowkase, 2021. [78] Bacon, 2005.
[79] E.g., Seligman, 2012. [80] Sternberg, 2021c.

It encompasses the ways in which creativity helps the creator. I think the odds are still strong that the benefits will trickle down and help the rest of the world be a better place. But the first step, in my view, is to highlight and pursue benevolent self-interest. Maybe I should be aiming for the stars and the moon instead of really nice views from terrace balconies. But I am in favor of attainable goals.

In the pages to come, I will propose five areas in which the creativity advantage can be seen across all the Cs: self-insight, healing, connection, drive, and legacy. First, however, as we reach the halfway mark, it is time to take a breath. Let us cleanse the palate with an aperitif of bile, malevolence, and madness. I must acknowledge the evil elephant in the room, or else others will do it for me.

A SMALL APERITIF: THE EVIL ELEPHANT

To be honest, I don't particularly feel like writing this bit. It's why I'm not calling it a chapter. But I also know that, if I don't, its absence will be too much of a focus. Whenever I talk about the benefits of creativity (in a talk, in a class, in a target article for a special issue, in a regular paper, to my pet rats), there is a kneejerk response: "What about all the bad stuff?"

I am not saying in any way that creativity is all good. It isn't. You could devote entire books to creativity's dark side[1] or its nuanced relationship with mental illness[2] – *and I have.* It's a bit baffling for me when someone pulls out the idea of malevolent creativity as a counterpoint to some "Yay, creativity!" argument I'm making; I coauthored the paper that coined the term "malevolent creativity."[3] I know it exists. The existence of evil outcomes does not preclude the existence – and prevalence – of good outcomes (and it is worth noting that artistic and cultural engagement was connected to fewer, not more, cases of antisocial behavior).[4]

Creative people have flaws. A lot of embezzlers, cheaters, con artists, and fraudsters are creative. There have been studies suggesting that creative work may come at the cost of quality,[5] company loyalty,[6] and adherence to rules;[7] that creative students may be more likely to be disruptive and impulsive;[8] and that creative people in

[1] Cropley et al., 2010. [2] Kaufman, 2014a. [3] Cropley et al., 2008.
[4] Bone et al., 2022. [5] Groeneveld et al., 2022; Miron et al., 2004.
[6] Madjar et al., 2011. [7] Miron et al., 2004. [8] Brandau et al., 2007.

general may be more likely to be dishonest.[9] Hell, creativity absolutely can be used for truly evil purposes. The terrorists who perpetrated the September 11 attacks were creative. Adolf Hitler, Ted Bundy, Jim Jones, and Charles Manson were creative. Hannibal Lecter, Lady Macbeth, Voldemort, and Cruella Deville were creative.

As I've briefly mentioned before, I see creativity as neutral. It's a tool, like a hammer. You can use a hammer to build a house for a family in need – but you can also use a hammer to bash someone's head in. Is a hammer benevolent or evil? Is being double-jointed good or bad? Almost nothing is truly just good or just bad. You can use your imagination to think up a cure for cancer or a way to steal children's spleens while they sleep. Here's another type of example: I absolutely love dogs. This sentiment includes the corgis and toy poodles we had growing up. It includes Pandora, the first dog I got as an adult with my then girlfriend, now wife Allison. She (Pandora, not Allison) was a hound mix and we've largely stuck to those big galoots, from our beagle mix Kirby, who would follow me around everywhere, to our bluetick hound Sweeney and to our recently passed drooly, smelly basset hound Gypsy. When I drive past someone walking a dog, I can't tell you anything about the person but I can tell you everything about the pup. But you know what? I still remember when we had one of my wife's friends over and I didn't know that he was terrified of dogs. To me, Pandora was pure good (not counting that one time I had leftover prime rib and went to get a knife and returned to find no prime rib and Pandora frantically swallowing). To him, she was a tail-wagging source of terror. Almost nothing is just good. I have to acknowledge that any piece of art I would call "my favorite," from David Bowie's "Life on Mars?" to Sondheim's *Sweeney Todd*, to the German Netflix show *Dark*, to Connie Willis's *Passage*, and to Tom Stoppard's *Arcadia*, has scores of people who can't stand it.

Here's another big question. Is creativity associated with mental illness? I have a lot of qualms about some of the most cited studies,[10] but there are so many different ones that it is hard for me to say that there's no connection. There is some evidence of a creativity–mental illness link at the Big-C level.[11] As much as I have reservations about any study (including mine) that relies on existing information about dead people (it's hard enough to study mental illness in living

[9] Beaussart et al., 2013; Kapoor & Khan, 2017.
[10] E.g., Andreasen, 1987; Jamison, 1993; see Schlesinger, 2009.
[11] Ludwig, 1995; Simonton, 2014c.

people who are cooperating), I respect Dean Keith Simonton and his work a great deal, and he and some others have done so many studies that I can't easily dismiss a connection.[12]

Most studies on living people are variations on giving little-c (occasionally Pro-c) folks a measure of creativity (typically, divergent thinking) and some measures of subclinical disorders.[13] Clinical disorders are the ones you know, such as schizophrenia or bipolar disorder. Subclinical disorders are studied under names that sound similar, such as schizotypy or hypomania.

However, as Christa Taylor explained to me (after only fifteen years of me teaching it incorrectly), subclinical disorders aren't actually disorders. They mean having symptoms associated with a disorder that by themselves don't meet the criteria for a diagnosis, and usually don't require therapy or medication. The difference between clinical and subclinical depression may not sound like it's a big deal. But clinical depression impacts your life in the same way as diabetes does; it requires attention and proper medication. Subclinical depression is more like being pre-diabetic. It certainly shouldn't be ignored, and there are actions (and medications) that can be taken to ensure it does not get worse, but it is much more manageable. A study of people with clinical depression would typically need to specifically seek them out as a specific population. A study of subclinical depression could mean giving college students a self-report depression inventory and comparing participants who score higher to participants who score lower.

There are many, many studies on this topic. It is very easy to find one with 100 college students that has given them a self-report measure of creativity, or maybe a divergent thinking test, along with some brief self-report measures of various subclinical disorders. The ones that don't find any correlation are harder to publish, so usually when you see something in print, they've found some type of significant connection. What happens when you try to aggregate?

Restricting my discussion to meta-analyses, there's no overall significant relationship between little-c and anxiety or depression[14] or mood disorders.[15] Creativity and schizotypy are related at $r = .07$... but schizotypy is complex. Positive and undefined schizotypy were related to creativity at $r = .14$, but negative schizotypy was negatively related, $r = -.09$[16]. That's a pretty important distinction, given positive schizotypy is more about odd beliefs whereas negative schizotypy is

[12] Simonton, 2014b, 2014c. [13] Silvia & Kaufman, 2010. [14] Paek et al., 2016.
[15] Taylor, 2017. [16] Acar & Sen, 2013.

associated with anxiety and isolation. Further, for all these meta-analyses, there were huge variations – depending on whose creativity was being measured, how it was measured, what domain of creativity was chosen, what specific subtype of disorder was being studied, and how moderating variables (such as gender, age, and intelligence) impacted the relationship.

Here's, to me, the essence.[17] Imagine that the studies were instead about what you eat and how much you weigh. One hypothetical study finds that children who ate pineapple gained weight over the next year (but compared to whom? you might ask). Another study looks at adults who eat steak versus adults who eat chicken, and concludes those who eat chicken lose a tiny bit of weight as opposed to the steak eaters. A third study has teenagers alternate between eating Cookie Crisp, Lucky Charms, and (weekends only) Frosted Flakes. On the weeks in which they eat Lucky Charms, they are more likely to lose weight (males only). A fourth study looks at prisoners who are served potatoes, by comparison with a population of non-imprisoned adults who eat whatever they want; the prisoners lose more weight and the authors propose the Simply Potatoes Ubiquitous Diet (SPUD). Finally, yet another study tangentially includes eating habits and weight, but only as a way to look at how they both impact a person's body odor. If you look carefully at the paper, you can see that they have categorized food into grains, dairy, meat, sweets, legumes, and miscellaneous (everything else); legume-consumers tend to be less smelly and lose weight.

What does it mean when you take hundreds and hundreds of studies like these and try to make sense of them? What can you conclude? I mean, my biggest suggested answer would be "not a whole hell of a lot." Notice that none of these imaginary studies looked at exercise, which might have just a bit of an effect as well. If in this mess you found six studies that showed an association between chocolate consumption and weight gain, you might agree that there's some evidence there. But every time I'm asked to summarize the creativity and mental health research literature,[18] I feel like I've been handed a random page from every Agatha Christie novel and asked to assemble a coherent mystery out of it.

Most importantly, we could go back and forth all day long pulling out competing and contrasting studies, and it wouldn't particularly change my point. Are creative people a little more likely to

[17] Adapted slightly from Kaufman, 2016a.

[18] Beaussart et al., 2014; Kaufman, 2014b, 2016b.

have this or that particular subclinical disorder? Maybe. Of course, the methodological elephant in the room (who is a little scared by the evil elephant and wishes I would just leave them alone) is that virtually no study shows that creative people have a mental illness or some subclinical disorder *because* they are creative. I'm not aware of any study that shows people engaging in a creative activity and then showing specific negative outcomes as a consequence (and I am sure that, if they do exist, I will find out about them as soon as this book is published and my mistake becomes a matter of public record). I don't mean people being creative and then killing someone (which would be malevolent creativity) but rather people being creative and then being more likely than a control group to be depressed or angry or prone to excessive sweating or to turning into werewolves.

However... I'll be talking a lot about associations with positive outcomes in the second half of this book, so I can't have my cake and chow down also. An association may be a random artifact; or it may be due to a third variable; or it may happen because one thing directly causes the other. Some of the happier findings I'll be discussing later fall into a category of "creative people tend to also have this good attribute," whereas others are framed as "when people do something creative, this happy result can happen." If I want to include the first category of good stuff, then I have to acknowledge that these types of studies, with negative mental health outcomes, also exist.

It's also important to note that, although I'm going to spend the next few chapters talking about how creativity benefits different facets of mental health and well-being, the direct relationship is fine but underwhelming. To give one example, an extensive survey of over 1,000 people examined how arts-related activities impacted their perceived quality of life. The authors looked at sixty-six different types of activities and used seven different scales, which measured an array of variables that ran from health through life satisfaction to well-being; and they had to ultimately acknowledge that "the relative impact of all of the arts-related activities and the satisfaction obtained from those activities ... contributed relatively little."[19] Such a statement is not a ringing endorsement.

Taking a broader view, a meta-analysis found a connection between creativity and overall positive well-being, but it was not an incredibly strong one (r = .14).[20] It's less than the connection that

[19] Michalos & Kahlke, 2008, p. 193. [20] Acar et al., 2020.

other meta-analyses have found between positive well-being and, for example, physical activity[21] and agreeableness.[22]

All these caveats must be noted, because data don't always end up telling the story we want them to tell; they tell whatever story they feel like telling. As much as I'd like to write a compelling polemic on how creativity makes you a happier and well-adjusted person, that view doesn't reflect the studies that are out there.

I acknowledge this fully. But I find it so much more interesting to talk about how, even if creative people may be more likely to have mental health issues (which, on a larger scale, I still do not fully believe), *it is their creativity that can also be their lifeboat.* Remember the Sylvia Plath effect? It's important to note that Plath herself saw her own writing as a form of therapy.[23] Some have argued that, in such an instance, her attempts to have her writing be therapeutic were a failure;[24] I don't know enough about Plath's life or clinical therapy to weigh in. But I think that coming to the conclusion that Plath's poetry was not enough to save her is quite different from viewing it as an associated symptom of any mental health issues she had.

A lot of this whole debate depends on where you want to focus and which story you find more compelling. A creative poet, or scientist, or cook, or entrepreneur who is more likely to have a particular mental health issue under particular conditions is a certain level of interesting – namely a low level (at least to me). It's the equivalent of a bad television movie about gangsters, the kind that Armand Assante used to star in about every other month.

If that same person, using that same creative interest or ability to climb out of depression, calms down, reaches an understanding about herself, cheers herself up, distracts herself, or finds a deeper purpose or calling? I find that storyline to be fascinating. That's *Goodfellas*. That's *The Sopranos*. If you feel this way too, even a tiny little bit, then come with me for the second half of *The Creativity Advantage*. It's like *The Godfather* movies (just the first two), but, instead of having to deal with folks like Marlon Brando, Al Pacino, or Robert DeNiro (yawn!), you get lots of cool empirical studies, theories, and syntheses.

I am hoping it will be an offer you can't refuse. On to Part II.

21 Buecker et al., 2021. 22 Anglim et al., 2020. 23 Berman, 2010.
24 Silverman & Will, 1986.

PART II
THE BENEFITS OF CREATIVITY

6 SELF-INSIGHT

A few years ago, my dad had a serious heart attack. I was stuck on the opposite coast, but my mom, my sister Jennie, and my niece Nicole all took amazing care of him. Before he was out of the woods with his heart, he was diagnosed with bladder cancer. First stage one, but more tests were needed. Then stage two, but more tests were needed. Then stage four and discussions of probabilities, options, and contingencies.

I have always been close to my parents. As some of you reading this book may know, they are Alan and Nadeen Kaufman. They develop IQ tests and are, both, legends in that field. Their first test, the Kaufman Assessment Battery for Children,[1] made a big splash in the field and in the press. I grew up going to conferences and seeing some people genuflect and others glare. It was an interesting childhood. My dad taught me about statistical analysis via baseball. Even as I learned factor analysis and multiple regression as a graduate student at Yale, I had to mentally go back to when the numbers stood for home runs and runs batted in for it all to make sense. When I switched from an MFA in creative writing to a PhD in psychology, I did so knowing the potential ramifications. The first time I attended a department social hour, I wanted to impress a girl and I suppose I did – but as Alan and Nadeen Kaufman's son: not the exact angle I was pursuing. As I moved from intelligence to creativity and began

[1] Kaufman & Kaufman, 1983.

to do my own scholarship, my need to establish my own identity faded into pride at continuing in the "family business."

A blogger once calculated that, by the time you move out of your parents' house, you've already spent 93 percent of all of the time you will ever spend with them.[2] I have no idea whether that is accurate (he makes a decent case, though), but upon my dad's diagnosis and with the whispered realization that we might be approaching his last summer, I made plans to change that percentage. With the strong and gracious encouragement of my wife, Allison, I flew out and spent most of the summer with my parents. I went to chemo appointments, joined them for breakfasts at their favorite spots, and watched ballgames and movies with them at home. I went on long dog walks with my dad, and we talked about life.

Discovering Meaning

I had time to think and explore after my parents would go to bed. I went back and reread some of the classics of humanism and positive psychology. I became fascinated with modern research on the meaning of life (at last, something even harder to study than creativity!). Whenever I discover any interesting corner of psychology, my immediate impulse is to see if I can connect it to creativity. It's like those old Reece's Peanut Butter Cup commercials; I'm a guy with a big chocolate bar trying to combine it with anything I see in case it's a good fit. I began the deep dive into how meaning might relate to creativity.

We'd been told that the odds on the chemo working were about 10 percent. Yet my dad kept saying that he felt okay (and, sometimes, that he felt great). Our family does not usually experience bouts of terrific luck; I'm not sure if I've ever gotten two items for the price of one from a vending machine. Yet somehow the scales worked to balance out here. My dad went into remission and, as I write these words, he is cancer-free. I have no idea what may happen tomorrow, but the last few years have been a gift. When that summer ended and I was back in Connecticut, I was still hooked on creativity and meaning. I spent the next several months going through several different versions of what would eventually become one of my favorite papers.[3] After two revise-and-resubmits, my overview of creativity and

[2] Urban, 2015. [3] Kaufman, 2018b.

meaning was accepted, pending minor changes. I had almost finished the last revisions after giving a seminar in Tallahassee, Florida. With just a few changes left to go, I boarded my flight back to Connecticut. I was flying barely ahead of a predicted snowstorm and I wanted to be home.

My flight was greatly delayed. I missed my intended connection but was able to get on standby for the last plane out. I ran as fast as I could to the gate, which wasn't wise, given that I was out of shape. I waited, panting, hoping to hear my name called to board. My chest was on fire; I assumed it was an asthma attack. Over the next hour, the flight departed without me. I kept calling Allison, oddly agitated and as fatigued as I had ever felt. She was able to get me booked on an early morning plane, depending on weather. With the help of a friendly employee, I assembled a tiny cot on the floor and tried to sleep. My chest was still thumping and I had a cold, sharp pain behind my jaw. I rolled over and felt a sudden numbness in my left arm.

At that point, some part of me knew exactly what was happening. But enough of me was in denial that I traipsed slowly toward the new gate. Allison, concerned, kept trying (and failing) to reach me, since all my effort was focused on the process of walking. Luckily, she intuitively realized that something was very wrong. She kept calling different offices at the airport until she found someone who called the paramedics. Allison then connected with me as I paused to rest, and she had me stay where I was.

I have told this story many times. I have told it for drama, for comedy, for extensions on overdue chapters, or as an excuse to say no to a request. How does the telling impact the tale? We know that sometimes, when you remember a specific bit of information, that very act can make related pieces harder to find again in your mind. Gloriously, this conundrum is called retrieval-induced forgetting.[4] It is a solid screw-you from your brain. Are you remembering a piece of information? Well, now it will be harder to do it again. Creative people may be more prone to this phenomenon.[5] Why? Well, consider the divergent thinking process. Sometimes your mind will forget the regular uses of an object, to let you come up with even more unusual uses.[6] False recognition and recall are associated with people who are better at divergent thinking.[7]

[4] MacLeod & Macrae, 2001. [5] Bristol & Viskontas, 2016. [6] Storm & Patel, 2014.
[7] Thakral et al., 2021.

Assuming that my memory is still reliable, I can tell you that an emergency medical technician located me, hooked me up to electrodes, and showed me a screen with indecipherable squiggles. Perhaps expecting a better reaction than my confused squint, he told me: "Sir, you are having a heart attack." As you might guess by this book's existence, it was not a fatal one. I recovered and learned to substitute brisk walks for yummy foods. My own brush with my mortality reinforced my interest in meaning. The first bit of work I tackled once I felt I was ready was to make the last few corrections and send in my creativity and meaning paper.

In that creativity and meaning paper, I followed a synthesis of the literature by Frank Martela and Michael Steger.[8] I found a lot of the papers on meaning to be well written, and this one may be my favorite. They outlined three broad categories for a tripartite model: coherence, significance, and purpose. I will explore these in great detail in the pages to come, but I'd like to offer a brief overview first. Coherence is understanding and making sense of your life, significance is feeling that your life is one that is worth living, and purpose is having specific goals for your future.[9]

My Creativity Advantage model began as I explored these three categories for my creativity and meaning paper. I found connections between components of these categories and creativity scholarship, although often in articles that did not necessarily use those terms (or the word "creativity," sometimes). I have taken my exploration of the existing research and theory and expanded into the five areas of self-insight, healing, connection, drive, and legacy.

This chapter will unpack self-insight. It is largely based on the coherence category of meaning, although (as in all of my areas) I have focused on some specific elements, included related components, and connected a variety of disciplines and studies. So I will first go into more depth about what coherence entails and how creativity can provide a pathway toward it and toward other aspects of self-insight.

Coherence

Coherence is a key part of feeling like your life has meaning. People with high coherence can see patterns in their lives that help them understand the bigger picture; it is a cognitively driven construct.[10]

[8] Martela & Steger, 2016. [9] See also King et al., 2016. [10] Heintzelman & King, 2014a.

It entails making sense of your life and of the events that happen to you.[11] Making sense does not mean understanding or being able to explain. Sometimes bad things just happen and there is no reason or explanation. But coherence enables us to see consistencies, patterns, and growth in our responses and future behavior. Unsurprisingly, higher coherence is associated with a strikingly varied array of good outcomes. They include (among many others) teenagers driving more safely,[12] cancer patients (regardless of differences in religion or disease progression) showing less distress,[13] and older adults recovering better from trauma.[14]

Coherence involves looking backwards. Whether that leads to negative feelings, such as regret, or to more positive moments of nostalgia can depend on your life choices and your current perspective on them. Erikson's[15] last stage of psychosocial development, for example, occurs when someone reflects back on their life. Depending on their decisions, accomplishments, and life circumstances, a person may feel either integrity and contentment or despair.

Positive nostalgia can give an impetus to both creativity and meaning. People who were induced into actively experiencing positive nostalgia were subsequently more creative than controls (one's inherent tendency toward being nostalgic was not related).[16] Some art making, such as scrapbooking, can specifically invoke positive nostalgia and comfort.[17] Aesthetic engagement, such as listening to music, can also specifically induce feelings of nostalgia.[18] Indeed, just the other day I was in the dentist's chair and Chris de Burgh's "Lady in Red" wafted through the air. For one brief second, I was awkwardly slow dancing at my eighth grade semi-formal, making sure my hands and feet were in the right place while I tried to think of anything to say.

Nostalgia has been proposed to increase one's meaning in life, in part by connecting one's past and one's present.[19] Nostalgia may also increase social connectedness and self-esteem, thereby enhancing meaning and potentially leading to inspiration.[20] Curiously, thinking of a nostalgia-provoking event is more associated with meaning in life than a recent pleasant event or a desired future experience.[21] I wonder how much of this finding is due to

[11] Heintzelman & King, 2014b. [12] Taubman–Ben-Ari, 2014. [13] Winger et al., 2016.
[14] López et al., 2015. [15] Erikson, 1982. [16] van Tilburg et al., 2015; Ye et al., 2013.
[17] FioRito et al., 2021. [18] Sedikides et al., 2022. [19] Sedikides & Wildschut, 2018.
[20] Stephan et al., 2015. [21] Routledge et al., 2012.

discrepancies between our experiencing self and our remembering self.[22] We are often able to selectively forget undesired memories,[23] which led some to compare personal memories to oral storytelling traditions.[24]

To make a brief tangent remark, nostalgia was associated not only with higher reported meaning but also with reduced searching for meaning.[25] That connection was interpreted positively; the investigators note that people who have a lower sense of meaning are more likely to search for it. My gut reaction was to balk, and I sought out some of the papers cited. One of them[26] compared presence of meaning and seeking meaning and, indeed, found a negative relationship. People seeking meaning also had lower psychological well-being, lower feelings of autonomy, and higher rumination (which is linked with anxiety and depression).[27] In addition, they were open to ideas and more likely to have artistic and investigative interests (all of which are linked with creativity).[28]

Uh-oh. I know what you're thinking. You read through the aperitif and thought you were done with the negativity. Yeah, I thought that, too. So I looked up the scale that measured searching for meaning in life as opposed to having it.[29] It's a fine scale, but I did notice one thing about how some of the items were worded. Many of the searching items included the word "always" – so instead of being asked if you were seeking meaning in your life, you'd be asked if you were always seeking meaning. Those questions are a bit different. I, for example, absolutely have meaning via my family, friends, dogs, writing, work, and collection of broken flash drives. But am I seeking meaning? Sure. There's always more that can enrich and add value to one's life. I feel as though saying that I'm in no way seeking meaning in life would be complacent and even arrogant.

When I talked with Todd Kashdan – one of the authors of the Steger et al. study (and of many more, amazing ones) – he used a great analogy, which helped me understand. Imagine that, instead of seeking meaning, we're talking about kids seeking extracurricular activities in school. Students who never join any activities, sports, or clubs are not going to be great examples of well-rounded kids (assuming that they don't spend their leisure time on out-of-school similar events).

22 Kahneman, 2011. 23 Kappes & Crockett, 2016. 24 Ross & Buehler, 1994.
25 Routledge et al., 2012. 26 Steger et al., 2008.
27 Nolen-Hoeksema et al., 1999; Nolen-Hoeksema et al., 1997. 28 Kaufman et al., 2013.
29 Steger et al., 2006.

But the student who joins a new club every week and ping pongs from the chess club to cheerleading, then to the key club, then to the rugby team, then to the science bowl, then to the theater, then to the student council won't have the time to actually become involved in those clubs. It's all appetizers and no main course.

There is seeking meaning and then there's taking the time to fully pursue finding meaning in a relationship, a hobby, a belief, or a pursuit. You need to throw yourself into it and allow that activity, person, thought, or value the chance to truly engage you. I love watching movies. Sometimes I give a movie my full attention, turning off the lights and putting away my phone and clearing my head. Other times I'll watch while I'm flipping between e-mail, social media, and a mobile game. There are several films that I've ended up starting over after twenty minutes, when I realized I might like them but had no idea of what was happening. Then there are films that I play on my phone throughout the whole running time, and I can't understand why I didn't enjoy them as much as everyone else did. Meaning requires a level of synthesis, processing, and reflection; otherwise it is like when my rats frantically scurry from their food to their sleep area over and over again, such that they don't actually end up either eating or sleeping.

The Writing Cure

Triggering nostalgic memories may be a bit difficult to do on a regular basis; I've highlighted the upside, but it can be bittersweet,[30] can stir feelings of loneliness,[31] and can stand in the way of seeking new experiences and opportunities.[32] How else might someone reach coherence? One way is through regular expressive writing. There is a very robust body of literature on its benefits (sometimes it's called "the writing cure") that has grown over the past thirty-five years,[33] much of it by James Pennebaker, his students, and scholars inspired by his work.[34] In this paradigm, people write for approximately twenty minutes about an emotional topic. Many early studies used a prompt that suggested trauma or negative emotions, but since then studies have indicated that writing about life goals[35] or positive

[30] Stephan et al., 2012. [31] Wildschut et al., 2010. [32] Iyer & Jetten, 2011.
[33] Pennebaker & Beall, 1986. [34] Lepore & Smyth, 2002. [35] King, 2001.

emotions[36] works equally well. This writing is done at least three times a week, usually for several weeks or more.

The benefits are striking. They include both self-reported physical health benefits and physiological markers such as increased antibody counts. Expressive writing was also linked to decreased anxiety and depression, higher grades, and enhanced ability to find work.[37] Such benefits have been found both in the short term and in the longer term.[38] I have to admit that it is an impressive body of research. I haven't written anything new about expressive writing in a few years. When I dove into PsycInfo for an update, I braced myself for a barrage of studies showing its flaws and shortcomings. I'm sure those are out there, but the literature I swam through was paper after paper showing the ways in which expressive writing helped an incredibly eclectic array of populations with a wide variety of outcomes. There was also discussion about how the writing therapy community has actually implemented this research into practice.[39]

Why does the writing cure work? One key component is the presence of a narrative.[40] More fragmented writing,[41] even if also emotionally focused, helps notably less. Poetry tends to not show any effect.[42] For example, people who wrote narratives over time reduced their anxiety and depression. In contrast, other folks who wrote poetry only increased their creativity; they remained just as depressed and anxious as ever.[43] Curiously, there is a Poetic Medicine movement aimed at having doctors and patients use poetry as a way to heal from trauma and improve resiliency;[44] perhaps other forms of writing might be better suited. Indeed, fiction seems to work just fine. People writing about an imagined trauma showed the same level of benefits as those writing about actual life events.[45] When given a choice of topics, people who chose to write about facing adversity and then shared their writing with others fared the best.[46]

The presence of a narrative in expressive writing may bring some cognitive benefits, such as higher self-regulation[47] and better working memory.[48] These can help organize your thoughts; traumatic incidents become easier to file into the back drawer of your

[36] Jones & Destin, 2021. [37] See reviews in Pennebaker, 1997; Smyth, 1998.
[38] Travagin et al., 2015. [39] Williamson & Wright, 2018.
[40] Pennebaker & Seagal, 1999. [41] Smyth et al., 2001. [42] Kaufman & Sexton, 2006.
[43] Stephenson & Rosen, 2015. [44] Kwok et al., 2022. [45] Greenberg et al., 1996.
[46] Hamby et al., 2016. [47] King, 2002. [48] Klein & Boals, 2001.

memory.[49] Think of it as the equivalent of having a closet filled with clothing all over the floor. Repeating your narrative is like getting many coat hangers, so you can tidy up. You have more closet space or, in this case, more brain space. That frees up your mind to process what has happened – and move on.

Rumination, as you may remember from a couple of pages ago, is associated with depression and anxiety.[50] Intrusive rumination, when you keep thinking about what happened without wanting to do so, is particularly undesirable. Ideally, this can shift to deliberate rumination, in which you intentionally think about what happened.[51] Here, again, the process of writing a narrative helps; in this case it increases the odds that your ruminations shift from being intrusive to being deliberate. Narratives can help you avoid brooding, but also keep the positive aspects of reflection.[52]

It is important to note how the element of narrative can help us across many different aspects of life. Some suggest that one reason why therapy can work is that it enables us to tell a coherent story about the key markers of our life.[53] Some therapies specifically use narratives for this purpose,[54] and patients can integrate the sessions into a larger narrative that helps them feel more in control.[55] More and more, the narrative has become a key component of how social workers help children heal after trauma. Often children are asked to tell their life story as they process events in therapy.[56] Another example is an elementary school intervention that drew on narrative components already present in fairy tales, alongside a creative storytelling task. Compared to controls, who learned about fairy tales in a more traditional way, the kids in the intervention showed higher well-being and lower depression and anxiety.[57]

We are a species that likes to perpetually tell and retell the stories of our own lives.[58] Such storytelling not only is tied to positive mental health,[59] but can become a core part of who we are. The narrative we weave out of our most salient life experiences becomes a large component of our identity, and the degree to which these narratives reflect coherence is associated with positive well-being and meaning.[60]

[49] Pennebaker & Seagal, 1999.
[50] Nolen-Hoeksema et al., 1999; Nolen-Hoeksema et al., 1997.
[51] Tedeschi & Calhoun, 2004. [52] Gortner et al., 2006; Sloan et al., 2008.
[53] Mahoney, 1995. [54] Suddeath et al., 2017. [55] Adler, 2012. [56] Booth, 2022.
[57] Ruini et al., 2020. [58] Stewart & Neimeyer, 2001.
[59] Baerger & McAdams, 1999; Sexton & Pennebaker, 2004. [60] Waters & Fivush, 2015.

Narratives and Identity

Narrative thought highlights our search for what has been and for what could be. With narrative thought comes the search for possible connections. Sometimes it is contrasted with paradigmatic thought, which tries to capture what actually is. Narrative thought is interested in stories, intentions, beliefs, and meaning, whereas paradigmatic thought is more logical, analytic, and factual.[61] My dissertation looked at narrative and paradigmatic thought in writers; I had people write captions to photographs, then had raters assess each one for both types of thought. Before I did so, I wrote to the estimable Jerome Bruner, the theorist, asking for his advice and approval. I was thrilled when he wrote back; that excitement decreased when he told me he thought it was a terrible idea. I nonetheless persisted (I wish I could claim resilience or passionate belief, but it was more likely inertia and wanting to finish my dissertation).

I found that creative writers were more likely to use narrative thought, whereas journalists were more likely to use paradigmatic thought. It wasn't ground-breaking, but it was an important early step for me.[62] It is easy to think of a journalist as representing the logical, paradigmatic way of thinking. Sportswriter Thomas Boswell put it beautifully when he wrote, "the beat journalist's ultimate goal isn't a dramatic or poetic effect, much as any writer lusts after such moments of luck ... 'That's right' is what we're after, more than 'That's beautiful.'"[63]

There is merit in both approaches, but narrative thinking can help shape your identity. Dan McAdams, a legend in studying narratives and how they relate to the self, has a three-stage model of how the self evolves over a lifespan.[64] In the beginning, when we are young, we figure out who we are by observing others; this stage is called being a social actor. As we progress through adolescence, we continue by becoming a motivated agent. We discover our own life goals and values. Young adults who encounter specific stressors or trauma may suffer identity distress; one study of young cancer patients found that narrative creativity helped mitigate such issues.[65]

These first two stages – actor and agent – continue throughout our life. The last stage, which begins in our teens and continues

[61] Bruner, 1986, 1990. [62] Kaufman, 2002b. [63] Boswell, 1989, p. xii.
[64] McAdams, 2013. [65] Barbot et al., 2021.

into adulthood, is that of the autobiographical author. Our self becomes a synthesis of our past, present, and future. We construct our life story as a narrative, and it becomes who we are. When it is consistent, we experience narrative continuity.[66] When that continuity is disrupted, we may experience an identity crisis.[67] Sometimes we can use narratives to look backwards and make sense of our lives; other times we can use these same basic concepts to look forward, at who we want to be. Identity is a construct that can be developed and shaped. As usual, creativity plays a role.

Identity Development and Creativity

What makes us who we are? When I was growing up, as I've discussed, being a writer was at the core of my identity. I considered myself a "writer." It was where I saw my value; it was who I was. Now I see myself as having many identities: a husband, a father, a professor, a psychologist, a mentor, a friend, a colleague... And a writer. Some things don't change.

Identity and creativity share similar processes. Think back to divergent and convergent thinking, in which you come up with many different ideas, and then select the best one to pursue.

Now remember when you were in high school (or earlier). You had to decide where you fit in. Were you a jock, a preppy, or a stoner? A geek, a goth, or a theater kid? Maybe you were actively trying out new outfits, vocabularies, and attitudes. After you generated and tried out different possible identities, you would eventually settle on who you wanted to be (at least for the time being). This process might keep repeating itself over and over again, as someone gets older and tries many different types of relationships, careers, and adult identities.

This whole cycle might require synthesizing many differently nuanced aspects of the self. Sometimes it can mean combining facets of the self that don't seem to go together. My friend and colleague Baptiste Barbot, an expert in creativity and identity (and where to find amazing hamburgers), offered as an example that some people may be outgoing with their close family but more reserved with their peer group. You have to be flexible to find a consistent story that fits the inconsistent strands of your life.[68]

[66] Prebble et al., 2013. [67] McAdams, 2013. [68] Barbot, 2018b.

Creativity and identity development are reciprocal, Barbot also told me. Expressing yourself in a creative way (whether it is a science experiment, new invention, or dramatic monologue) can help you channel your identity. When you think of being personally creative, isn't *self*-expression one of the first concepts to come to mind? It is not exclusively positive; figuring out who you are can be confusing and even distressing. But, on the whole, it is a time of exploration and discovery. Finally, the creative outlets that you choose help define who you are. Even if the process is not as explicit as my younger self equating himself completely with his ability to write, your passions, hobbies, and goals shape who you are.

It is important to emphasize that creativity is not a magical cure-all. A study of creativity and identity in adolescents looked at whether participants were inclined to choose creative responses to situations (what you might do if you forgot a spoon with your lunch), and then looked at the valence of each response (neutral, positive, or negative). Neutrally creative kids, who gave not particularly creative answers that were neither good nor bad (e.g., the kids who answered that they would just eat their lunch anyway), showed solid identity development. Those who were more likely to respond in a negatively creative way were also more likely to show identity diffusion (i.e., being confused about who you are), anxiety, and depression. As I was reading, I was primed to find that the positively creativity adolescents would be doing great; but they were also high on anxiety and depression.[69] Damn. This last group was also high on rumination, which you may remember is connected to depression. Perhaps their inclination to be creative in a positive way represented a response to internal struggles?

A relevant idea is that of a creative personal identity.[70] How important is your creativity to who you are? Imagine that someone asked you to pick five adjectives to describe yourself. Would "creative" be one of them? If not, would it be in the top ten or twenty? Or maybe it would feature in a specific creative pursuit, such as "painter" or "cook" or "builder"?

Self-Insight and beyond

There are so many other areas I could explore – I've been largely talking about self-insight as understanding one's own self, but

[69] Sica et al., 2022. [70] Karwowski, 2016; Karwowski et al., 2013.

creative people are also more likely to want to understand the world. People who are creative tend to also have a higher need for cognition.[71] Relatedly, there is significant empirical[72] and theoretical[73] support for the idea that curiosity is strongly related to creativity. Curiosity has a number of different components, however. One scale (created, among others, by Todd Kashdan)[74] splits curiosity along five dimensions. One of them, joyous exploration, is all about wanting to learn, grow, and think; it would fit perfectly with self-insight. Another dimension, thrill seeking, focuses on taking risks and going on adventures; it would be a better match for a later area, drive.

Many of the positive outcomes of the Creativity Advantage model are a bit cyclical: creativity leads to these good things, and often the good things can end up reinforcing and supporting creativity. We use our creativity to help develop our identity, and these identities may be shaped by seeing ourselves as creative. As we do so, we are essentially determining our own future narrative. At any point, we can enhance our coherence through regular, narrative-driven writing that channels our emotions. As we age, we can continue benefiting from articulating and shaping our narratives by writing a memoir (or by conveying our story in any form). These are not only good outcomes, they can help us be creative, too.

As you understand who you are, who you were, and who you want to be, you can heal. There are many sources of pain and trauma in this world, and I'm not about to turn creativity into some kind of cosmic superhero of a construct. It can only go so far, and it may not always be the best way to heal; every person, every situation is different. But, as I'll explain in the next chapter, creativity is certainly one pathway toward healing.

[71] Dollinger, 2003. [72] Schutte & Malouff, 2020. [73] Gross et al., 2020.
[74] Kashdan et al., 2020; Kashdan et al., 2018.

7 HEALING

When we think about creativity and mental health, most people gravitate toward the image of the mad genius.[1] If creativity and mental health struggles are associated, what might be the underlying reasons? I have yet to read or hear any serious creativity scholar suggest that partaking in creative activity actually causes any type of mental illness. The most common arguments and explorations deal with whether creative people are more prone to being mentally ill or whether mentally ill people are more likely to be creative. There is also the theory that the two constructs have traits in common (which is a neat idea, just a topic for a different book).[2]

There is also the thought that personal struggles and negative experiences may provide fodder for artistic or general inspiration.[3] For example, Red Smith is commonly credited with saying: "Writing is easy. You just open a vein and bleed."[4] I do find that maxim reflected in my own memories of creative writing. My first true heartbreak led to a pretty decent short story. The imprint of my brother's extensive mental health issues led to many early short stories. The general apprehension and uncertainty I felt about him, along with my experience as a mental health worker in college, led to my first musical, *Discovering Magenta* (with music composed by Michael Bitterman). It premiered in New York after my brother's early death. I'm pondering whether my decision to turn such life events

[1] Kaufman et al., 2006, although see Alabbasi et al., 2020. [2] Carson, 2011, 2019.
[3] Forgeard, 2013. [4] Eubanks, 2016.

into stories and plays represents my trying to heal myself by writing my own version of events... Or if it's simply mining my own demons for creative fodder.

But what about flipping the question on its head? As Marie Forgeard has suggested, could it be that people who suffer from mental health issues or have experienced trauma seek out creative activities because of their potentially healing properties?[5] Maybe creativity helps you feel better, so people who are struggling with their mental health may gravitate (consciously or not) toward being creative?

Much of what I'm going to talk about in this chapter comes from the world of arts therapy. A large part of the research is qualitative in nature, with many case studies or narratives of specific interventions. Samples are usually small, which is generally good because it means that few people are suffering. But, although such studies offer valuable insights, there are some limits that should be acknowledged before we extrapolate too much to larger populations. Many people who have extensive training in art therapy may not have taken high-level coursework in quantitative research methods (and vice versa).[6] Reviews of the existing literature have noted many flaws and have suggested that future studies use follow-up testing, better control groups, and more specific outcome assessments[7] and focus on the specific mechanisms that underly positive change.[8] There is much more work to be done, but I am still excited about what is here.

Creativity and Post-Traumatic Growth

There is quite a bit of support for creativity's ability to help people heal. One place to start is with the worst moments of people's lives. As discussed in the last chapter, one core creativity advantage is that it helps us make sense of our lives. Our lives typically include tragic happenings. When the unthinkable happens, it is utterly human to want to believe that there is some benefit behind the event.[9] This need can be a reason why many people try to form a charity or foundation in a lost loved one's name. Our need to achieve insight or silver lining from trauma is an intense one.[10]

[5] Forgeard, 2019; Forgeard & Elstein, 2014. [6] van Westrhenen & Fritz, 2014.
[7] Maujean et al., 2014. [8] Baker et al., 2018. [9] Lichtenthal et al., 2010.
[10] McAdams et al., 2001.

We hear a lot about post-traumatic stress disorder (PTSD) and other rippling effects that can occur after people experience terrible life events. What we hear about a little less is that sometimes, after we experience trauma, it is possible to undergo beneficial psychological changes.[11] Such post-traumatic growth does not come from the actual terrible event – so there is no need to actively pursue tragedy in hopes of becoming a better person. Rather it is the aftermath of reflection, sensemaking, and coping that can give rise to an improved identity or life.[12] It is important to note that believing that you have grown and evolved as a person does not mean that you actually have done so; indeed, there is a chance that some people may report post-traumatic growth because they are in denial about the damage their life event has caused.[13]

There are many ways in which people may display such growth: interpersonally, spiritually, or through enhanced gratitude.[14] My dad, after his recovery from heart attack and cancer, experienced a great deal of post-traumatic growth. He's always been a "glass half-full" type of person, but now he can sound so happy when we chat that if it were anyone else I would worry I reached someone while they were being held hostage.

As you may have guessed from the fact that I'm writing about this topic in the present book, post-traumatic growth can be associated with creativity. Specifically, creative people seem to be more likely to report growth or to show resilience after traumatic situations. This connection has been found in survivors of the Rwandan genocide,[15] Hurricane Katrina,[16] and the Lushan earthquake[17] (among other disasters). Creativity has also been linked to post-traumatic growth in people with chronic illnesses or disabilities.[18]

Why would creativity help people after trauma? The diversifying experiences theory argues that encountering (and surviving) adversity requires someone to think in new ways in order to adapt,[19] with a particular emphasis on cognitive flexibility.[20] Others have suggested that creativity may help enhance self-esteem.[21] In such cases, creativity may simply be required in order to have survived. But what about creativity helping people not just survive, but to thrive?

[11] Tedeschi et al., 2018. [12] Joseph & Linley, 2006. [13] Boerner et al., 2017.
[14] Forgeard, 2019; Tedeschi & Calhoun, 2004. [15] Forgeard et al., 2014.
[16] Metzl, 2009. [17] Liang et al., 2021. [18] Tolleson & Zeligman, 2019.
[19] Damian & Simonton, 2014, 2015. [20] Ritter et al., 2012.
[21] Thomson & Jaque, 2016.

Some have suggested that certain creative therapies may activate components of the brain to unearth buried memories or emotions.[22] Others note that imagination and PTSD itself can be found in overlapping spaces in the brain.[23] An investigation that interviewed Holocaust survivor artists found that some saw their art as a safe space where it was okay to think about their trauma.[24] Emotions may well be the key; emotional creativity – being able to express and experience emotions in a creative way[25] – has been found to be an important mediator between exposure to trauma, mental health symptoms, and post-traumatic growth.[26] A study on mental health during the COVID-19 pandemic also emphasized the importance of emotional creativity.[27]

There have been other studies that looked at how arts-based interventions and workshops can help people in times of crisis. Participants include women who survived an ISIS attack,[28] asylum-seeking children living in shelters,[29] victims of domestic violence,[30] and combat veterans.[31] I admit to my own emotional self-preservation limiting how deeply I can dive into this sometimes dark literature; there are other, great books that focus on the intersection of creativity and trauma.[32] Instead of continuing down this path, then, I'm going to pivot to how creativity can heal under less profoundly tragic circumstances.

Emotional Equilibrium

Healing can also mean maintaining emotional equilibrium. Rebounding from major trauma is a huge benefit, but there are also everyday blahs begging to be overcome. Thankfully, you can use your creativity to raise yourself up from simply feeling sad or down in a number of different ways. There is a large body of work on how being creative in the arts can help regulate or simply improve your emotional state. In general, women, people of lower socioeconomic status, and people with the relevant background or training are more likely than others to turn to the arts for emotional strength.[33]

A very high percentage of the research I'm about to discuss is centered on the arts. I'm not ignoring a huge stream of nonarts work;

[22] Belkofer & Konopka, 2008; Perryman et al., 2019. [23] Rubinstein & Lahad, 2022.
[24] Diamond & Shrira, 2022. [25] Averill, 1999; Ivcevic et al., 2007.
[26] Orkibi & Ram-Vlasov, 2019. [27] Zhai et al., 2021. [28] Abdulah & Abdulla, 2020.
[29] de Freitas Girardi et al., 2020. [30] Hernández-Ruiz, 2005. [31] Bensimon et al., 2008.
[32] E.g., Thomson & Jaque, 2019. [33] Fancourt et al., 2020.

there just isn't much out there.[34] There are some small, initial studies on domains that fit well into everyday life, such as cooking[35] or gardening.[36] There is also some work that is more in the leisure studies arena than in that of creativity but is nonetheless relevant – for example some papers suggest that psychological benefits come from participating in the Makerspace and Do It Yourself movements[37] or from playing video games such as Animal Crossing.[38] I wonder whether this trend might continue, in part because the ongoing aftereffects of the COVID-19 pandemic lockdown make us hyperaware of anything that brings the smallest amount of joy. For now, however, we'll largely be sticking to the arts.

With this caveat in place, there are many different strategies that can be used to regulate your emotions. One analysis narrowed them down to three broad types.[39] The first is focused on improving self-related factors. These can include building up your identity (which was discussed in the last chapter), self-efficacy, or self-esteem. The second, which I will highlight in a moment, is to avoid negative emotions or issues. The third is approach-focused and can include creatively solving your problem or cognitively reappraising the situation.

Cognitive reappraisal is a process in which we are able to think in different ways about an incident, often in the service of changing how we feel.[40] Someone can use cognitive reappraisal to see a silver lining in a past trauma, or even to be able to think about an emotionally charged past incident without becoming upset all over again. One of my favorite examples is in Amy Hempel's short story "The Man from Bogota." An unnamed narrator sees someone who is threatening to commit suicide and imagines what would be the best thing to say to get the person to climb off the ledge. She decides it would be the story of a wealthy industrialist in Bogota who is kidnapped and held for ransom. Unlike in the movies, it takes his family a long time to raise the money and the kidnappers need to make sure he stays alive. So they make him exercise, quit smoking, and eat healthy meals. When eventually the money is paid and he is released, his doctor says he is in the best health he has been in for years. The narrator then concludes that she hopes "that the woman

[34] Grossman & Drake, 2023. [35] Güler & Haseki, 2021; Mosko & Delach, 2021.
[36] Sunga & Advincula, 2021. [37] Collier & Wayment, 2018.
[38] Barr & Copeland-Stewart, 2022. [39] Fancourt et al., 2019.
[40] McRae & Gross, 2020; McRae et al., 2012.

on the ledge will ask herself a question, the question that occurred to that man in Bogota. He wondered how we know that what happens to us isn't good."[41]

Someone who is strong on cognitive reappraisal should be able to think of many different ways of interpreting or processing an upsetting life event. Having this ability may sound a bit similar to being able to think of many different possible uses for a tin can, and... actually, it's not too far off. High cognitive reappraisal skills are linked to higher divergent thinking,[42] although cognitive control is more important in cognitive reappraisal.[43] People who are more creative than others in how they cognitively reappraise a situation – as long as it is in a positive way – will generally be better at also bringing themselves to equilibrium;[44] indeed, creative reappraisals were better able to turn negative emotional arousal into positive emotional arousal than ordinary reappraisals.[45] Presumably being able to generate all the potentially terrible interpretations of a negative event is less good for you.

Another way of thinking about cognitive reappraisal is that events that might normally trigger feelings of unhappiness can be shifted to be oddly motivating instead. People who have an independent self-concept (in other words, are less focused on the group or collective goals) are able to take social rejection and to use that negative experience as inspiration to be more creative.[46] Being pissed off – if it's related to the task at hand – can help you generate more ideas.[47] In addition, although being rejected can increase fluency in divergent thinking, being ignored can also enhance convergent thinking.[48]

Diving into Distraction

Let's go back to avoiding your emotions, which sounds like it belongs on a list of "things that your therapist will yell at you for doing." It turns out that there's actually a wide body of research about the positive power of distraction and the arts that I find absolutely fascinating. I feel like we all saw the power of positive distraction during the COVID-19 pandemic lockdown, when the creativity of viral videos,

[41] Hempel, 1986, p. 98. [42] Weber et al., 2014.
[43] Fink et al., 2017; Rominger et al., 2018. [44] Wu et al., 2017, 2019.
[45] Zhang et al., 2022. [46] Kim et al., 2013. [47] Strasbaugh & Connelly, 2022.
[48] Sun et al., 2020.

craft projects, culinary exploits, and finding fun ways to socially distance kept many of us sane.[49] Indeed, creative activity was linked to higher subjective well-being,[50] optimism, and positive affect.[51]

So there is an extensive base of research that could have tipped us off about the power of the arts (and beyond) to distract us. The initial studies, led by Ellen Winner and her colleagues, began innocuously, by checking whether art therapy actually worked. First, they wanted to test whether the actual process of drawing helped people feel better. We often assume that some treatments or interventions help – for example, basic therapy – when the actual data may not be as supportive as we'd prefer.[52]

Therefore the first study along these lines induced people to feel sad. In this case, it was through a brief video with images of the Holocaust, funerals, the 9/11 attacks, and other terrible things. The researchers had some people draw a picture and others copy shapes; the ones who actually drew a picture showed a more improved mood. Next, the researchers had some people draw and others complete a word puzzle. Those who drew showed improved mood, but not the people who did the puzzle.[53]

Okay, so art helps. Which is cool. But the next question is to figure out *why* it helps. In a subsequent study, participants were again showed a sad and upsetting movie clip (war films are always a good bet). Afterwards, some were asked to make a drawing that expressed how they were currently feeling; others were asked to draw something happy. Those who drew the short straw to be in the control group got a dull task designed to measure attention. The results surprised me when I first read them. The participants who were distracted with the happy drawing showed a short-term increase in mood. Those who expressed their feelings were no better off than the controls.[54]

There have been a wide array of studies, most of them conducted by Jennifer Drake, which have expanded, refined, and clarified the question of how the arts can help short-term mood repair. One paper presented several studies in which children were ask to draw after they thought about a disappointing event. Drake's findings suggest that kids who draw with the goal of feeling distracted can better enjoy and be absorbed by drawing.[55] The content (real or

[49] Kapoor & Kaufman, 2020. [50] Kyriazos et al., 2021. [51] Brosowsky et al., 2022.
[52] Watkins, 2011. [53] De Petrillo & Winner, 2005. [54] Dalebroux et al., 2008.
[55] Drake, 2021.

imaginary) of the drawings and the age of the children did not impact the results, although younger kids generally enjoyed the task more (so would I, if I did not have to concern myself with bladder control – although a more likely reason, as Drake suggested to me, is that younger kids are less critical of their own drawings). Also irrelevant was the presence of instructions. She noted that, when children were simply told to draw whatever they wanted, they were instinctually more likely to draw to distract themselves, as opposed to drawing to express themselves.

Many more studies examined specific dimensions. For example, the basic expression–distraction comparison has been revisited multiple times. One study allowed participants to express their feelings by drawing a picture related to the sad film clip they had just seen, whereas others were distracted by being made to draw something unrelated, and, again, distraction was more effective than expressive drawing.[56] Another study reported the same core effect with children (having had them think about a disappointing event instead of showing them sad images).[57] Next, drawing was compared to coloring, the fundamental idea being that drawing would be a higher cognitive demand (with mild apologies to all of those people who flock to the adult coloring books). After an induced sad mood, people colored a design, drew a design, or drew to express themselves. Both coloring and drawing a design (forms of distraction) improved affect more than expressive drawing.[58]

Well, you may wonder, sadness is all well and good, but what about other negative emotions? One study examined the "coloring versus drawing" and "expression versus distraction" questions by using surveys and by measuring heart rate, respiratory sinus arrhythmia (higher levels are associated with being better able to regulate one's emotions),[59] and skin conductance (which I used to know as galvanic skin response in my youth). People were first made anxious (for me, that would just mean asking me to talk to someone) and then asked to color, to draw to distract, or to draw to express. It turns out that in all three groups anxiety – as measured through both psychological and psychophysiological methods – was reduced, although the participants who drew for the purpose of distraction enjoyed the task more.[60] Coloring was explored in more detail, to see whether it matters if you can choose which colors to use or there's forced choice

[56] Drake & Winner, 2012. [57] Drake & Winner, 2013. [58] Forkosh & Drake, 2017.
[59] Beauchaine, 2001. [60] Turturro & Drake, 2022.

(think of paint by numbers). Being able to pick your colors helped reduce anxiety more, and also led to people persevering on a subsequent impossible anagram task.[61] Anxiety's more extraverted cousin, anger, inspired another study. When sadness and anger were compared, the same results were found. Drawing to distract improved the negative emotion, regardless of which one, better than expressive drawing.[62]

Further studies have explored how much the domain matters; is art the sole pathway to a happier, distracted you? The most common comparison is with writing. We already know, from the last chapter, that expressive writing helps across a longer period of time.[63] How about mood repair? First, distraction helps more than expression in the short term, regardless of domain. Second, drawing seems to help more than writing,[64] even among people (like me) who prefer writing over drawing.[65] One study asked people to think about the saddest thing they had ever experienced, then either asked them to express themselves about that sad topic or gave them a distracting activity focused on what they were doing for the rest of the day. They were then directed to express or distract themselves by drawing, writing, thinking, or talking.[66] Distraction reduced negative affect across all domains more than expression. Positive affect stayed the same for the people who talked or wrote but increased for those who used distraction by drawing or thinking (although, in eyeballing the numbers, it looks like writing was just on the wrong side of significance and drawing was just on the right side).

You may remember from the last chapter that narratives activated the writing cure but, in general, poetry did not.[67] One study I mentioned compared the longer-term effects of (expressively) writing narratives to those of writing poetry. Its authors found that narratives helped with anxiety and depression, but poetry did not.[68] A similar comparison was made between narratives and poetry, except this time focusing on writing for distraction versus expressive writing. The authors of this study found that writing for distraction helped more than expressive writing, regardless of format, although people enjoyed writing poetry more.[69] Finally, drawing was compared to calculating (as in adding numbers together), as a way of recovering from sad or angry moods. Drawing helped more than calculating

[61] Eaton & Tieber, 2017. [62] Genuth & Drake, 2021. [63] Pennebaker, 1997.
[64] Drake et al., 2011. [65] Drake & Hodge, 2015. [66] James et al., 2018.
[67] Kaufman & Sexton, 2006. [68] Stephenson & Rosen, 2015. [69] Fink & Drake, 2016.

toward becoming less sad, but there was no difference between the two when it cxame to anger.[70] It's a little funny, because calculating usually makes me sad and angry.

What happens as the length of time increases? The comparison between expressive drawing and distracted drawing has been studied in contexts where these activities were pursued over a longer period of time. An initial study that had people draw over four consecutive days found, just like past work, that distraction led to a better mood than did expression.[71] Another study had people draw over a month (they were allowed to eat, too) and looked at psychological (including self-reported mood) and psychophysiological benefits (including respiratory sinus arrhythmia, RSA, which is considered a proxy for emotion regulation).[72] People who drew to distract showed more of an increase in positive affect and decrease in negative affect than people who drew to express themselves after a single session. Both groups showed increased RSA (better emotion regulation). After the full month, the people in the distraction condition showed more of an increase in positive affect than those in the expression condition (although not, curiously, those in the control group). The drawing-to-distract group had significantly higher RSA than the control group, but the difference between it and the drawing-to-express group was not significant. The picture of the longer-term impact of distraction-based art therapy is a bit murkier. So, too, is the question of how your aptitude at art is a possible factor.

Benefits of Active and Passive Arts Engagement

Even experiencing the arts as a user – aesthetic engagement – can help, including by giving you emotional benefits. Indeed, the emotions that the arts can inspire in us are distinct from our aesthetic appreciation or judgement of a piece.[73] I hope I am not the only one who can be moved to tears by a sappy movie or a poignant *Cold Case* episode, or even by a particularly moving Thai life insurance commercial. When we process art that engages our emotions, we show increased activity in the areas in our brains that are used when we get rewards.[74] It may not be surprising that, although "beauty" and "wellness" are still considered fully separate concepts, there is substantial overlap in our mental word maps between the ideas that

[70] Yan et al., 2021. [71] Drake et al., 2016. [72] Drake, 2019. [73] Leder et al., 2004.
[74] Mastandrea et al., 2019.

surround them, and it is found across generations (with slightly more convergence in younger people).[75] Engaging with the arts in person is even more beneficial.[76]

A great deal of the research on music and emotion regulation, particularly via distraction, is focused on listening to music. Of course, there is work on actively creating music. Music therapy interventions that encompassed composing, singing, or listening to music have been shown to improve perceived mental health across twenty-six studies.[77] In general, music helps lower anxiety in younger people, elevate mood in adults, and increase coping for those with health issues[78] – and is associated with lower mortality risk.[79] Both virtual and live singing in groups help emotion regulation, for example, although the former is not as effective as the latter.[80] During the worldwide COVID-19 lockdown, singing – as well as dancing, which also broadly helps improve emotions[81] (listening to music and reading also helped)[82] – was among the most effective emotion regulation strategies... But these were also the ones most likely to have been stopped because of the pandemic.[83] Even singing together remotely has mental health benefits.[84]

The distraction approach to emotion regulation, unsurprisingly, works well when we listen to live music.[85] Yet recorded music also works; one underlying mechanism that helps explain the connection is that the medial prefrontal cortex, which can activate when we get rid of emotions we don't want to be experiencing, increases when people listen to music to distract themselves.[86] I should also note that, curiously, general neuroticism moderates whether people choose in the first place to regulate their emotions with music.[87] Make of that what you will; I'm just sitting here listening to Bowie's "Life on Mars" to feel better.

It is important to note that listening to angry or sad music to express, ruminate on, or discharge your feelings can be maladaptive and lead to more anxiety (particularly for men),[88] although those with musical training were less likely to have this pattern translate into depression or anxiety.[89] It is interesting to explore the literary

[75] Kenett et al., 2021. [76] Totterdell & Poerio, 2021. [77] McCrary et al., 2022.
[78] Daykin et al., 2018. [79] Story et al., 2021. [80] Fancourt & Steptoe, 2019.
[81] Zimmerman & Mangelsdorf, 2020. [82] Drake et al., 2022. [83] Kiernan et al., 2021.
[84] Bind et al., 2022. [85] Theorell et al., 2019. [86] Carlson et al., 2015.
[87] Miranda, 2020; Miranda & Blais-Rochette, 2020.
[88] Carlson et al., 2015; Miranda, 2021. [89] Miranda, 2022.

roots of the belief that small bursts of anger or sadness can inure you to future suffering. A. E. Housman's poem "Terrence, this is stupid stuff"[90] features a poet who defends writing melancholic verse by giving the example of Mithridates the Great, king of Hellenistic Pontus (135–63 BC). According to legend, the king was afraid of being poisoned. As a result, he added a tiny bit of every imaginable variety of poison into his own food for years. Whenever someone tried to assassinate him with poison, it didn't affect him. The eponymous Terrence ends the poem by noting that Mithridates died old. Alas, even classic poetry should bear a "Don't try this at home" label.

Healthy versus unhealthy music use is also associated with better (or worse) coping skills.[91] Another study of cancer patients and caregivers showed that, after singing in choirs, both groups indicated an increase of positive emotions and a decrease of negative emotions. In addition, cytokines (which build up your immune system) increased, while oxytocin and cortisol (hormones associated with stress) decreased.[92] Finally, if you were wondering about music genres, there's some evidence for the particular strength of soul and funk.[93] Perhaps I need to switch from David Bowie to James Brown?

Cognitive Healing

There is a vast amount of research on creativity (particularly in the arts) in older adults. I've touched very slightly on this population in the last chapter, and will continue to pepper in relevant studies throughout the book. Of interest here is the role that creative activities can have in helping those at risk of dementia or those who already have it. Before we start, at the risk of completely neutering the cheery news to follow, I should note three very important caveats. First, although there have been many studies along these lines, quite a few of them have had key methodological flaws (such as limited evaluation methods, samples, and timespans).[94] Second, many of the studies that have strong research methods in place may find affective benefits (such as improved mood or self-esteem), but no cognitive benefits.[95] Finally, even in studies with solid methodology that find cognitive benefits, such improvements are typically temporary and for the short term.[96]

[90] Housman, 1932. [91] Silverman, 2021. [92] Fancourt et al., 2016.
[93] Cook et al., 2019. [94] Zeilig et al., 2014. [95] Young et al., 2016.
[96] Särkämö, 2018.

All of that said, being creative can reduce the odds of developing cognitive difficulties in the first place. One longitudinal study of older adults that took place over more than twenty years found that those who were more likely to read, play music, or dance were less likely to develop dementia.[97] A different long-term study found the key activities to be related to participation in arts and crafts.[98] Another study compared older adults who showed signs of dementia or cognitive impairment to older adults who did not. Reading books and doing crafts were more commonly found in the unimpaired group; playing music and making art just lacked statistical significance.[99] One nicely thorough long-term study broke down leisure activities into five categories (typically there are three or fewer): individual cognitive, group cognitive, social, physical, and creative (or, more accurately, activities traditionally perceived as being creative; any of these can be creative). This last category placed a nice emphasis on writing (articles, letters, stories, and poems), along with arts, crafts, and sewing. All activities were related at least slightly to less eventual cognitive impairment, but creative activities specifically showed additional predictive power above and beyond the other types.[100]

Creative, artistic, or aesthetic activities can also help those who already have dementia (typically, mild or moderate cases).[101] Studies have found specific cognitive benefits from creating and appreciating visual art and music. For example, one study found that both singing and listening to music can improve personal episodic memory (i.e., stories from one's life), orientation (i.e., knowing one's location, the date, and other core information), and (mildly) basic cognition. Singing, in addition, was found to improve short-term and working memory,[102] and this result has been replicated in other studies.[103] Dance interventions (but not playing an instrument) have also been found to help short-term memory.[104] Interventions for people with dementia that include both making and viewing visual art have found slightly longer-term but inconsistent benefits to episodic memory[105] and verbal fluency.[106] In addition, listening to music as a group can encourage collective reminiscence and, thus, allow

[97] Verghese et al., 2003. [98] Roberts et al., 2015. [99] Geda et al., 2011.
[100] Hansdottir et al., 2022. [101] Ward et al., 2020. [102] Särkämö et al., 2009.
[103] Davidson & Fedele, 2011; Särkämö et al., 2016. [104] Doi et al., 2017.
[105] Eekelaar et al., 2012; Lee et al., 2019. [106] Young et al., 2015.

those with dementia to remember the songs.[107] Similar arts-based reminiscence activities (which can encompass other domains) show more affective short-term benefits as well.[108]

There has been a call to expand this type of work beyond arts-based interventions and to also focus on everyday creativity.[109] Unsurprisingly, I completely agree and would push it further. There are so many creative domains that have nothing or very little to do with the arts, from the hard sciences to engineering, business, computer science, academic scholarship, and technology. Would it be possible to look at how being creative in these areas might help stave off or slow down cognitive decline?

Well, most people aren't going to discover a late-in-life passion for creative nuclear physics. There are many reasons both obvious and less obvious, why such a pursuit would be rare, and they do shed some light on which nonartistic domains might or might not be legitimate possibilities. As I mentioned when I first discussed creativity across domains, there are some areas that do not lend themselves to hobby pursuits. In this case, someone would need access to extensive material resources, relevant knowledge and expertise, and likely collaborators. It is difficult to make a novel professional contribution in a specific field (including in many hard sciences) late in life,[110] in part because our ability to solve new problems drops sharply as we reach middle age and beyond.[111]

However, there absolutely are people who stay active in their careers late in life – and such individuals are less likely to develop dementia.[112] Such a connection should not shock you; nor should hearing that people who are more educated and more successful at work are less likely to develop dementia. One theory posits that they are better able to use cognitive reserve, drawing from their past intellectual activities to process their current responsibilities and thus taking much longer before their functionality is impacted.[113]

However, what I would love to see explored more is nonartistic mini-c and little-c activities. Older people who frequently pursued cognitively demanding hobbies, such as playing games, solving puzzles, or reading, were less likely to develop Alzheimer's disease[114] or other types of dementia.[115] Three factors tend to be found in these types of hobbies that can help avoid cognitive impairment, and one is

[107] Dowlen et al., 2018. [108] Keating et al., 2020. [109] Bellass et al., 2019.
[110] Simonton, 1994, 1997. [111] Kaufman, 2000, 2001. [112] Dufouil et al., 2014.
[113] Stern, 2006. [114] Wilson et al., 2002. [115] Carlson et al., 2008.

novelty seeking (along with exchanging ideas and being social). The descriptors of such activities include learning new skills or knowledge, problem solving, and finding mental challenges.[116] Many non-artistic domains are quite cognitive; I'd love to see more investigations of such possible interventions. What about computer coding or programming, for example? A study of older men found that regular computer use reduced dementia risk.[117] In addition, there have been initial studies about the use of computer-based programs[118] and activities that suggest that they, too, may help people with mild cognitive impairment.[119] One study compared younger and older adults at their ability to program computers and found that the older group's extra experience compensated for the members' additional stress when working under pressure; as a result, age had no overall effect[120]... except that "older" meant being as ancient as fifty-four years old. There has been preliminary work describing a successful course designed to teach adults over sixty with no prior experience how to program computers.[121] I'd be thrilled to see more studies and interventions that look at how creative coding might prevent or delay dementia.

I realize that the percentage of people who perform creative science, technology, engineering, and mathematics (STEM) activities for fun is likely low. However, after examining some of the various surveys used to measure leisure activities, I think there's room for improvement and even for adding more types of recreation. The items scored as "intellectual leisure" can include having a hobby (any hobby, which could include collecting your toenail clippings) and using a cell phone (for any purpose).[122] Some activities seem a bit oddly specific, although it might just be me (it wouldn't occur to me to ask about people picking mushrooms).[123] I know that very often these studies use huge datasets that often are focused on other topics, and you take what you can get. But what about cooking? I found some case studies but little else – except a paper reporting that caretakers and hospital staff noted that, presented with a number of possible leisure options, people with dementia seemed to engage in cooking last.[124] Magic? Sports strategizing? 3D printing? Animal training?

[116] Stern & Munn, 2009. [117] Almeida et al., 2012. [118] Faucounau et al., 2010.
[119] Tak et al., 2015. [120] Kock et al., 2018. [121] Sayago & Bergantiños, 2021.
[122] Almeida-Meza et al., 2021. [123] Wang et al., 2021.
[124] Cohen-Mansfield et al., 2019.

Finding legal loopholes? Building a better mousetrap? What about creatively analyzing data – everyone loves that, right?

Small Good Things

There is a wonderful short story by Raymond Carver in which a baker, attempting to make amends to a couple, offers them bread that is hot out of the oven. As they eat it, he tells them that such food can be a small, good thing.[125] I've always loved that story, in part because it is easy to overlook the small, good things in our own lives. If someone asked me about the best day of my life, I'd likely gravitate to capital-B Big events, like my wedding or the birth of my kids. But it is essential to not overlook the everyday moments, like the weekend family movie and pizza days with the boys and dogs hanging out on the bed with me and my wife.

Small, good things... When I planned out this chapter on creativity and healing, I started with how creativity can help overcome major trauma. The next big section focused on emotion regulation, which is a huge area, and then I covered a bit on how creativity can (slightly) cognitively help those who might be at risk or in decline. Now I want to highlight a few small, good things that creativity can do to help us feel better. I've already talked about how pretend play can help us cope.[126] Another component to consider is stress reduction. On the one hand, most studies of stress and creativity emphasize how stress can make us more or less creative.[127] However, there are some that look from the reverse perspective. Although the relationship between relaxation and creativity disappeared when past ability and experience were controlled in one empirical study, there was nonetheless a broader association found between having more creative experience and being able to relax more thoroughly.[128] Other research, by Nicola Holt, has examined arts workshops that are given as part of someone's mental healthcare (sometimes called "arts on prescription," which I love). They're not quite classes or therapy, Holt told me, but emphasize play, exploration, and the enjoyment of the artistic process itself (mistakes and all). Among other benefits, participating in these workshops reduced tense arousal (which includes lowered nervousness, anxiety, and stress), leading directly to higher global well-being.[129]

[125] Carver, 1982. [126] Fiorelli & Russ, 2012. [127] Byron et al., 2010.
[128] Meier et al., 2020. [129] Holt, 2020.

Creativity can also help us replenish ourselves. Employees who participated in creative activities over the weekend were better able to recover from the stress of work and subsequently to show higher performance than those who did not do so.[130] This relationship is stronger for those people who work in jobs that are not stereotypically creative.[131] It is also worth noting that workdays that are considered toxic (low on resources, freedom, and support, yet also high-pressure) or disengaged (simply low on everything) are the least conducive to creativity in the workplace.[132] A series of studies had college students write about either a big or a small secret, engage in a generation task that emphasized either creative or practical ideas, and then either throw a beanbag at a distant target or carry stacks of books. The underlying idea was that holding on to secrets can burden us both psychologically and physically, and creativity might be a way of finding release. Indeed, those participants who wrote about big secrets and generated creative ideas threw farther and carried more.[133] It is, perhaps, not surprising that initial studies have suggested that creativity is associated with reduced burnout in nurses,[134] occupational therapists,[135] and teachers,[136] or that creative activities helped buoy resilience during the COVID-19 pandemic lockdown.[137] Another COVID-19 study found that people who saw themselves as more creative were more likely to have positive emotions, which was associated with reduced stress and having a globally more positive view of their experience during the pandemic.[138]

Creativity in general can be seen as a small, good thing that can grant us self-insight and help us heal. Moving forward, it can also connect us to others. As we will see in the next chapter, we can feel connected with others by engaging in creative activities, by experiencing the creative work of others, or through the traits and attributes associated with a creative individual.

[130] Eschleman et al., 2014. [131] Eschleman et al., 2017. [132] McKay et al., 2022.
[133] Goncalo et al., 2015. [134] Li et al., 2019. [135] Derakhshanrad et al., 2019.
[136] Ghanizadeh & Jahedizadeh, 2016. [137] Elisondo, 2021. [138] Fiori et al., 2022.

8 CONNECTION

Self-insight encompasses making sense of your past. Healing is moving from the past to the present. Connection may be rooted in the past but lives in the present. Creativity can enhance feelings of connection in ways that are both obvious and a bit less direct. I'll start by breaking down a stream of research that seems at first to be suggesting that creativity may not build community. I believe, however, that this research reveals a more complex relationship.

Terror Management Theory and Creativity

If you start investigating creativity and meaning, you quickly encounter terror management theory (TMT).[1] TMT is an evolutionary, psychology-based approach centered around the basic idea that, as human beings, we know that we're going to die. This knowledge can be so overwhelmingly painful as to induce pure terror. One proposed buffer for this existential dread is to emphasize one's cultural worldview and self-esteem.[2] Each culture, typically, has its own value system and sets of rituals designed to address mortality, from a belief in the afterlife to the broad idea that one's people (from children to compatriots) will still live on. This focus helps assuage our fears by making us hope that, even if – or, rather, when – we stop living physically, some aspect of our being will continue.

[1] Greenberg, et al., 1990; Routledge & Vess, 2018. [2] Greenberg et al., 1997.

This central idea has been studied in many ways; most involve the concept of mortality salience, or getting people to think about death. I am reminded of one of my favorite Facebook moments, one that I've seen circling the Internet. Someone first posts that life is precious and that we need to remember our mortality, then suggests that you call the people you love and tell them. In response, someone else posts that they have called four people to remind them that they are going to die, and none of them appreciated it. TMT posits that, when you remind people of death, they will respond by seeking out others who are like them and, presumably, share their worldview. They would then have their beliefs reinforced, which bolsters their feelings of belongingness and esteem.

So where does creativity fit in? The first study of TMT and creativity[3] turned to the ideas of psychoanalyst Otto Rank.[4] Rank argued that being creative comes from our rejecting society and pursuing our own path, which is reflected in early childhood rebellions. As a result, he proposed that creativity comes at a cost, namely that of feeling connected to other people. Rank's point about creativity entailing a certain amount of defiance against the status quo has been echoed in current work.[5] His ideas about creativity and death anxiety will be discussed in the last chapter.

Anyway, in a series of TMT experiments, a team led by Jamie Arndt primed people for mortality salience by having them write about their emotions about death and what they thought would physically happen when they die. The control condition wrote about dental pain. As someone who spent two years getting my four front teeth replaced by implants, I am not sure which one I would pick. All participants then read a *New York Times* article about dreaming and were asked to write a story about dreams that incorporated characters from the article (I can't explain why they used that). The people in the mortality salience condition reported more guilt after their creativity writing task than those in the control condition and, after a comparable second study, higher levels of social projection (trying to fit in).[6]

I have to admit that this angle isn't one that I would have deemed to be superimportant; but the study was published in a high-impact factor journal that wouldn't consider my work if I were dressed up as Daniel Kahneman, so who am I to judge? Subsequent work built on this finding and emphasized how these negative effects

[3] Arndt et al., 1999. [4] Rank, 1989. [5] Sternberg, 2018; Sternberg & Lubart, 1995.
[6] Arndt et al., 1999.

of being creative in the face of death anxiety could be reduced. If people received (randomly assigned) feedback that they tended to have a conforming personality, their guilt about being creative was reduced.[7]

In another study, participants were primed for mortality salience and then asked to design a T-shirt that was (a) creative, (b) appealing to others, or (c) reflective of shared values. People in the creative condition were less compelled to defend their worldview after being reminded of death, although the authors continued to argue that one couldn't completely dismiss the view that creative activity could nevertheless increase defensiveness.[8] Subsequent studies pushed against the idea that mortality salience might be worsened by being creative, finding that creativity could have a positive impact on death anxiety (including in times of COVID-19)[9] and help people avoid cultural dogmatism.[10]

Other studies looked at how mortality salience ("You're going to die, ha!") might increase or decrease creativity. People were primed to think about death or dental pain and then asked to do a problem-solving task that was either self-focused or other-focused. In the mortality salience condition, self-focused work was less creative but other-focused work was more creative.[11] A similar effect was found on a creative assignment that either did or did not involve the idea of leaving a legacy.[12] Both studies were described as dealing with how focus on another and legacies could undo the negative effects of mortality salience on creativity, as opposed to how self-focus and no-legacy could undo the positive effects of mortality salience on creativity. I get that, according to the tenets of TMT theory, creative activity in the wake of mortality salience should lead to negative effects and death anxiety should decrease creativity... But I'm not seeing that pattern in the data. Perhaps, as a wider point, I see the ultimate message that emerges from this work as being less "creativity makes you feel guilty and bad when you're primed to think about death because it makes you move away from other people" and more "creativity is its own thing, and people who are creative or engaged in creative actions simply react differently to being primed to think about their death."

[7] Arndt et al., 2005. [8] Routledge et al., 2004. [9] Cui et al., 2020.
[10] Routledge & Arndt, 2009. [11] Routledge et al, 2008. [12] Sligte et al., 2013.

For example, some people have a high personal need for structure, which means they prefer tasks that are ordered and clear.[13] There are some very specific scenarios under which such individuals are more creative;[14] however, in taking a broader view, such a need for structure would not seem to be a desirable attribute for creativity. When people with a low personal need for structure were asked to think about death, they became more creative. Not only that, but the mortality salience priming mechanism was less effective for these people in the first place.[15] A different study found that people with more creative achievements were less likely to gravitate around thoughts of death when primed with mortality than were people with fewer creative achievements.[16] A third study found that people who score high on emotional stability are more likely to gravitate around creative interests when primed for mortality salience.[17] Let's also note that there are cultural differences in responses to mortality salience. Eastern cultures are more likely to enjoy life and to engage in favorite activities, whereas western cultures are less so and have opposite tendencies.[18] Putting all these pieces together makes me question the practical significance of applying any of the negative TMT creativity studies to people who care about being creative.

There is also a theoretical model that distinguishes death anxiety from death reflection, arguing that death reflection can have many benefits (including a boost to generativity).[19] One extensive study on life during COVID-19 found that death reflection was positively related to creativity.[20] Indeed, creative activities in general blossomed during the COVID-19 pandemic lockdown,[21] and developed the remarkable feature that a high number of intergenerational family members were working together.[22]

I suppose these past few paragraphs may seem an odd way to begin a chapter on creativity and connection. I took this angle because, if you start off by looking at the literature on meaning and creativity, one of the first places you will likely stumble upon suggests that creativity can be a specifically negative thing in terms of feeling connected to other people. Yet not only does the evidence not bring me to this conclusion but – as I will discuss – other research makes me

[13] Neuberg & Newsom, 1993. [14] Rietzschel et al., 2007; Rietzschel et al., 2014.
[15] Routledge & Juhl, 2012. [16] Perach & Wisman, 2019. [17] Xu & Brucks, 2011.
[18] Ma-Kellams & Blascovich, 2012. [19] Grant & Wade-Benzoni, 2009.
[20] Takeuchi et al., 2021. [21] Karwowski et al., 2021. [22] de Guzman et al., 2022.

believe that creativity may often have the opposite characteristic. Creativity can bring us together. Let's talk about how.

Creativity and Connection

Remember the Martela and Steger tripartite model of coherence, significance, and purpose?[23] In case you don't, significance can mean feeling as though you have a life worth living[24] or (more commonly) as though you are a part of something larger than just yourself.[25] People need to feel as though they matter. Feeling insignificant can lead to a host of bad outcomes, from suicide[26] to active malevolence.[27]

One straightforward way to feel significant is to feel connected to other people, and creativity can help. My friend Jeffrey Smith has proposed "the museum effect,"[28] which says that, when people visit an art museum, they bring their own experiences, beliefs, and knowledge as they interact with each work of art. Art can serve as a mirror, in essence,[29] and allow viewers to reflect upon themselves and the world. Studies have shown that, when people view works of art, they are able to identify the emotions that the artist intended to convey, and even feel those emotions themselves.[30]

Smith found empirical evidence to support the museum effect. He surveyed visitors to an art museum on their connections to other people and to the world in general and on their own striving to be a better person. He found that most people peaked in the middle of their visit and showed a slight regression to the mean as they left (but were still feeling more interconnected than when they first arrived).[31] Perhaps one reason for the slight dip by the end is that a museum's ability to make people feel restored and refreshed declines if a visit is perceived as going on for too long.[32] Smith reinforced these ideas to me; that moment of intense connection starts to fade when someone begins to think instead about where they parked and what they are having for dinner. When Smith conveyed these findings, a colleague at the Metropolitan Museum of Art responded magnificently: "Well that only makes sense," the colleague said. "If it

[23] Martela & Steger, 2016. [24] Kaufman, 2018b.
[25] King & Hicks, 2021; Steger & Dik, 2010. [26] Kleiman & Beaver, 2013.
[27] Kruglanski et al., 2009. [28] Smith, 2014. [29] Tinio, 2013.
[30] Pelowski et al., 2020, 2022. [31] Smith, 2014. [32] Aeschbach et al., 2022.

maintained, then curators would be the most wonderful people in the world, and we have empirical evidence that that isn't so."

Another way to look at creativity and being connected to others is to ask whether creative people have more friends. Well, popular kids are likely to be rated as being more creative than unpopular ones,[33] but I can think of a number of completely unrelated reasons why that might be the case. Self-reported creative achievement was associated with having a high number of primary friends (people you actually know), although not with having a broader social group (people who feature on your list of "those I should send a holiday card to, even though I never will").[34]

In other studies, friendships have been examined by looking at real-life social networks, in which students are asked to rate or classify their classmates on how much they would want to hang out with them. Being commonly listed by peers as a friend was associated with creative performance[35] and with being perceived as creative by your peers.[36] It is also interesting to note that programs focused on the arts have been shown to help combat loneliness in young adults who have learning disabilities[37] and mental health issues.[38]

Most studies of interpersonal relationships and creativity in the workplace focus on what factors increase team creativity. For example, one commonly studied variable is psychological safety. Psychological safety occurs when there is a mutual understanding between you, your co-workers, and your boss that it is okay to take risks.[39] It requires communication and trust and is a solid indicator that you work in a good place. When employees feel psychologically safe, they are more likely to be creative;[40] this finding is not especially surprising. The vast majority of the research is on how psychological safety mediates or moderates the relationship between a particular type of leadership style or management philosophy and team innovation. Such a pattern is understandable, given that much of organizational psychology is focused on tangible outcomes. The question of whether creative employees are more likely than others to both feel and encourage psychological safety has been much less explored. Similarly, interpersonal conflict is associated with lower team

[33] Lau & Li, 1996. [34] Kéri, 2011. [35] McKay et al., 2017. [36] Hopp et al., 2019.
[37] Datlen & Pandolfi, 2020. [38] Salomon-Gimmon et al., 2022. [39] Edmondson, 1999.
[40] Ford & Sullivan, 2004; Han et al., 2019.

creativity,[41] but to my knowledge the reverse implication (might creative workers get along better?) has not been studied in depth.

Then there's the question of how creativity is related to romance or sex (or both). Creative people were found to be more likely than others to hold on to passion in a relationship, perhaps because creativity was associated with entertaining the illusion that your partner was more attractive than more objective ratings might have suggested.[42] Further, self-assessed creativity and everyday creative behaviors predicted passion, intimacy, and commitment in romantic relationships – although, curiously, artistic creativity was a negative predictor of the same variables.[43] One possible reason is that everyday creativity is inherently easy to share with other people (such as a partner), as it can be social.[44] Or perhaps artistic creativity offers other pathways to connection, or other emotional rewards. Interestingly, however, people specifically find artistic creativity to be sexy.[45] Creative people report having more sex, too (presumably they are not simply exercising their imagination).[46]

Love can also enhance creativity. Lovers working together on a creative task scored higher on originality and fluency than did pairs of strangers – and they also showed more interpersonal brain synchronization.[47] Hell, seeing pictures of people you're attracted to can make you more creative.[48] Nevertheless, a study of creativity in the workplace found that love (in the companionate sense) could reduce creativity, but anger turned out to be a better booster.[49] Make of that what you will.

The Soul of Creativity

We talk a lot about what makes up a creative person, from cognitive strengths to work habits, to childhood development, and to access to resources. A huge part of a creative person is their personality, but I'm not going to dive into a straightforward discussion of the creative personality. There is already a massive body of work on this topic,[50] but my reasons go beyond that. Much of the research is fascinating. Conscientiousness is differentially related to creativity depending on

41 De Clercq & Belausteguigoitia, 2021; Kurtzburg & Amabile, 2000.
42 Carswell et al., 2019. 43 Campbell & Kaufman, 2017.
44 Ivcevic & Mayer, 2009; Zielińska, 2020. 45 S. B. Kaufman, Kozbelt et al., 2016.
46 Beaussart et al., 2012; Clegg et al., 2011. 47 Duan et al., 2020.
48 Griskevicius et al., 2006. 49 Yang & Hung, 2015. 50 Feist et al., 2017.

the domain, being positively related to science and negatively related to the arts.[51] This relation can even show nuances within the same domain; for example, contemporary and modern dancers display lower levels of conscientiousness than more traditional dancers.[52] There are also differences within conscientiousness itself; the facet of being industrious is positively associated with creativity, but the facet of orderliness is negatively associated. Such dichotomies lead to a suppression effect, such that it may appear that general creativity and conscientiousness simply aren't related.[53] Cool stuff, but this is not where I'm going.

The personality factor most related to creativity is openness, which is, broadly, being interested in and seeking out new experiences, ideas, and sensations. There are lots of studies of how openness is associated with creativity;[54] their findings are remarkably unsurprising, especially given how many openness items on personality measures explicitly reference creativity, imagination, or art.[55] This connection is found across domains such as creative writing,[56] photographic essays,[57] and humor production,[58] and even in a Minecraft building task.[59] Openness is also linked to creativity across most types of measures, including self-report,[60] divergent thinking,[61] actual creative achievement,[62] experience sampling or daily diaries,[63] and also the Remote Associates Test[64] – albeit at a much lower level, since the latter not truly a creativity measure. Openness can be split along two facets. One is experiential and focuses on appreciating nature, beauty, and art, whereas the other is rather centered on ideas, intellectual challenges, and deep thinking.[65] Broadly, the experiential facet is predominantly associated with artistic creativity and the intellect facet is predominantly associated with scientific creativity and actual measured intelligence.[66]

The personality factor of openness is the most prominent trait or characteristic of creative people, but there are several others that are broadly related both to creativity and to each other. For example, there is perspective taking, which is a mix between an ability and an inclination. It is not unlike empathy and compassion[67] but, whereas

[51] Feist, 1998; Feist et al., 2017. [52] Fink & Woschnjak, 2011.
[53] Reiter-Palmon et al., 2009. [54] Puryear et al., 2017. [55] Martindale, 1989.
[56] Maslej et al., 2017. [57] Dollinger & Clancy, 1993. [58] Sutu et al., 2021.
[59] Shaw, 2022. [60] Karwowski & Lebuda, 2016. [61] Asquith et al., 2020.
[62] Grosul & Feist, 2014. [63] Conner & Silvia, 2015. [64] Harris, 2004.
[65] DeYoung, 2015; DeYoung et al., 2007.
[66] Kaufman, 2013; S. B. Kaufman, Quilty, et al., 2016. [67] Bengtsson et al., 2016.

empathy is feeling how someone feels[68] and compassion is being moved by someone else's feelings to the point of action,[69] perspective taking is cognitively understanding and perceiving someone else's thoughts, opinions, and points of view.[70] In his perspectival model, Vlad Glăveanu highlights the need to understand, listen to, and ultimately adapt to and grow from other people's beliefs as part of the creative process.[71] If little-c is akin to an "I-paradigm" and Big-C is a "S/He-paradigm," he argues, then there is also a "We-paradigm"[72] to consider. It is here that we create and collaborate with one another, ideally connecting to people across cultures and domains. Perspective taking enables this possibility.

There are a few other creativity-related traits that I would include as fitting into this general pattern. One is cognitive flexibility, which is being able to shift one's thinking and produce different types or categories of responses to a situation.[73] Another is tolerance of ambiguity, which is being able to cope with uncertainty and not knowing exactly what is going happen;[74] its opposite equivalent trait is having a high need for structure and closure.[75] There is also the ability to take sensible risks, at least socially[76] and intellectually,[77] accompanied by a proclivity for doing so.

All these different openness-related traits help form a rough cluster that is, indeed, related to creativity, but they are not necessarily its most predictive, essential, or epitomizing factors. They are rather what I might call the soul of creativity. I am exploring different dimensions of this broad concept in ongoing theoretical and empirical work with colleagues, who include my graduate student Sarah Luria[78] and Vlad Glăveanu.[79] In essence, the "creativity soul" variables also connect to a lot of "good human being" variables – such as the desire to live in an equitable world, to care for other people, and to be free from prejudice, bias, and hatred.[80]

There is a vast body of research that supports this last statement.[81] There are subcomponents of openness whose names vary depending on the exact model:[82] values/liberalism, aesthetics/artistic

[68] Decety & Jackson, 2006; Goetz et al., 2010. [69] Cuff et al., 2016.
[70] Batson et al., 1997; Stietz et al., 2019. [71] Glăveanu, 2015. [72] Glăveanu, 2010.
[73] Nijstad et al., 2010; Pringle & Sowden, 2017. [74] Zenasni et al., 2008.
[75] Leone et al., 1999. [76] Tyagi et al., 2017. [77] Beghetto, 2009.
[78] Luria & Kaufman, 2017a; Luria et al., 2017. [79] Kaufman & Glăveanu, in press.
[80] Corazza et al., 2021; Groyecka, 2018; Kaufman, 2017a.
[81] Crawford & Brandt, 2019; Sibley & Duckitt, 2008.
[82] Costa & McCrae, 1992; Goldberg, 1992.

interests, feelings/emotionality, fantasy/imagination, ideas/intellect, and actions/adventurousness. In general, people who are high on openness are less prejudiced and more tolerant, the specific components of values, feelings, and fantasy being most significant.[83] There are many ways in which openness can help increase tolerance; to take one example, people who are more open are better able to develop trust with people who come from different cultures.[84] In contrast, low openness and a high need for closure are associated with right-wing authoritarianism.[85] In general, being high on openness is associated with prosocial behavior.[86]

Growing Work on Interventions

One line of research has developed interventions to enhance creativity that are comparable to those designed to increase tolerance and decrease prejudice.[87] These interventions ask people to think about examples such as a female mechanic – that is, examples that run against a prevailing stereotype. Thus primed, participants are likely to perform better on a divergent thinking task than participants who have been given a stereotypical exemplar. Openness,[88] cognitive flexibility,[89] and a low need for structure[90] can help moderate this connection. There are circumstances under which these interventions don't work. For example, a counter-stereotype related to creativity, such as a dull poet, isn't effective.[91] The intervention may even decrease creativity for people who are inherently curious, perhaps because a counter-stereotype is less stimulating and provocative to people who already enjoy thinking.[92] On the flip side, incidentally, priming people to endorse a racial essentialist view (i.e., the belief that race is biological and unalterable) reduces their creativity.[93]

Does this kind of intervention work in the reverse direction? We need more research – although I hate writing that out, even if it's true, since when am I ever going to say "we have the exact amount of research we need"? But there are some good studies to discuss. Telling people to "think different" made them less likely to engage in (unconscious) stereotype activation (and, presumably, to buy an iMac).[94]

[83] Ng et al., 2021. [84] Saef et al., 2019. [85] Onraet et al., 2011.
[86] Mlčák & Záškodná, 2008. [87] Gocłowska & Crisp, 2013. [88] Gocłowska et al., 2017.
[89] Gocłowska et al., 2013; Zuo et al., 2019. [90] Gocłowska et al., 2014.
[91] Wen et al., 2019. [92] Damer et al., 2019. [93] Tadmor et al., 2013.
[94] Sassenberg & Moskowitz, 2005.

Studies have found relationships between openness and lower levels of prejudice[95] and, in conjunction with perspective taking, higher beliefs in multiculturalism.[96] A reanalysis of data from a creativity and intercultural sensitivity training study[97] suggested that increased creativity was the driving force behind the experimental group's increased intercultural sensitivity by comparison with that of the control group.[98]

An experimental study explicitly designed to examine this issue found that two interventions, one focused on imagination and one on divergent thinking, led to decreased social distance toward three different minority groups.[99] Curiously, participants had stereotypical and counter-stereotypical stimuli for the divergent thinking study – yet only the stereotypical stimuli reduced prejudice, which is inconsistent with the series of studies I discussed earlier. I promise that I am not stealthily trying to increase your own creativity by going against your expectation! The authors suggest that perhaps the participants did not have the necessary resources to handle the schema-breaking suggestions,[100] which is as good an explanation as I can come up with at the moment.

Self versus Others

This last part of the chapter is one of the few places where I talk about research on how creativity can help the world. Most of the five dimensions of the Creativity Advantage model are primarily focused on the ways in which creativity helps the creator. I think that this section still fits in. Certainly, there are benefits to the world if people are less racist, sexist, homophobic, antisemitic, and so on. But increased tolerance can bring cognitive benefits.[101] More generally, prosocial behavior is associated with increased well-being[102] and positive affect.[103] As I'll explore in the next chapter, a desire to help others can also be a reason that motivates people to create.

Much as I feel (or at least part of me feels) that using the argument "be nice to other people because it will have positive benefits for you" is a little icky, I do want to emphasize that I have not wandered too far astray from the core tenets of this book.

[95] Sparkman & Blanchar, 2017; Sparkman et al., 2016. [96] Sparkman et al., 2019.
[97] Dziedziewicz et al., 2014. [98] Groyecka et al., 2020.
[99] Groyecka-Bernard et al., 2021. [100] Gocłowska et al., 2018. [101] Prati et al., 2015.
[102] Martela & Ryan, 2016a. [103] Martela & Ryan, 2016b.

Sometimes it is not just that being a good person is its own reward, but that being a good person can bring additional rewards.

Doing an activity for its own sake and doing it for a specific reward represent the twin poles of intrinsic and extrinsic motivation, which form the backbone of the next chapter, drive (just as personality was the backbone of this chapter). Let's explore how creativity can provide joy and inspiration and guide our interests and general advancement in life.

9 DRIVE

The story of the blind men and the elephant is used so often that it has become cliché. The idea of a number of people who cannot see one another, each examining a different part of an elephant (trunk, ears, tail, and so on) and coming to drastically different conclusions about what constitutes an elephant, serves as a nice analogy for scientists who approach large problems from narrow perspectives and miss the point. But I can also see it illustrating the exact opposite point with creativity.[1] Most scholars focus on their own particular slices of the creativity cake, but so many of them are absolutely crucial. For example, when I wrote "motivation" on the previous page, it was the first time I used that word in the entire book. Yet motivation is a topic that many creativity scholars spend their whole career studying – and that's not for some kind of myopic reason, but because motivation is so incredibly important to creativity.

Going back to the tripartite model of meaning,[2] we've covered coherence and significance. Purpose, as you may remember, is having specific goals for your future that are important to you. This concept is so important that some conceptions of meaning are largely just focused on purpose.[3] My original intention for this book was to focus on creativity and meaning, in which case delving into purpose so late in the game and for such a brief spell would be inexcusable. As I shifted the idea for this book around, meaning remained important

[1] Sternberg et al., 2022. [2] Martela & Steger, 2016. [3] King & Hicks, 2021.

but was not the sole point of emphasis. This chapter, on drive, encompasses elements of both significance and purpose – what makes life worth living and how we strive toward the future. I see both of these issues as being closely tied to motivation.

Intrinsic and Extrinsic Motivation

Having intrinsic motivation means doing an activity because it is enjoyable, fulfilling, or interesting. It might offer a challenge, or growth, or fun. For example, I have a bluetick coonhound. He was a shelter dog, rescued from a southern state where hound dogs are often treated more like property than like living beings. When we got him, he was severely underweight, had trouble standing, and his skin was so covered with scabs, bruises, and mange that we weren't sure what color of fur he had. I convinced my wife to name him Sweeney, after Sweeney Todd (aka the demon barber of Fleet Street); I had visions of him rising up and seeking vengeance against all those who would hurt dogs. Instead, the time when he was abandoned outside, with no food, in freezing temperatures may have left him with a little brain damage – but he is also the sweetest, least malicious creature I have ever known. It may take him an extra minute to remember how to lie down if he stands up suddenly, but all he wants from life is to be near someone and get his head or belly scratched.

Every night we have a little ritual where Sweeney noses me until I relent and pet him. I am not getting compensated for the petting. He may not even remember my efforts as one day passes into the next. I have the vague idea that, every time I enter my house, he thinks, "Who's this guy? Well, he seems nice, whoever he is!" There is no identifiable reason why I spend so much time reassuring Sweeney that he is a good boy except that I truly enjoy it. I am intrinsically motivated.

Then there is extrinsic motivation, which is what you have when you need to do an activity for some kind of outside reason such as money or extra credit. Any reward would qualify, although some are subtle (such as praise).[4] When I was a kid, my folks paid me twenty-five cents for every toilet I cleaned (in our house, not in Grand Central Station). I felt no satisfaction or pride of accomplishment. I did not take any delight in the task. These toilets became

[4] Deci & Ryan, 1985, 2000; Ryan & Deci, 2000.

(somewhat) clean for the singular reason that there was a quarter waiting for me when each one was finished, and that could buy *Choose Your Own Adventure* or *Three Investigators* books.

In graduate school I would occasionally volunteer to take part in a medical study. I would have my brain scanned in an enormous MRI machine in exchange for about $50. That could, in turn, translate into nearly a week's worth of food (back then, before I began worrying about cholesterol, I could get an eggplant and sausage calzone for five straight days with the payment). Such motivation is purely extrinsic.

Sometimes, of course, you are driven by both motivations. I am writing this book with the expectation that it will get published and people will read it – and that's an external reason. Theoretically, if I were driven only by enjoyment, I would be okay with writing this book and then never showing it to anyone. But I'm not – I am writing this very sentence with the expectation that at some future date you will read these words. I am also aware that there will be some level of royalties and (paid) speaking invitations. I cannot deny that I would be happy with that (and even happier with higher royalties).

However, I am not primarily driven by extrinsic motivations. I know there is a decent chance that any money I make will end up being less than whatever the current minimum wage rate is, given the number of hours that will be consumed by this project. If my goal were only money, consulting pays much better. Further, I genuinely enjoy writing this book. I sometimes use my writing time as a reward, if I have been good about answering emails, grading papers, or editing and revising my other academic work. This aspect of my motivation is intrinsic.

Like most good things in life, intrinsic motivation is hard to cultivate and easy to kill. Extrinsic motivation can be increased, typically at the expense of intrinsic motivation, if you're being observed by an audience and if rewards are particularly salient.[5] Competition and time pressure are among the additional variables that can trigger extrinsic motivation.[6] Other external factors, such as praise, would theoretically seem to make someone more extrinsically motivated;[7] in practice, it does not seem quite so straightforward.[8]

A vast number of studies, many by the legendary Teresa Amabile, have shown that intrinsic motivation is associated with higher creativity.[9] If you think about it, it's not terribly surprising.

[5] Lepper & Greene, 1975. [6] Hennessey, 2015. [7] Kohn, 1993.
[8] Bear et al., 2017. [9] Reviewed in Amabile, 1996; Hennessey, 2019.

If you are interested in and enjoy a task, then you will be more creative when doing it. Extrinsic motivation can hurt creativity at times, but often it turns out to be complicated. If someone worries that they would be evaluated and would look incompetent, that may hurt,[10] but if someone is specifically trying to be creative, then the expectation of evaluation can help.[11] Similarly, rewards have been shown to decrease creativity.[12] However, there are many conditions under which rewards can be neutral, or even beneficial,[13] for instance when they are specifically tied to creative performance.[14] To make a sweeping generalization, most of the research carried out in schools concludes that extrinsic motivation can be harmful to creativity. In contrast, most studies coming from business arrive at the opposite viewpoint that extrinsic motivation can help facilitate creativity.

I've always been somewhere in the middle. I think you need both. If I rely too much on intrinsic motivation, then invariably I will hit a snag when I come to a dull, challenging, or upsetting part. Every article or book I've written has had a time when I had to respond to specific criticism, overcome a block, or go through something boring like copyediting. There will always be some part in any process where intrinsic motivation is going to wane and some kind of carrot is needed to incentivize you to muddle through. On the other hand, when I find myself emphasizing extrinsic motivation too much, I can end up dreading the activity so much that it will take three hours to do ten minutes of work. I think that being able to shift back and forth helps, depending on the stage of the process and the task at hand.

Needing to Create

Self-determination theory represents the leading view on why we do what we do. It proposes three key needs that underlie intrinsic motivation: autonomy, competence, and relatedness.[15] In addition, intrinsic motivation is associated with having learning goals as opposed to performance goals[16] and growth mindsets (i.e., believing that you can get better at an ability or task) as opposed to fixed mindsets.[17] I have always been drawn to the question of why people create. Too often the conversation ends up in a debate between intrinsic and extrinsic

[10] King & Gurland, 2007. [11] Shalley, 1995. [12] Amabile et al., 1986.
[13] Eisenberger & Shanock, 2003. [14] Byron & Khazanchi, 2012.
[15] Deci & Ryan, 2010; Ryan & Deci, 2017. [16] Midgley, 2014. [17] Dweck, 2000.

motivation, which is fascinating but a different question. I like self-determination theory, but I have always felt that the motivation to create is a little different from our motivation for other activities.

So what is out there? Certainly, researchers have studied the relationship of needs, values, and interests to creativity. Having a high need for uniqueness (wanting to be different from everyone else)[18] and a high need for cognition,[19] for example, is associated with increased creative activity and performance.[20] Vocational interests have traditionally been divided into categories labeled realistic, investigative, artistic, social, enterprising, and conventional.[21] Unsurprisingly, artistic and (to a lesser extent) investigative interests are associated with creativity.[22] The work on values is also generally straightforward. Those who value independent thought and new challenges and care about all people tend to be creative, whereas those who value security, conformity, and tradition are less so.[23] There are notable variations depending on domains,[24] but no stunning reversal.

These topics are all interesting, but not exactly what I had in mind. I had actually sketched out extensive notes for a model for creative needs many years ago, when my laptop completely crashed. I lost about four months of work. Coincidentally, I had emailed my working draft of the revised *Creativity 101*[25] to a colleague the day before the crash; if not for that bit of fortuitous luck, I might have dropped the book entirely. My creative needs model, however, was gone – vanished from my hard drive and my brain.

I explored the question in a coauthored chapter[26] in which we analyzed interviews with famous creators and discerned six underlying needs: beauty, power, discovery, communication, individuality, and pleasure. A study of why people create developed a scale with nine needs on the basis of a synthesis of the literature: enjoyment, expression, challenge, coping, social, prosocial (i.e., altruism), recognition, material (i.e., money), and duty.[27] Another model, which uses the term "work orientation," describes how people approach work. Its authors outline six orientations: job (money), career (advancement), calling/service (helping others or feeling like your work has a higher

[18] Snyder & Fromkin, 1977. [19] Cacioppo et al., 1996.
[20] Dollinger, 2003; Watts et al., 2017. [21] Holland, 1997.
[22] Kaufman et al., 2013; Perrine & Brodersen, 2005.
[23] Dollinger et al., 2007; Kasof et al., 2007.
[24] Lebedva et al., 2019; Taylor & Kaufman, 2020. [25] Kaufman, 2016a.
[26] Luria & Kaufman, 2017b. [27] Benedek et al., 2019.

purpose), kinship (valuing your colleagues), craftsmanship (aiming for high quality), and passion.[28] Although not explicitly tied to creativity, this model suggested that career, calling/service, craftsmanship, and (especially) passion would be more likely to enhance creativity.[29]

Let's put these ideas together. Some (power; material and recognition; job and career orientations) are extrinsic. We've already talked a bit about discovery/challenge and individuality/expression in the self-insight chapter, about coping in the healing chapter, and about kinship/communication in the connection chapter.

Calling/service and prosocial are more in line with Sternberg's transformational creativity idea[30] than with this book's primary focus on the benefits of creativity for the creator. Nonetheless, I think that these motivations are important to note. Prosocial motivation can increase the link between intrinsic motivation and creativity,[31] while altruism can boost both prosocial behavior and creativity.[32] The two-dimensional framework overlays the intrinsic–extrinsic split with the distinction between whether one's creativity is self-oriented and whether it's other-oriented (the latter would be related to prosocial motivation).[33] The resultant four categories are the four Gs, where gain (extrinsic-self) and growth (intrinsic-self) are relatively similar to extrinsic and intrinsic, as I've described. Giving (extrinsic-other) is helping people toward a specific outcome, and guidance (intrinsic-other) is mentoring people to help them learn. An example of giving would be knitting a nice sweater for someone to wear, whereas an example of guidance would be teaching that person to knit.

Recent work in the tradition of the two-dimensional framework used interviews to develop a new motivation-for-creativity scale. Three different types of motivations emerged: prosocial, intellectual (akin to intrinsic, but cognitively focused), and emotional. In addition, a process factor of having a sense of one's audience was also found. Prosocial motivation had three subfactors: connection with others, offering others new perspectives, and wanting to change others' lives. Intellectual motivation was associated with working more hours than normal and valuing other people's opinion more. Interestingly, emotional motivation in artists was associated with

[28] Lepisto & Pratt, 2017; Pratt et al., 2013. [29] Amabile & Pratt, 2016.
[30] Sternberg, 2021b. [31] Grant & Berry, 2011. [32] Lin et al., 2023.
[33] Forgeard & Mecklenburg, 2013.

working fewer hours than normal and valuing other people's opinions less.[34]

Prosocial motivations can also work with creativity to help people find meaning in life. Children who scored high on a measure of being creative for prosocial purposes were likely to show more positive emotions and higher life satisfaction than did children with lower scores.[35] A different study of college students emphasized the link between creative expression and higher meaning of life; interviews with the participants often highlighted their desire to use their creativity to help others.[36]

What other needs are there? A dedication to craft, an appreciation for beauty, and passion, pleasure, or enjoyment. In the previous chapter I talked about how significance can mean feeling as though you matter or feeling that your life is worth living. That cluster of creative needs sure sounds like the type of experiences that make life worth living. My original concept for this part of the model was joy; indeed, when people are asked why they engage in creative activity, relaxation and fun are very common responses.[37] I nonetheless switched to drive for a couple of reasons. Although I chose the term after a fruitful conversation with my friend and colleague Matthew Worwood, drive is also the first phase of the dynamic creativity framework.[38] It is nicely described there as the cluster of motivational and emotional forces that spur creativity on.

So why did I abandon joy? One reason was the mixed findings out there on creativity and well-being that I have already discussed.[39] Another was that ultimately I felt as though the positive emotion aspect was less essential than the elements of passion, engagement, striving, mastery, and growth.[40] Consider one study that had people sort different emotions related to aesthetics and found that, although there was a positive emotion–negative emotion distinction, a more interesting and nuanced cluster emerged. It was comprised of emotions related to being captivated, interested, driven, and appreciative. Although generally such emotions were positively skewed, they represented feelings that were more complicated than just "good" or "bad."[41] Finally, in reflecting on my own experience of getting tremendous pleasure from my intellectual and career progression, I can also see ways in which drive could encompass joy – and much more.

[34] Forgeard, 2022. [35] Shoshani & Russo-Netzer, 2017. [36] Nell, 2014.
[37] Benoit-Bryan et al., 2022. [38] Corazza et al., 2022. [39] Acar et al., 2020.
[40] Holinger & Kaufman, 2023. [41] Hosoya et al., 2017.

One concept that covers both the ideas of joy and drive is Mihaly Csikszentmihalyi's "flow."[42]

Flow and Passion

Some ideas are immediately appealing and intuitive. For me (and for many of the students I teach), flow is one of them. Also called "optimal experience" (or, informally, "being in the zone"), flow is the state you enter when you are intensely immersed in an activity. It is a moment of complete absorption when you lose track of time. You might even forget to eat. In Raymond Carver's story "Cathedral," the main character is trying to explain what a cathedral is to a visually impaired acquaintance. He ends up drawing a cathedral with his friend holding onto his hands, and he gets so caught up in the activity that he ultimately thinks: "I was in my house. I knew that. But I didn't feel like I was inside anything."[43]

Flow is rarely entered passively; this type of extreme focus and energy is less likely to be needed when relaxing or watching something.[44] Further, in order to enter flow, there needs to be a balance between your abilities and the requirements of the task. As in what J. McV Hunt[45] called "the problem of the match," you need to feel challenged, but not overwhelmed. There is a reason why one of Csikszentmihalyi's books was called *Between boredom and anxiety*.[46] If you are attempting a task that is too easy or too hard, you won't be engaged at the right level to enter flow.

Flow can come from an extreme physical activity; it can be considered comparable to the feeling of a runner's high. Of course, my interest is in how creative pursuits can lead to flow. On a good day, I feel flow when I am writing. When I ask my students, most of them have been in flow. People most commonly mention playing music, visual art, or writing, although I think you can enter flow in virtually any domain. Most essentially, flow is fun and makes people happy.[47] Csikszentmihalyi argued that "[t]he best moments [in our lives] usually occur when a person's body or mind is stretched to its limits in a voluntary effort to accomplish something difficult and worthwhile."[48] It is not surprising that people high on openness[49] and

[42] Csikszentmihalyi, 1990, 1996. [43] Carver, 1984, p. 228.
[44] Csikszentmihalyi & Csikszentmihalyi, 1988. [45] Hunt, 1961.
[46] Csikszentmihalyi, 2000. [47] Csikszentmihalyi & LeFevre, 1989.
[48] Csikszentmihalyi, 1990, pp. 3–4. [49] Ilies et al., 2017.

intrinsic motivation[50] will be more creative and happier when they can enter flow at work. A study of artists found that regularly entering flow was related to both positive affect and markers of longer-term happiness (such as having a sense of meaning and purpose).[51]

Similarly, the connection between flow, passion, and creativity makes sense.[52] In passion research, there is obsessive passion and harmonious passion. Obsessive passion is internalized pressure that can end up controlling someone. I'm not talking about that type of passion. I mean harmonious passion, which is when people freely choose to care about and pursue an activity.[53] One of these passions is positively associated with health and well-being and the other is negatively associated with them, and I will let you decide which is which.[54] Interestingly, however, a study conducted right as the pandemic lockdown began found that the lowest to score in life satisfaction were people who felt virtually no passion at work but both harmonious and obsessive passion for non-work activities. A follow-up done over a year later found a regression to the mean for that group – but also a large increase in the percentage of people who fell into this category, which suggests that one impact of the pandemic lockdown was a general reduction in passion for work.[55]

Passion is associated with creative self-efficacy[56] and creative behavior,[57] and also serves as a moderator between other variables and creativity.[58] One series of studies of creative artists found that passion achieved these effects by facilitating moderately activated levels of positive emotions throughout the creative process.[59] In other words, artists with higher passion felt an activated positive emotion (such as joy or elation), but not at such an extreme level that it might interfere with the cognitive ability needed.[60] The connection with emotion was strongest during the initial problem identification phase. In general, people experience activated positive emotions when they are being creative[61] – whereas when they feel deactivated and have negative emotions such as feeling sleepy, bored, or dull, they are less likely to feel creative.[62] Passion also makes us more likely

[50] Moneta, 2012. [51] Holt, 2018. [52] Amabile et al., 2005; Amabile & Fisher, 2009.
[53] Vallerand et al., 2003. [54] St-Louis et al., 2015. [55] Astakhova et al., 2022.
[56] Puente-Díaz & Cavazos-Arroyo, 2017. [57] Grohman et al., 2017; Lafrenière et al., 2012.
[58] Ivcevic & Brackett, 2015; Liu et al., 2011; Luh & Lu, 2012.
[59] St-Louis & Vallerand, 2015. [60] De Dreu et al., 2008.
[61] Conner et al., 2018; Karwowski et al., 2017. [62] Zielinska et al., 2022.

to savor and stay in the moment when something good happens (or is imagined), as opposed to dampening its positive feeling.[63]

One example of how the power of passion and creativity can be practically put into action is in the work of my dear friends and colleagues at the University of Connecticut, Joe Renzulli and Sally Reis. Passion (which they sometimes call enthusiasm) is a key part of their giftedness models and programs. The Enrichment Triad[64] and the Schoolwide Enrichment Model[65] are based on decades of research and practice.[66] One core aspect is the focus on the three Es of what they call investigative learning: enjoyment, engagement, and enthusiasm.[67]

Growth and Progress

Flow is in the moment and of the moment. It can be intense, ephemeral, and addictive. Then there is the more long-term perspective of personal development, growth, and progress. As you may remember, a few chapters back I discussed positive psychology and its emphasis on balance strengths (such as wisdom) at the expense of focus strengths (such as creativity).[68] In contrast, humanism embraced focus strengths. Humanism emphasized values such as identity development, freedom, and personal growth.[69]

Just as positive psychology encompasses but does not especially value creativity, humanism places creativity smack in the middle of many of its most prominent theories. Rollo May considered creativity to be a pinnacle of life.[70] Creativity was one of the seven traits of a fully functioning person according to Carl Rogers,[71] and a way to reach self-actualization, the height of Abraham Maslow's hierarchy of needs.[72]

One of the leading theorists in humanism was Viktor Frankl, an Auschwitz survivor who used his experiences to develop a type of psychotherapy called logotherapy.[73] The core focus of his approach was on how we find meaning in our lives. Frankl proposed three ways. One, the manner in which we face inevitable suffering, is certainly linked to Frankl's personal circumstances and everything he witnessed in the concentration camps. The other two ways are more

[63] Schellenberg & Gaudreau, 2020. [64] Renzulli, 1977; Reis & Renzulli, 2003.
[65] Renzulli & Reis, 1997, 2021. [66] Reis & Peters, 2021. [67] Renzulli, 2012.
[68] Bacon, 2005. [69] Waterman, 2013. [70] May, 1994. [71] Rogers, 1961.
[72] Maslow, 1943. [73] Frankl, 2006.

clearly connectable to creativity: we discover meaning first by creating works and performing deeds, and second by having experiences and connections. The first way ties into any creative activity; the second has links to flow and interpersonal relationships (which can be enriched through creativity). A scholar who followed Frankl's tradition was Irvin Yalom, an existential psychiatrist who highlighted a number of secular behaviors that could fight feelings of meaninglessness: altruism, dedication to a cause (which could be political, religious, or familial), hedonism, self-actualization, self-transcendence, and, of course, creativity.[74]

In addition to personal growth, there is also professional growth. People who feel as though their work is meaningful are more likely to innovate than people who don't feel this way, and both these elements – the feeling and the attribute of innovating – are connected with career satisfaction.[75] Longitudinal studies have found creativity to be associated with career satisfaction.[76] This link can occur even when employees are not explicitly aware that their creativity is a significant predictor of satisfaction.[77] Flow has been identified as a mediating variable.[78] There are some very practical benefits, too. Thus the creativity and job satisfaction combination is also associated with lower absenteeism[79] and, alongside lower job stress, with a reduced intention to switch jobs.[80]

Consider also the progress principle, which was developed by Teresa Amabile and colleagues as an extension and development of her work on intrinsic motivation.[81] Although it is applicable to any type of creative effort, its roots are in business and organizational psychology. It speaks to the power of small wins. When people make progress on a creative project, these incremental successes lead to a number of positive outcomes. Creators feel higher creative self-efficacy and intrinsic motivation, which then helps them double down on their involvement. This renewed engagement makes additional progress more likely, thereby starting the cycle anew. Progress on creative work is often accompanied by increased positive affect[82] and subjective well-being.[83] In order for the progress principle to be

[74] Yalom, 1980. [75] Allan et al., 2019; Boldt & Kaufman, 2023. [76] Kim et al., 2009.
[77] Duffy & Richard, 2006. [78] Mihelič & Aleksić, 2017. [79] Mayfield et al., 2020.
[80] Tongchaiprasit & Ariyabuddhiphongs, 2016.
[81] Amabile & Kramer, 2011; Kramer & Amabile, 2011.
[82] Amabile et al., 2005; Tavares, 2016. [83] Sherman & Shavit, 2018.

fully activated, however, creators should be making meaningful work that aligns with their own values.[84]

I've experienced the progress principle during the course of this book. I tend to write in bursts that are related not so much to any feelings of inspiration as to how many emails I have to answer, how much student work to grade, or how many other papers to write or edit. There were a few times when I blinked and a month or two flew by without my moving forward a paragraph. When I was able to get back it was slow going at first, but then I would find my voice again. Rather than feeling like I was merely trudging toward the finish line, I felt that it was a rush. There is a wonderful concept for which Pulitzer Prize-winning author Robert Olen Butler has coined the term "sumo Zen."[85] It is based on his observation that, when sumo wrestlers are interviewed by the media after a match, they all give a variation of the same answer. They do their style of sumo and they do their best, and that is all they can do. I hoped I was applying my own version of sumo Zen – doing my particular style of scholarship and doing it to the best of my abilities. It's invigorating, it's fun, and it brings a sense of accomplishment.

In fact the feeling of making progress is so intoxicating that I'm going to finish this chapter right now, to give myself the thrill of starting the next one. Woo hoo!

[84] Allan et al., 2019; Lysova et al., 2019. [85] Butler, 2005.

10 LEGACY

Animals don't particularly understand the idea of death. Before you tell me about elephants and how they seem to change the way they act when a member of their herd dies,[1] I have a couple of important responses: (a) I don't care; and (b) I'm not actually interested in the question of whether animals understand death. I've delved into animal cognition before,[2] but this point is intended as a metaphor.

We have a house full of animals: Sweeney the bluetick coonhound, Pickles the beagle puppy, Eliza the African gray parrot, four rats, and an axolotl (a salamander-like creature that is two thirds smile). At various times we have also had cats, rabbits, iguanas, snails, chameleons, Madagascar hissing cockroaches, toads, fish, and millipedes. None of them was worried about dying. Sweeney's worldly concerns are vast; they include whether he has been fed, when he might next be fed, whether he is on a comfy couch or bed, whether there is a squirrel anywhere in the vicinity, whether he is under a blanket, whether that might be food on the floor, whether someone is petting him, whether Pickles is too close, and whether he is going to be fed soon. He's not big on existential dread or death anxiety, or wondering about the meaning of life (unless it is food).

In contrast, anyone reading this book knows they're going to die (or, if not, my sincere apologies for spilling the beans). Although I'm writing a bit lightly about it, death anxiety is a real issue.[3] When

[1] Rutherford & Murray, 2021. [2] A. B. Kaufman et al., 2021. [3] Iverach et al., 2014.

I was a kid, I was prone to asking too many questions about what would happen if I died (my favorite response was: "A fat man visiting the Salvation Army would be very happy"). How do we handle this Pandora-like knowledge that we have a limited amount of life? Earlier I referenced T. S. Eliot's J. Alfred Prufrock[4] and his overwhelming question of why creativity matters. The larger context of that question (and poem) is asking why anything at all matters. Why does living matter, if we're going to die?

Symbolic Immortality

We're getting well above my pay grade here. But people have been grappling with these issues since the beginning of time. Otto Rank, whose work inspired terror management theory, also argued that the desire for immortality was humankind's driving need.[5] Given that we have yet to conquer death (although searches for a literal or medical fountain of youth are certainly pervasive), we must settle for the next best thing: finding ways in which we can kind of live on after we die. We can't be immortal, but we can engage in actions or beliefs that can offer some sort of survival after death – what Rank called symbolic immortality. He saw three possible ways, one genetic (by having biological children) and another religious (by believing in an afterlife). Particularly relevant for this book is that he also highlighted how some people can strive for immortality by creating a work that might survive them.[6] Years later, Stephen Sondheim would synthesize two of these three pathways in "Children and art," a song in *Sunday in the Park with George.*

Rank's ideas have been adapted and added to by many other scholars. Ernest Becker's *Denial of Death*,[7] which somewhat grimly won him a posthumous Pulitzer Prize, talks about *causa sui*, or hero projects. People create or contribute to works that they believe will outlive them – which, again offers some kind of immortality. Robert Jay Lifton[8] outlined five ways in which people might achieve symbolic immortality. The first three parallel Rank's, although with some differences of nuance. Rank's genetic pathway is broadened to accommodate the knowledge that any in-group one associates with, from organization to nation to culture, will survive. The religious pathway is comparable, if a bit more inclusive of spirituality. Lifton also

[4] Eliot, 1915. [5] Rank, 1989, 1998. [6] Kainer, 1984. [7] Becker, 1973.
[8] Lifton, 1979, 2011.

describes a nature-oriented pathway, drawing on the dust-to-dust parallel as well as on the idea of having a natural habitat that lives on. Another new pathway is experiential transcendence, which is reminiscent of the peak optimal experiences one finds in flow (although Lifton also mentions hallucinogenic drugs).

Going through some of the research and writings on the topic of legacies, it is interesting to note that creativity is not always mentioned, even when it is clearly present. One typology, developed from interviews, proposed three types of legacy: biological, values, and material.[9] The biological legacy is quite similar to the pathways articulated by Rank and Lifton. Quite often values were prosocial, but also reflected the person's culture or personality. Most notably, material legacy could certainly take the form of worldly goods, possessions, and heirlooms, but just as important, if not more, were family stories and creating a book, a work of art, or some other testament to one's life. Yet creativity was explicitly mentioned only once. One reason why I kept gravitating back to Lifton's conceptions was his emphasis on creativity. He also expanded what constituted creativity in his work. For example, he specifically highlighted creative service (such as the contributions of teachers and doctors).[10]

Another related concept is the contrast, in Erikson's theory of psychosocial development, between feelings of generativity and feelings of stagnation in adulthood.[11] Generativity involves moving beyond one's own interests in order to nurture, guide, and booster future generations.[12] It is akin to Dan McAdams' autobiographical author stage, in which we see our life as a narrative that entwines our past, present, and future.[13] Stagnation, or the absence of such goals and desires, is associated with lower well-being.[14] This generativity can be boosted with an adulthood narrative that contains the theme of redemption.[15] Indeed, priming people to think about death can encourage them to allocate more resources for future generations than they would otherwise.[16] This concept is sometimes called legacy motivation.[17]

Generativity is closely tied to creativity.[18] It is often[19] – but not always[20] – associated with higher life satisfaction, particularly when it works in tandem with symbolic immortality[21] and with

[9] Hunter & Rowles, 2005. [10] Lifton & Olson, 2004. [11] Erikson, 1982.
[12] Erikson, 1974. [13] McAdams, 2013. [14] Newton et al., 2020. [15] McAdams, 2006.
[16] Wade-Benzoni et al., 2012. [17] Wade-Benzoni, 2019. [18] Peterson & Stewart, 1996.
[19] McAdams et al., 1993. [20] Newton et al., 2020. [21] Huta & Zuroff, 2007.

having close ties to one's community.[22] It is important to note that feeling a high need for generativity is not necessarily altruistic; an element of narcissism can always be found in the desire to make an impact on future generations.[23]

So creativity can help people reach symbolic immortality (and generativity). As you may remember, the studies on mortality salience and creativity tried to suggest that priming people to think about death made them *less* creative,[24] although any negative relationship dissipated when they thought about the idea of a legacy.[25] But what else is out there? I suppose I should note first of all that the specific interaction of creativity and symbolic immortality has not been explored in great detail. A literature search on all my library databases turned up five articles, which include the one I just cited and one of my own papers. But let's try to spread out a bit more.

One question is whether it is reasonable to hope that your creative work would earn you symbolic immortality. A sociologist surveyed the expectations of prominent fellow sociologists for their own legacy, and their awareness of those who came before them. More than half of those who taught at active PhD-granting institutions thought that they would end up among the top ten leaders in their field. More than 60 percent in that same group thought that their writings would survive them. In contrast, about one half of the first twenty presidents of the American Sociological Society (later renamed the American Sociological Association, presumably for acronym-related reasons) had been forgotten by about a half of those surveyed.[26] A follow-up study of retired sociologists found that beliefs in the impact and worthiness of one's work do not diminish with age.[27]

Something important to consider, though, is what it means to have our creative work survive us. Obviously, Big-C creativity constitutes a legacy. Imagine a ten-minute period in which someone deplanes at Chicago's O'Hare airport, buys a Coke and a chocolate chip cookie, and walks through the terminals to baggage claim. In that short time, this person is using the creative spirit of the Wright brothers, John Pemberton (inventor of the Coke formula), Ruth Wakefield (who, at the Toll House Inn, invented chocolate chips and chocolate chip cookies), and George Gershwin (whose "Rhapsody in Blue" famously plays at O'Hare). Maybe that same person is wearing

[22] McAdams & Guo, 2015. [23] Newton et al., 2014. [24] Arndt et al., 1999.
[25] Sligte et al., 2013. [26] Westie, 1972. [27] Westie & Kick, 1980.

blue jeans (from Levi Strauss) and is holding a copy of *The Turn of the Screw* (by Henry James).

Some Big-C efforts are the result of hundreds or thousands of Pro-c creators. Indeed, the idea of the lone genius toiling by him- or herself and being fully responsible for his or her brilliant creation is largely a myth.[28] Soon after the Wright brothers, for example, the world saw further experimentation and development of flight by Traian Vuia, Jacob Ellehammer, Alberto Santos-Dumont, Gabriel Voisin, and Henri Farman. All these people have Wikipedia entries and I imagine are well-known in aviation circles, but I've never heard of them before now.

It's important to emphasize, however, that the creative work of all of these people lives on in some way. You may not know your great-great-great-grandmother's name or anything about her, but her biological legacy lives on in you. Similarly, even if you don't know the composer, inventor, writer, artist, or scientist behind a work, their creative legacy continues. Our friend in the airport could be using a rolling suitcase. Even if this person doesn't know that Bernard Sadow was the one who added the wheels, Sadow's ideas continue to have an impact.

Similarly, we may not know the Pro-c people who all contributed to a known Big-C work, but their efforts are also a form of immortality. The Hoover Dam is a National Historical Landmark and considered a tremendous feat of civic engineering. One study coded speeches and newspaper articles about the Hoover Dam for the language used by people involved in its creation. Its authors found evidence that the words conveyed emotions and thoughts associated with mortality salience, positive valence and reduced anxiety being particularly pronounced in the years after its construction. These researchers argue the Hoover Dam could be considered an example of Becker's hero project for those who worked on it.[29] Indeed, it is suggested that the desire to control water itself may be rooted in mortality salience.[30] Perhaps beavers are more self-aware than we may think?

Even if you're a Pro-c creator who isn't at work on a large group project that aims to harness the natural power of Poseidon, there are many ways in which you can experience symbolic immortality through your creativity. Many Pro-c creators' efforts will survive

[28] Montuori & Purser, 1995; Plucker et al., 2004. [29] Ross & Wolfe, 2016.
[30] Wolfe & Brooks, 2017.

their death, even if not by the generations and generations that Big-C requires. At a very basic level, simply go through this book with an eye for how many scholars are cited who have passed away. Some are Big-C, but many are Pro-c researchers and theorists whose contributions still resonate and have value. I love mystery stories; when I tackle a new anthology, I find in it, alongside the living writers and long-dead legends, enjoyable works by Jeremiah Healy, Margaret Maron, John Lutz, Edward D. Hoch, and many others who passed away in the twenty-first century and may still be read a hundred years from now. . . but also may not.

Similarly, if I consider the musical theater composers and librettists we've lost since 2020, there are some on whose being Big-C I would bet a lot of money, most notably Stephen Sondheim. But there are others who remain on my playlists, yet are not at that level of renown or accomplishment. Keith Herrmann composed a musical I truly love, *Romance Romance*, but I admit he's probably closer to Pro-c than to Big-C. Yet does it matter? The four Cs have been reasonably criticized for not having enough gradations,[31] so perhaps there should be another category or two, or twelve. But consider the larger issues. How many Big-C creators do you think are guaranteed to be remembered a hundred or a thousand years from now? What happens if theater as we know it is completely gone? The novel and mini-series *Station Eleven* posits a post-apocalyptic world where theater still survives, but in many scenarios even Shakespeare might be forgotten.

Lifton himself, incidentally, questioned whether the threat of nuclear holocaust would impact how people pursue symbolic immortality. Several decades ago, he wondered whether some people may not feel psychically numb and gravitate more toward the experiential path than toward biological and creative modes, which rest on the assumption that humanity will survive.[32] This argument prompted some discussion and studies, in which some largely agree that this kind of change is happening,[33] but others point to evidence that people are still focused on non-experiential symbolic immortality pathways.[34] If I look at today's world, we still have the ever-present threat of nuclear war, but now there is so much more. We also have fears over the lingering threat of COVID-19 (or a new plague), over the ever-increasing effects of climate change, and over so many more

[31] Beghetto & Kaufman, 2015; Runco, 2014. [32] Lifton, 2012.
[33] Mathews & Mister, 1988. [34] Schmitt, 1983.

ways in which the world might end. Yet given how much creativity we saw developing during the pandemic in so many different forms,[35] I remain hopeful that symbolic immortality continues being a comfort, even if our species' chances for survival do not always seem to be as high as they once were.

Whispers of Creative Immortality

I would argue that it is possible for people across all levels of the four Cs to have some type of creative immortality, although with a wide variety of gradation in its impact. I think of the Pixar movie *Coco*, which is a brilliant conceptualization of symbolic immortality. Being remembered is how your soul survives. When someone in the Land of the Dead is truly forgotten, this state is seen as akin to a second death. The beautiful thing, to me, is that you can be remembered by fans (as is the fictional singer Ernesto de la Cruz, who is famed yet duplicitous) just as well as by your loved ones. Both count.

Big-C can reach creative symbolic immortality through the sheer power of its impact, whether on a whole field or on a small audience – even an audience of one. Pro-c can continue to exert some influence or elicit some corner of appreciation. It may be too much to ask that little-c be able to live on for complete strangers, although the possibility certainly exists; I am sure that some readers have a thrift store delight that holds a place of honor in their house.

Little-c and even mini-c can live on, however, for those who love us or whom we love. My favorite examples are my grandmother's paintings; I grew particularly close to my grandma in the last decade of her life. As an aside, I was fascinated that her younger brother Eddie Levine had died a hero in World War II, in the Battle of the Bulge (in the antiaircraft division). She had his Purple Heart and ended up giving it to me when I expressed an interest. My great uncle Eddie's Purple Heart is hanging proudly on my wall today, more than twenty years later (and many more after his own death), offering him, too, some symbolic immortality.

Back to the main story. Grandma was a character. When I met my then girlfriend, now wife Allison, my grandma was in the hospital, with the heart ailment that would unexpectedly take her from us less than a month later. I took Allison to meet her, and they

[35] Brosowsky et al., 2022; Kapoor & Kaufman, 2020; Kyriazos et al., 2021.

immediately clicked. When the nurse came to check in, my grandma introduced her to "my grandson, James... and his fiancé, Allison." Upon seeing my slightly panicked raised eyebrow, she shrugged and added to me: "Girlfriend seemed so boring."

My grandma took up painting later in life. After her death, I was offered my choice of her creations, and I picked two still lifes of flowers. Both were brightly colored; one was yellow and one was red. We later found in China (by pure happy coincidence) some pretty woven tapestries that were also yellow and red, so now the two sets are paired by matching color and are on opposite sides of my living room. Are my grandma's paintings high art? Heck, I'm not even sure they're low art. But they're bright and pleasant and they make me think of her. That makes me smile.

I have many other little-c-type works around my house, from family members or other loved ones, and I imagine that many of us do. One could argue that most forms of nostalgia related to our past (old cards, childhood drawings, or craft projects) qualify. Many of the stories that pass down from generation to generation, whether funny or poignant, are another way in which we keep people's memory alive by remembering their creative actions.

When I have my undergraduates present their semester-long creativity projects, I always note how many creations are related to the path of symbolic immortality. Many of these students are young enough for their grandparents to be still alive, and so they have the chance to work directly with an older loved one on preserving a creative legacy. Some make a family cookbook or prepare favorite recipes. Others build bookcases or furniture with a handy parent or grandparent. I remember two undergraduates who teamed up with their fathers; one made an instructional video on how to repair cars and the other set up an elaborate domino chain reaction trick. There were several others who learned from beloved aunts and grandmothers how to knit, quilt, and make jewelry. Some projects were in memory of lost loved ones; thus a student put together a beautiful art project in tribute to a late cousin. Another had lost a friend at a young age and devoted a big project to taking pictures of the kinds of cars that that friend had loved.

Others relate to symbolic immortality in different ways. There are students whose projects are designed to be given to the ones they love, from parents and grandparents to boyfriends and girlfriends. Many students are seniors and try to capture the best of their senior year in a journal, video, or art project. I remember one student constructed a signpost in her native language using the colors from her country's flag and ended up donating the sign to the local club on campus. The club was devoted to that culture and used the sign to mark its office. Another student noticed that his country of birth didn't have an official Twitter account for tourism and set one up; the account was later adopted as that country's official account.

Creating Legacies

The need to leave a legacy, particularly as one begins to ponder the end of one's life, can be a powerful motivator. One increasingly popular activity is to write a memoir or life story.[36] I tend to think of a person who writes a memoir as being someone who is a brilliant writer, survived an astounding life event, had an accomplished career, or perhaps is simply a complete narcissist. But you can reap the benefits of writing a memoir without any of that. You can write for your family (current or future) or for yourself. A memoir does not need to be a complete life history. It can be a series of stories that revolve around a particular theme or around crucial life decisions.[37] Similar benefits can be found in alternative techniques designed to also encourage reviewing and coming to terms with one's life, such as making a time capsule, a memory book, or a life map.[38] Some even see their funeral as a chance to creatively leave a legacy.[39]

An entire industry of life history businesses has come to be, and it ranges from ghostwriters to workshops designed to facilitate the process. One study found that people engage in these services for reasons of generativity, reminiscence, and death preparation, and that what they termed a collective communal motivation was a driving force. In other words, people who hire others to help them with a life history are driven by the idea that their memoir or similar project might reach others beyond their immediate family.[40]

Life histories are often used as a part of palliative end-of-life care. One analysis of some life stories found four central themes: specific life events, personal values, one's family or support system, and one's specific medical struggles.[41] Interventions such as Memory Banking have been developed that aim to improve cognition and social connections while also helping patients feel as though they

[36] McAdams & Pals, 2006. [37] Germeten, 2013; Riessman, 2003. [38] Caldwell, 2005.
[39] Hunter, 2008. [40] Guillemot & Urien, 2016. [41] Skinner et al., 2019.

were leaving a legacy.[42] Such techniques can also be used for patients with mental health or addiction disorders who are not facing the end of their life; they can improve life satisfaction.[43]

It is heartbreaking to consider that some palliative treatments are not designed for adults. One strategy for pediatric cancer patients is to have them work with their parents on legacy making activities, which often revolve around the creative arts.[44] These activities can range from digital storytelling to blogs, crafts projects, and drawing, and sometimes patients perform them together with their parents. Such projects help the children cope and, in worst-case scenarios, help the parents grieve.[45]

We're nearing the home stretch. After all, once you've covered creativity at the end of one's life, where else is there to go?

[42] Zanjani et al., 2015. [43] Franklin & Cheung, 2017. [44] Foster et al., 2012.
[45] Schaefer et al., 2020.

AFTERWORD

Because I have no ability for (or affinity with) Microsoft Word and because I like everything in one very big document, I began having difficulty locating where I was after I went to the end of the document to add in a reference. So I added the word "spatula" at the end of the text, before the references, so I could quickly do a search and find my place. I figured it was a word I was unlikely to use (and this is the first time I'm using it). It feels weird to go and delete my little placeholder after all this time. Goodbye, spatula. Run free.

It has been fun and interesting for me to learn, review, synthesize, and explore these ideas with you. Along the way, I've thought about these topics myself. Throughout the book I've looked backwards on my own development as a writer and psychologist. I've considered how creativity can help bring self-insight, healing, connection, drive, and legacy. Some recurring themes keep popping up across these chapters, from the power of stories to the need to find joy in any way, shape, or form we can.

I've been thinking a lot about how to come to terms with the inherent contradictions of creativity's valence. How can we balance creativity's potential for malevolence and connection with unpleasant or maladaptive traits with the message about the positive power of creativity that I want to convey? Certainly there is Frank Barron's famed observation that a creative person is filled with contradictions.[1] But I also wonder how much of it can also be found in the four Cs and in the four Ps, and what we mean by creativity.

Many quotes from great artists emphasize how hard it is to create. "Writing is not a profession but a vocation of unhappiness," writer Georges Simenon once said.[2] I could easily run through another dozen. More complexly, Kurt Vonnegut explores his trauma of surviving the Dresden bombings during World War II in his classic *Slaughterhouse Five*. In the first chapter he talks about how, after Sodom and Gomorrah were destroyed, Lot's wife was told to not look back – yet, as we know, she could not help it and was turned into a pillar of salt. "People aren't supposed to look back," Vonnegut wrote. "I'm certainly not going to do it anymore. I've finished my war book now . . . [it] is a failure, and had to be, since it was written by a pillar of salt."[3]

Now contrast that to the benefits I've described of coherence[4] and of the writing cure,[5] both of which involve looking back. What's the difference? Is reflecting and considering past life events, including trauma, an activity that is good for your mental health, or one that is bad? I think one place of divergence is whether we are talking about the product or about the process. Do we mean mini-c, little-c, Pro-c, or Big-C? I think there is one scenario in which a creator would mine every painful, embarrassing, or upsetting memory for the sake of the end result, emphasizing the product and aiming for a higher C level. I do not see creativity being helpful in this case; it may even have a negative impact on that creator's mental health. In contrast, there is a scenario in which a different creator would explore her past issues and struggles with the intention of understanding them, of making peace with them, and of accepting what her life experience has been. Such a creator's goal would be the process, and a mini-c or little-c would be absolutely fine as a final outcome (even if Pro-c would be welcome). In these cases I believe that creativity offers quite an advantage.

Only 20 percent of articles about creativity look at what the construct predicts; in contrast, nearly three quarters of them want to find out how other variables impact creativity.[6] We, as a field, place a very strong emphasis on how to get people to be more creative. We are less concerned about whether they should be creative or when, or what types of creativity lead to the most positive outcomes.

[1] Barron, 1963. [2] Quoted in Collins, 1955, n.p. [3] Vonnegut, 1991, p. 22.
[4] Martela & Steger, 2016. [5] Pennebaker, 1997. [6] Forgeard & Kaufman, 2016.

I understand this tendency. Most of us in the creativity research community have devoted our lives to studying the topic. When I talk about creativity, it's usually to people who are in the field, too (or in a related one), or else to people who specifically want to learn about it. One of the few times when I've addressed a more hostile audience was during one memorable job talk (I didn't get the position) in which someone asked point blank why creativity mattered in education. Most of us don't need to defend creativity; besides, as I've already discussed, such an action is comparable to defending pizza and ice cream.

But the attributes and behaviors needed to climb the ladder from little-c to Pro-c, then to have a shot at Big-C, are not necessarily best for the creator. Howard Gardner spoke of the Faustian bargain that many creators of genius make,[7] placing their work above everything in life – family, friends, personal happiness, physical health. I used to understand and seek to emulate that ambition. If you read Joe Posnanski's book on the greatest baseball players, a recurring theme is that most of them had fathers who pressured them intensely, from early childhood on; they devoted their entire life and being to playing ball.[8] In such cases, he notes, having a larger perspective on life in any way whatsoever can hurt someone's chances of success.

Indeed, I remember that, back in 1987, Mark McGwire had forty-nine home runs in his rookie year. Players were about to hit fifty or more homers on a regular basis, but not yet; George Foster was the only player to do it in my lifetime. McGwire missed the last day of the season, and I was incensed and astounded. How could someone give up their shot at the record books for something as minor and petty as being there for the birth of their first child? In my defense, I was barely a teenager and could still envision being a ballplayer more easily than I could being a father. But that was my mindset.

When I wanted to be a writer, I felt that the work was what mattered; I did not. I was so obsessed with an eventual creative legacy that I forgot that, if you wanted to leave behind some evidence that you were once alive, you have to *live* first. As I switched to psychology, even as I fell in love with creativity research, I was less obsessed. I still worked hard, I still had specific, concrete goals for myself, and I still strived for an upward momentum. I hit some of these mental

[7] Gardner, 1993. [8] Posnanski, 2021.

milestones (tenure, full professorship, position at a top research university). I also got married and had my two boys (to whom this book is dedicated). I wouldn't say that I've made a 180-degree turn (otherwise I'd just keep revising this book and never send it to my publisher), but I am much more focused on the process. I want to enjoy what I do. I want to work with people I like and respect. I want my creativity to serve my life – to let me understand myself, heal from past traumas, connect with other people, get the joy and growth that come from drive, and, if I'm lucky, leave behind a legacy of some kind. I am less preoccupied with sacrificing anything and everything in order to boost my creative output to its maximum value. I know I have the luxury of these values, since I enjoy an uncommon level of autonomy and security, so I also aim to give back with my creative work as well.

To merge the underlying message of the first half of the book (it all counts) with that of the second half (small, good things): *All small, good things count (and creativity can help)*. I would be very happy if that is your takeaway from this book.

REFERENCES

Abadi, M. (2018, June 24). 14 vegetables that are actually fruits. *Business Insider*. Retrieved from www.businessinsider.com/fruits-and-vegetables-difference-2018-6.

Abdulah, D. M., & Abdulla, B. M. O. (2020). Suicidal ideation and attempts following a short-term period of art-based intervention: An experimental investigation. *The Arts in Psychotherapy*, **68**, 101648.

Abdulla, A. M., Paek, S. H., Cramond, B., & Runco, M. A. (2020). Problem finding and creativity: A meta-analytic review. *Psychology of Aesthetics, Creativity, and the Arts*, **14**, 3–14.

Acar, S., Berthiaume, K., Grajzel, K. et al. (2021). Applying automated originality scoring to the verbal form of Torrance Tests of Creative Thinking. *Gifted Child Quarterly*, **67**(1). https://journals.sagepub.com/doi/10.1177/00169862211061874.

Acar, S., & Runco, M. A. (2017). Latency predicts category switch in divergent thinking. *Psychology of Aesthetics, Creativity, and the Arts*, **11**(1), 43–51.

Acar, S., & Runco, M. A. (2019). Divergent thinking: New methods, recent research, and extended theory. *Psychology of Aesthetics, Creativity, and the Arts*, **13**, 153–158.

Acar, S., & Sen, S. (2013). A multilevel meta-analysis of the relationship between creativity and schizotypy. *Psychology of Aesthetics, Creativity, and the Arts*, **7**, 214–228.

Acar, S., Tadik, H., Myers, D., Sman, C., & Uysal, R. (2020). Creativity and well-being: A meta-analysis. *Journal of Creative Behavior*. http://doi.org/10.1002/jocb.485.

Adler, J. M. (2012). Living into the story: Agency and coherence in a longitudinal study of narrative identity development and mental health over the course of psychotherapy. *Journal of Personality and Social Psychology*, **102**, 367–389.

Adobe (2016). *State of Create: 2016*. Retrieved from https://s23.q4cdn.com/979560357/files/doc_events/2016/11/1/AdobeStateofCreate_2016_Report_Final.pdf.

Aeschbach, V. M., Schipperges, H., Braun, M. A. et al. (2022). Less is more: The effect of visiting duration on the perceived restorativeness of museums. *Psychology of Aesthetics, Creativity, and the Arts*. Advance online publication. http://dx.doi.org/10.1037/aca0000475.

Agogué, M., Poirel, N., Pineau, A., Houdé, O., & Cassotti, M. (2014). The impact of age and training on creativity: A design-theory approach to study fixation effects. *Thinking Skills and Creativity*, **11**, 33–41.

Alabbasi, A. M. A., Sumners, S. E., Paek, S. H., & Runco, M. A. (2020). Association, overlap, and inhibition: A study of implicit theories of creativity. *Creativity: Theories–Research–Applications*, **7**(2), 251–283.

Albert, A., & Kormos, J. (2011). Creativity and narrative task performance: An exploratory study. *Language Learning*, **61**, 73–99.

Aljughaiman, A., & Mowrer-Reynolds, E. (2005). Teachers' conceptions of creativity and creative students. *Journal of Creative Behavior*, **39**, 17–34.

Allan, B. A., Batz-Barbarich, C., Sterling, H. M., & Tay, L. (2019). Outcomes of meaningful work: A meta-analysis. *Journal of Management Studies*, **56**(3), 500–528.

Allen, W. (dir.) (1986). *Hannah and her sisters [motion picture]*. Los Angeles, CA: Orion Pictures.

Almeida, O. P., Yeap, B. B., Alfonso, H. et al. (2012). Older men who use computers have lower risk of dementia. *PLoS One*, **7**(8), e44239.

Almeida-Meza, P., Steptoe, A., & Cadar, D. (2021). Is engagement in intellectual and social leisure activities protective against dementia risk? Evidence from the English Longitudinal Study of Ageing. *Journal of Alzheimer's Disease*, **80**(2), 555–565.

Amabile, T. M. (1996). *Creativity in context: Update to "The social psychology of creativity."* Boulder, CO: Westview Press.

Amabile, T. M., Barsade, S. G., Mueller, J. S., & Staw, B. M. (2005). Affect and creativity at work. *Administrative Science Quarterly*, **50**(3), 367–403.

Amabile, T. M., & Fisher, C. M. (2009). Stimulate creativity by fueling passion. In E. Locke (ed.), *Handbook of principles of organizational behavior* (2nd ed., pp. 481–497). West Sussex: Wiley.

Amabile, T. M., Hennessey, B. A., & Grossman, B. S. (1986). Social influences on creativity: The effects of contracted-for reward. *Journal of Personality and Social Psychology*, **50**(1), 14–23.

Amabile, T. M., & Kramer, S. (2011). *The progress principle: Using small wins to ignite joy, engagement, and creativity at work*. Boston, MA: Harvard Business Press.

Amabile, T. M., & Pratt, M. G. (2016). The dynamic componential model of creativity and innovation in organizations: Making progress, making meaning. *Research in Organizational Behavior*, **36**, 157–183.

Andreasen, N. C. (1987). Creativity and mental illness. *American Journal of Psychiatry*, **144**, 1288–1292.

Anglim, J., Horwood, S., Smillie, L. D., Marrero, R. J., & Wood, J. K. (2020). Predicting psychological and subjective well-being from personality: A meta-analysis. *Psychological Bulletin*, **146**, 279–323.

Arndt, J., Greenberg, J., Solomon, S., Pyszczynski, T., & Schimel, J. (1999). Creativity and terror management: The effects of creative activity on guilt and social projection following mortality salience. *Journal of Personality and Social Psychology*, **77**, 19–32

Arndt, J., Routledge, C., Greenberg, J., & Sheldon, K. M. (2005). Illuminating the dark side of creative expression: Assimilation needs and the consequences of creative action following mortality salience. *Personality and Social Psychology Bulletin*, **31**(10), 1327–1339.

Arnheim, R. (2001). What it Means to be creative. *British Journal of Aesthetics*, **41**(1), 24–25.

Asquith, S. L., Wang, X., Quintana, D. S., & Abraham, A. (2020). Predictors of creativity in young people: Using frequentist and Bayesian approaches in estimating the importance of individual and contextual factors. *Psychology of Aesthetics, Creativity, and the Arts*, **16**(2), 209–220.

Astakhova, M., Ho, V., & McKay, A. S. (2022). Passion amid the pandemic: Applying a person-centered approach to examine cross-domain multi-passion profiles during a crisis. Article under review.

Augustin, D., & Leder, H. (2006). Art expertise: A study of concepts and conceptual spaces. *Psychology Science*, **48**(2), 135–156.

Averill, J. R. (1999). Individual differences in emotional creativity: Structure and correlates. *Journal of Personality*, **67**, 331–371.

Bacon, S. F. (2005). Positive psychology's two cultures. *Review of General Psychology*, **9**, 181–192.

Baer, J. (1994). Divergent thinking is not a general trait: A multi-domain training experiment. *Creativity Research Journal*, **7**, 35–46.

Baer, J. (1998). The case for domain specificity in creativity. *Creativity Research Journal*, **11**, 173–177.

Baer, J. (2011a). How divergent thinking tests mislead us: Are the Torrance Tests still relevant in the 21st century? *Psychology of Aesthetics, Creativity, and the Arts*, **5**, 309–313.

Baer, J. (2011b). Four (more) arguments against the Torrance Tests. *Psychology of Aesthetics, Creativity, and the Arts*, **5**, 316–317.

Baer, J. (2015). *Domain specificity of creativity*. San Diego, CA: Academic Press.

Baer, J., & Kaufman, J. C. (2005). Bridging generality and specificity: The Amusement Park Theoretical (APT) Model of creativity. *Roeper Review*, **27**, 158–163.

Baer, J., & Kaufman, J. C. (2017). The Amusement Park Theoretical Model of creativity: An attempt to bridge the domain specificity/generality gap. In J. C. Kaufman, V. P. Glăveanu, & J. Baer (eds.), *Cambridge handbook of creativity across domains* (pp. 8–17). New York: Cambridge University Press.

Baer, J., & Kaufman, J. C. (2019). Assessing creativity with the Consensual Assessment Technique. In I. Lebuda & V. P. Glăveanu (eds.), *The Palgrave handbook of social creativity research* (pp. 27–37). Basingstoke: Palgrave Macmillan.

Baer, J., Kaufman, J. C., & Gentile, C. A. (2004). Extension of the consensual assessment technique to nonparallel creative products. *Creativity Research Journal*, **16**, 113–117.

Baer, J., Kaufman, J. C., & Riggs, M. (2009). Rater-domain interactions in the Consensual Assessment Technique. *International Journal of Creativity and Problem Solving*, **19**, 87–92.

Baerger, D. R., & McAdams, D. P. (1999). Life story coherence and its relation to psychological well-being. *Narrative Inquiry*, **9**(1), 69–96.

Baker, F. A., Metcalf, O., Varker, T., & O'Donnell, M. (2018). A systematic review of the efficacy of creative arts therapies in the treatment of adults with PTSD. *Psychological Trauma: Theory, Research, Practice, and Policy*, **10**(6), 643–651.

Barbot, B. (2018a). The dynamics of creative ideation: Introducing a new assessment paradigm. *Frontiers in Psychology*, **9**, 2529.

Barbot, B. (2018b). "Generic" creativity as a predictor or outcome of identity development? *Creativity: Theories–Research–Applications*, **5**, 159–164.

Barbot, B. (2019). Measuring creativity change and development. *Psychology of Aesthetics, Creativity, and the Arts*, **13**, 203–210.

Barbot, B. (2020). Creativity and self-esteem in adolescence: A study of their domain-specific, multivariate relationships. *Journal of Creative Behavior*, **54**, 279–292.

Barbot, B., Besançon, M., & Lubart, T. (2016). The generality–specificity of creativity: Exploring the structure of creative potential with EPoC. *Learning and Individual Differences*, **52**, 178–187.

Barbot, B., & Heuser, B. (2017). Creativity and identity formation in adolescence: A developmental perspective. In M. Karwowski & J. C. Kaufman (eds.), *The creative self* (pp. 87–98). San Diego, CA: Academic Press.

Barbot, B., Piering, K., Horcher, D., & Baudoux, L. (2021). Creative recovery: Narrative creativity mitigates identity distress among young adults with cancer. *Journal of Psychosocial Oncology*. http://doi.org/10.1080/07347332.2021.1907498.

Barr, M., & Copeland-Stewart, A. (2022). Playing video games during the COVID-19 pandemic and effects on players' well-being. *Games and Culture*, **17**(1), 122–139.

Barrett, G., & Dotinga, R. (2010, July 21). Fact check: Wild Animal Park's naughty line. *Voice of San Diego*. Retrieved from www.voiceofsandiego.org/topics/news/fact-check-wild-animal-parks-naughty-line.

Barron, F. (1955). The disposition toward originality. *Journal of Abnormal and Social Psychology*, **51**, 478–485.

Barron, F. (1963). *Creativity and psychological health*. Princeton, NJ: Van Nostrand.

Bathroom Readers' Institute. (1989). *Uncle John's second bathroom reader*. New York: St. Martin's Press.

Batson, C. D., Early, S., & Salvarani, G. (1997). Perspective taking: Imagining how another feels versus imaging how you would feel. *Personality and Social Psychology Bulletin*, **23**(7), 751–758.

Bauer, P. J. (2007). *Remembering the times of our lives: Memory in infancy and beyond*. Mahwah, NJ: Erlbaum.

Bear, G. G., Slaughter, J. C., Mantz, L. S., & Farley-Ripple, E. (2017). Rewards, praise, and punitive consequences: Relations with intrinsic and extrinsic motivation. *Teaching and Teacher Education*, **65**, 10–20.

Beaty, R. E., & Silvia, P. J. (2012). Why do ideas get more creative across time? An executive interpretation of the serial order effect in divergent thinking tasks. *Psychology of Aesthetics, Creativity, and the Arts*, **6**, 309–319.

Beauchaine, T. (2001). Vagal tone, development, and Gray's motivational theory: Toward an integrated model of autonomic nervous system functioning in psychopathology. *Development and Psychopathology*, **13**(2), 183–214.

Beaussart, M. L., Andrews, C. J., & Kaufman, J. C. (2013). Creative liars: The relationship between creativity and integrity. *Thinking Skills and Creativity*, **9**, 129–134.

Beaussart, M. L., Kaufman, S. B., & Kaufman, J. C. (2012). Creative activity, personality, mental illness, and short-term mating success. *Journal of Creative Behavior*, **46**, 151–167.

Beaussart, M. L., White, A. E., Pullaro, A., & Kaufman, J. C. (2014). Reviewing recent empirical findings on creativity and mental illness. In J. C. Kaufman (ed.), *Creativity and mental illness* (pp. 42–59). New York: Cambridge University Press.

Becker, E. (1973). *The denial of death*. New York: Free Press

Becker, G. (2014). A socio-historical overview of the creativity–pathology connection: From antiquity to contemporary times. In J. C. Kaufman (ed.), *Creativity and mental illness* (pp. 3–24). New York: Cambridge University Press.

Beghetto, R. A. (2007). Ideational code-switching: Walking the talk about supporting student creativity in the classroom. *Roeper Review*, **29**(4), 265–270.

Beghetto, R. A. (2009). Correlates of intellectual risk taking in elementary school science. *Journal of Research in Science Teaching*, **46**(2), 210–223.

Beghetto, R. A. (2014). Creative mortification: An initial exploration. *Psychology of Aesthetics, Creativity, and the Arts*, **8**, 266–276.

Beghetto, R. A., & Kaufman, J. C. (2007). Toward a broader conception of creativity: A case for "mini-c" creativity. *Psychology of Aesthetics, Creativity, and the Arts*, **1**, 73–79.

Beghetto, R. A., & Kaufman, J. C. (2009). Intellectual estuaries: Connecting learning and creativity in programs of advanced academics. *Journal of Advanced Academics*, **20**, 296–324.

Beghetto, R. A., & Kaufman, J. C. (2015). Promise and pitfalls in differentiating amongst the Cs of creativity. *Creativity Research Journal*, **27**, 240–241.

Beghetto, R. A., Kaufman, J. C., & Baer, J. (2014). *Teaching for creativity in the common core classroom*. New York: Teachers College Press.

Belkofer, C. M., & Konopka, L. M. (2008). Conducting art therapy research using quantitative EEC measures. *Art Therapy: Journal of the American Art Therapy Association*, **25**, 56–63.

Bellass, S., Balmer, A., May, V. et al. (2019). Broadening the debate on creativity and dementia: A critical approach. *Dementia*, **18**(7–8), 2799–2820.

Benedek, M., Beaty, R. E., Schacter, D. L., & Kenett, Y. N. (2023). The role of memory in creative ideation. *Nature Reviews Psychology*. https://doi.org/10.1038/s44159-023-00158-z.

Benedek, M., Bruckdorfer, R., & Jauk, E. (2020). Motives for creativity: Exploring the what and why of everyday creativity. *Journal of Creative Behavior*, **54**(3), 610–625.

Benedek, M., Christensen, A. P., Fink, A., & Beaty, R. E. (2019). Creativity assessment in neuroscience research. *Psychology of Aesthetics, Creativity, and the Arts*, **13**(2), 218–226.

Benedek, M., Karstendiek, M., Ceh, S. M. et al. (2021). Creativity myths: Prevalence and correlates of misconceptions on creativity. *Personality and Individual Differences*, **182**, 111068.

Bengtsson, H., Söderström, M., & Terjestam, Y. (2016). The structure and development of dispositional compassion in early adolescence. *Journal of Early Adolescence*, **36**(6), 840–873.

Benoit-Bryan, J., Smith, M., & Linett, P. (2022). *Rethinking relevance, rebuilding engagement*. Slover Linett. https://sloverlinett.com/insights/rethinking-relevance-rebuilding-engagement-findings-from-the-second-wave-of-a-national-survey-about-culture-creativity-community-and-the-arts.

Bensimon, M., Amir, D., & Wolf, Y. (2008). Drumming through trauma: Music therapy with post-traumatic soldiers. *The Arts in Psychotherapy*, **35**(1), 34–48.

Berman, J. (2010). The talking cure and the writing cure. *Philosophy, Psychiatry, & Psychology*, **17** (3), 255–257.

Bilalić, M., McLeod, P., & Gobet, F. (2008). Inflexibility of experts: Reality or myth? Quantifying the Einstellung effect in chess masters. *Cognitive Psychology*, **56**, 73–102.

Bind, R. H., Estevao, C., Fancourt, D. et al. (2022). Online singing interventions for postnatal depression in times of social isolation: A feasibility study protocol for the SHAPER-PNDO single-arm trial. *Pilot and Feasibility Studies*, **8**(1), 1–12.

Boden, M. A. (2004). *The creative mind: Myths and mechanisms*. New York: Routledge.

Boerner, M., Joseph, S., & Murphy, D. (2017). Reports of post-traumatic growth and well-being: Moderating effect of defense style. *Journal of Social and Clinical Psychology*, **36**, 723–737.

Boldt, G. (2019). Artistic creativity beyond divergent thinking: Analysing sequences in creative subprocesses. *Thinking Skills and Creativity*, **34**, 100606.

Boldt, G., & Kaufman, J. C. (2023). Creativity and meaning at work. In R. Reiter-Palmon & S. T. Hunter (eds.), *Handbook of organizational creativity* (2nd ed.). San Diego, CA: Academic Press.

Bone, J. K., Bu, F., Fluharty, M. E. et al. (2022). Arts and cultural engagement, reportedly antisocial or criminalized behaviors, and potential mediators in two longitudinal cohorts of adolescents. *Journal of Youth and Adolescence*, **51**, 1463–1482.

Booth, R. (2022). Helping us heal: How creative life story work supports individuals and organisations to recover from trauma. *Journal of Social Work Practice*, **36**(1), 119–127.

Brosowsky, N. P., Barr, N., Mugon, J. et al. (2022). Creativity, boredom proneness and well-being in the pandemic. *Behavioral Sciences*, **12**(3), 68.

Boswell, T. (1989). *The heart of the order*. New York: Doubleday.

Bowden, E. M., & Jung-Beeman, M. (2003). One hundred forty-four compound remote associate problems: Short insight-like problems with one-word solutions. *Behavioral Research, Methods, Instruments, and Computers*, **35**, 634–639.

Bowers, R. (2012). *Superman versus the Ku Klux Klan: The true story of how the iconic superhero battled the men of hate*. Washington, DC: National Geographic Books.

Boyle, T. C. (1993). *The road to Wellville*. New York: Viking Press.

Brandau, H., Daghofer, F., Hollerer, L. et al. (2007). The relationship between creativity, teacher ratings on behavior, age, and gender in pupils from seven to ten years. *Journal of Creative Behavior*, **41**, 91–113.

Brannigan, A., & Wanner, R. A. (1983). Historical distributions of multiple discoveries and theories of scientific change. *Social Studies of Science*, **13**, 417–435.

Bristol, A. S., & Viskontas, I. V. (2016). Dynamic processes within associative memory stores: Piecing together the neural basis of creative cognition. In J. C. Kaufman & J. Baer (eds.), *Creativity and reason in cognitive development* (2nd ed., pp. 187–210). New York: Cambridge University Press.

Bruner, J. (1986). *Actual minds, possible worlds*. Cambridge, MA: Harvard University Press.

Bruner, J. (1990). *Acts of meaning*. Cambridge, MA: Harvard University Press.

Brown, T. (2008). Design thinking. *Harvard Business Review*, **86**, 84–92.

Buecker, S., Simacek, T., Ingwersen, B., Terwiel, S., & Simonsmeier, B. A. (2021). Physical activity and subjective well-being in healthy individuals: A meta-analytic review. *Health Psychology Review*, **15**, 574–592.

Butler, R. O. (2005). *From where you dream: The process of writing fiction*. New York: Grove Press.

Byron, K., & Khazanchi, S. (2012). Rewards and creative performance: A meta-analytic test of theoretically derived hypotheses. *Psychological Bulletin*, **138**, 809–830.

Byron, K., Khazanchi, S., & Nazarian, D. (2010). The relationship between stressors and creativity: A meta-analysis examining competing theoretical models. *Journal of Applied Psychology*, **95**(1), 201–212.

Cacioppo, J. T., Petty, R. E., Feinstein, J. A., & Jarvis, W. B. G. (1996). Dispositional differences in cognitive motivation: The life and times of individuals varying in need for cognition. *Psychological Bulletin*, **119**(2), 197–253.

Calaprice, A. (2000). *The expanded quotable Einstein*. Princeton, NJ: Princeton University Press.

Caldwell, R. L. (2005). At the confluence of memory and meaning: Life review with older adults and families: Using narrative therapy and the expressive arts to re-member and re-author stories of resilience. *Family Journal*, **13**(2), 172–175.

Callahan, C. M., Hunsaker, S. L., Adams, C. M., Moore, S. D., & Bland, L. C. (1995). Instruments used in the identification of gifted and talented students. *American Educational Research Journal*, **45**, 150–165.

Campbell, K., & Kaufman, J. C. (2017). Do you pursue your heart or your art? Creativity, personality, and love. *Journal of Family Issues*, **38**, 287–311.

Carlberg, I. (2016). *Raoul Wallenberg: The heroic life and mysterious disappearance of the man who saved thousands of Hungarian Jews from the Holocaust*. London: MacLehose Press.

Carlson, E., Saarikallio, S., Toiviainen, P. et al. (2015). Maladaptive and adaptive emotion regulation through music: A behavioral and neuroimaging study of males and females. *Frontiers in Human Neuroscience*, **9**, 466.

Carlson, M. C., Helms, M. J., Steffens, D. C. et al. (2008). Midlife activity predicts risk of dementia in older male twin pairs. *Alzheimer's & Dementia*, **4**(5), 324–331.

Carson, S. H. (2011). Creativity and psychopathology: A shared vulnerability model. *Canadian Journal of Psychiatry / Revue Canadienne de Psychiatrie*, **56**, 144–153.

Carson, S. H. (2019). Creativity and mental illness. In J. C. Kaufman & R. J. Sternberg (eds.), *The Cambridge handbook of creativity* (2nd ed., pp. 296–318). New York: Cambridge University Press.

Carson, S. H., Peterson, J. B., & Higgins, D. M. (2005). Reliability, validity and factor structure of the Creative Achievement Questionnaire. *Creativity Research Journal*, **17**, 37–50.

Carswell, K. L., Finkel, E. J., & Kumashiro, M. (2019). Creativity and romantic passion. *Journal of Personality and Social Psychology*, **116**(6), 919–941.

Carver, R. (1982). A small, good thing. *Ploughshares*, **8**(2/3), 213–240.

Carver, R. (1984). Cathedral. In R. Carver, *Cathedral* (pp. 209–228). New York: Vintage.

Ceci, M. W., & Kumar, V. K. (2016). A correlational study of creativity, happiness, motivation, and stress from creative pursuits. *Journal of Happiness Studies*, **17**, 609–626.

Cerasoli, C. P., Nicklin, J. M., & Ford, M. T. (2014). Intrinsic motivation and extrinsic incentives jointly predict performance: A 40-year meta-analysis. *Psychological Bulletin*, **140**, 980–1008.

Chamorro-Premuzic, T., & Reichenbacher, L. (2008). Effects of personality and threat of evaluation on divergent and convergent thinking. *Journal of Research in Personality*, **42**, 1095–1101.

Chassell, L. M. (1916). Test for originality. *Journal of Educational Psychology*, **7**, 317–328.

Chen, Q., Beaty, R. E., & Qiu, J. (2020). Mapping the artistic brain: Common and distinct neural activations associated with musical, drawing, and literary creativity. *Human Brain Mapping*, **41**, 3403–3419.

Choi, D., & Kaufman, J. C. (2021). Where does creativity come from? What is creativity? Where is creativity going in giftedness? In R. J. Sternberg & D. Ambrose (eds.), *Conceptions of giftedness* (pp. 65–81). Cham: Springer Nature.

Chrysikou, E. G., Motyka, K., Nigro, C., Yang, S.-I., & Thompson-Schill, S. L. (2016). Functional fixedness in creative thinking tasks depends on stimulus modality. *Psychology of Aesthetics, Creativity, and the Arts*, **10**, 425–435.

Clegg, H., Nettle, D., & Miell, D. (2011). Status and mating success amongst visual artists. *Frontiers in Psychology*, **2**, 1–4.

Cohen, L. M. (1989). A continuum of adaptive creative behaviors. *Creativity Research Journal*, **2**, 169–183.

Cohen-Mansfield, J., Gavendo, R., & Blackburn, E. (2019). Activity preferences of persons with dementia: An examination of reports by formal and informal caregivers. *Dementia: The International Journal of Social Research and Practice*, **18**(6), 2036–2048.

Collier, A. F., & Wayment, H. A. (2018). Psychological benefits of the "maker" or do-it-yourself movement in young adults: A pathway towards subjective well-being. *Journal of Happiness Studies*, **19**(4), 1217–1239.

Collins, C. (1955). George Simenon: The art of fiction. *The Paris Review*. Retrieved from www.theparisreview.org/interviews/5020/the-art-of-fiction-no-9-georges-simenon.

Connelly, B. S., McAbee, S. T., Oh, I.-S., Jung, Y., & Jung, C.-W. (2022). A multirater perspective on personality and performance: An empirical examination of the trait–reputation–identity model. *Journal of Applied Psychology*, **107**, 1352–1368.

Conner, T. S., DeYoung, C. G., & Silvia, P. J. (2018). Everyday creative activity as a path to flourishing. *Journal of Positive Psychology*, **13**(2), 181–189.

Conner, T. S., & Silvia, P. J. (2015). Creative days: A daily diary study of emotion, personality, and everyday creativity. *Psychology of Aesthetics, Creativity, and the Arts*, **9**(4), 463–470.

Cook, T., Roy, A. R. K., & Welker, K. M. (2019). Music as an emotion regulation strategy: An examination of genres of music and their roles in emotion regulation. *Psychology of Music*, **47**(1), 144–154.

Coon, D. J. (1982). Eponymy, obscurity, Twitmyer, and Pavlov. *Journal of the History of the Behavioral Sciences*, **18**, 255–262.

Cooper, R. A., Kensinger, E. A., & Ritchey, M. (2019). Memories fade: The relationship between memory vividness and remembered visual salience. *Psychological Science*, **30**, 657–668.

Corazza, G. E., Agnoli, S., & Mastria, S. (2022). The dynamic creativity framework: Theoretical and empirical investigations. *European Psychologist*, **27**, 191–206. https://doi.org/10.1027/1016-9040/a000473.

Corazza, G. E., Glăveanu, V., & Kaufman, J. C. (2021). Injecting creativity in society for possible futures of improved ethics and equity. In C. Mullen (ed.), *Handbook of social justice interventions in education* (pp. 635–652). Cham: Springer Nature.

Corrigan, P. W. (2000). Mental health stigma as social attribution: Implications for research methods and attitude change. *Clinical Psychology: Science and Practice*, **7**, 48–67.

Costa, P. T., & McCrae, R. R. (1992). *NEO PI–R: Professional manual*. Odessa, FL: Psychological Assessment Resources.

Coyle, T. R. (2015). Relations among general intelligence (g), aptitude tests, and GPA: Linear effects dominate. *Intelligence*, **53**, 16–22.

Cramond, B., Matthews-Morgan, J., Torrance, E. P., & Zuo, L. (1999). Why should the Torrance Tests of Creative Thinking be used to access creativity? *Korean Journal of Thinking & Problem Solving*, **9**(2), 77–101.

Crawford, J. T., & Brandt, M. J. (2019). Who is prejudiced, and toward whom? The big five traits and generalized prejudice. *Personality and Social Psychology Bulletin*, **45**(10), 1455–1467.

Crockett, Z. (2020, August 16). The man who has created 100+ pointless inventions. *The Hustle*. Retrieved from http://thehustle.co/the-man-who-has-created-100-pointless-inventions.

Cropley, A. J. (2006). In praise of convergent thinking. *Creativity Research Journal*, **18**, 391–404.

Cropley, D. H. (2015a). *Creativity in engineering: Novel solutions to complex problems*. San Diego, CA: Academic Press.

Cropley, D. H. (2015b). Teaching engineers to think creatively. In R. Wegerif, L. Li, & J. C. Kaufman (eds.), *The Routledge international handbook of research on teaching thinking* (pp. 402–410). London: Routledge.

Cropley, D. H., & Cropley, A. J. (2010). Functional creativity: Products and the generation of effective novelty. In J. C. Kaufman & R. J. Sternberg (eds.), *Cambridge handbook of creativity* (pp. 301–320). New York: Cambridge University Press.

Cropley, D. H., Cropley, A. J., Kaufman, J. C., & Runco, M. A. (eds.). (2010). *The dark side of creativity*. New York: Cambridge University Press.

Cropley, D. H., Kaufman, J. C., & Cropley, A. J. (2008). Malevolent creativity: A functional model of creativity in terrorism and crime. *Creativity Research Journal*, **20**, 105–115.

Cropley, D. H., & Marrone, R. L. (2022). Automated scoring of figural creativity using a convolutional neural network. *Psychology of Aesthetics, Creativity, and the Arts*. Advance online publication. http://doi.org/10.1037/aca0000510.

Cseh, G. M., & Jeffries, K. K. (2019). A scattered CAT: A critical evaluation of the consensual assessment technique for creativity research. *Psychology of Aesthetics, Creativity, and the Arts*, **13**, 159–166.

Csikszentmihalyi, M. (1990). *Flow: The psychology of optimal experience*. New York: Harper & Row.

Csikszentmihalyi, M. (1996). *Creativity: Flow and the psychology of discovery and invention*. New York: HarperCollins.

Csikszentmihalyi, M. (1998). Reflections on the field. *Roeper Review*, **21**, 80–81.

Csikszentmihalyi, M. (1999). Implications of a systems perspective for the study of creativity. In R. J. Sternberg (ed.), *Handbook of creativity* (pp. 313–335). New York: Cambridge University Press.

Csikszentmihalyi, M. (2000). *Between boredom and anxiety: Experiencing flow in work and play*. San Francisco, CA: Jossey-Bass.

Csikszentmihalyi, M., & Csikszentmihalyi, I. S. (1988). *Optimal experience*. New York: Cambridge University Press.

Csikszentmihalyi, M., & LeFevre, J. (1989). Optimal experience in work and leisure. *Journal of Personality and Social Psychology*, **56**, 815–822.

Cuff, B. M. P., Brown, S. J., Taylor, L., & Howat, D. J. (2016). Empathy: A review of the concept. *Emotion Review*, **8**, 144–153.

Cui, Y. X., Zhou, X., Zu, C. et al. (2020). Benevolent creativity buffers anxiety aroused by mortality salience: Terror management in COVID-19 pandemic. *Frontiers in Psychology*, **11**, 3705.

Dai, D. Y., & Niu, W. (in press). Looking at intelligence, creativity, and wisdom in the Chinese way: A troika model of mind power. To appear in R. J. Sternberg, J. C. Kaufman, & S. Karami (eds.), *Intelligence, creativity and wisdom: Exploring their connections and distinctions*. London: Palgrave Macmillan.

Dalebroux, A., Goldstein, T. R., & Winner, E. (2008). Short-term mood repair through art-making: Positive emotion is more effective than venting. *Motivation and Emotion*, **32**(4), 288–295.

Damadzic, A., Winchester, C., Medeiros, K. E., & Griffith, J. A. (2022). [Re]thinking outside the box: A meta-analysis of constraints and creative performance. *Journal of Organizational Behavior*. https://doi.org/10.1002/job.2655.

Damer, E., Webb, T. L., & Crisp, R. J. (2019). Diversity may help the uninterested: Evidence that exposure to counter-stereotypes promotes cognitive reflection for people low (but not high) in need for cognition. *Group Processes & Intergroup Relations*, **22**(8), 1079–1093.

Damian, R. I., & Simonton, D. K. (2014). Diversifying experiences in the development of genius and their impact on creative cognition. In D. K. Simonton (ed.), *The Wiley handbook of genius* (pp. 375–394). Oxford: Wiley Blackwell.

Damian, R. I., & Simonton, D. K. (2015). Psychopathology, adversity, and creativity: Diversifying experiences in the development of eminent African Americans. *Journal of Personality and Social Psychology*, **108**, 623–636.

Datlen, G. W., & Pandolfi, C. (2020). Developing an online art therapy group for learning disabled young adults using WhatsApp. *International Journal of Art Therapy*, **25**(4), 192–201.

Davidson, J. W., & Fedele, J. (2011). Investigating group singing activity with people with dementia and their caregivers: Problems and positive prospects. *Musicae Scientiae*, **15**(3), 402–422.

Daykin, N., Mansfield, L., Meads, C. et al. (2018). What works for wellbeing? A systematic review of wellbeing outcomes for music and singing in adults. *Perspectives in Public Health*, **138**(1), 39–46.

De Clercq, D., & Belausteguigoitia, I. (2021). The links among interpersonal conflict, personal and contextual resources, and creative behaviour. *Canadian Journal of Administrative Sciences / Revue Canadienne des Sciences de l'Administration*, **38**(2), 135–149.

De Dreu, C. K. W., Baas, M., & Nijstad, B. A. (2008). Hedonic tone and activation in the mood–creativity link: Towards a dual pathway to creativity model. *Journal of Personality and Social Psychology*, **94**, 739–775.

de Freitas Girardi, J., Miconi, D., Lyke, C., & Rousseau, C. (2020). Creative expression workshops as psychological first aid (Pfa) for asylum-seeking children: An exploratory study in temporary shelters in Montreal. *Clinical Child Psychology and Psychiatry*, **25**, 483–493.

de Guzman, A. B., Mesana, J. C. B., Manuel, M. E., Arcega, K. C. A., Yumang, R. L. T., & Miranda, K. N. V. (2022). Examining intergenerational family members' creative activities during COVID-19 lockdown via manifest content analysis of YouTube and TikTok videos. *Educational Gerontology*, **48**, 458–471.

De Petrillo, L., & Winner, E. (2005). Does art improve mood? A test of a key assumption underlying art therapy. *Art Therapy*, **22**(4), 205–212.

De Stobbeleir, K. E., Ashford, S. J., & Buyens, D. (2011). Self-regulation of creativity at work: The role of feedback-seeking behavior in creative performance. *Academy of Management Journal*, **54**, 811–831.

Decety, J., & Jackson, P. L. (2006). A social-neuroscience perspective on empathy. *Current Directions in Psychological Science*, **15**(2), 54–58.

Deci, E. L., & Ryan, R. M. (1985). *Intrinsic motivation and self-determination in human behavior.* New York: Plenum.

Deci, E. L., & Ryan, R. M. (2000). The what and why of goal pursuits: Human needs and the self-determination of behavior. *Psychological Inquiry*, **11**, 227–268.

Deci, E. L., & Ryan, R. M. (2010). *Self-determination.* New York: Wiley.

Derakhshanrad, S. A., Piven, E., & Zeynalzadeh Ghoochani, B. (2019). The relationships between problem-solving, creativity, and job burnout in Iranian occupational therapists. *Occupational Therapy in Health Care*, **33**(4), 365–380.

DeYoung, C. G. (2015). Cybernetic Big Five theory. *Journal of Research in Personality*, **56**, 33–58.

DeYoung, C. G., Quilty, L. C., & Peterson, J. B. (2007). Between facets and domains: 10 aspects of the Big Five. *Journal of Personality and Social Psychology*, **93**, 880–896.

Diakidoy, I. A. N., & Spanoudis, G. (2002). Domain specificity in creativity testing: A comparison of performance on a general divergent-thinking test and a parallel, content-specific test. *Journal of Creative Behavior*, **36**(1), 41–61.

Diamond, S., & Shrira, A. (2022). From "a nothing" to something special: Art as a space of holding attunement in the creative experience of Holocaust survivor artists. *Psychology of Aesthetics, Creativity, and the Arts*, **16**, 318–331.

Diedrich, J., Jauk, S. J., Gredlein, J. M., Neubauer, A. C., & Benedek, M. (2018). Assessment of real-life creativity: The inventory of creative activities and achievements (ICAA). *Psychology of Aesthetics, Creativity, and the Arts*, **12**, 304–316.

Dimitropoulos, A., Zyga, O., Doernberg, E., & Russ, S. W. (2021). Show me what happens next: Preliminary efficacy of a remote play-based intervention for children with Prader-Willi syndrome. *Research in Developmental Disabilities*, **108**, 103820.

Doernberg, E., Russ, S. W., & Dimitropoulos, A. (2021). Believing in make-believe: Efficacy of a pretend play intervention for school-aged children with high-functioning autism spectrum disorder. *Journal of Autism and Developmental Disorders*, **51**, 576–588.

Doi, T., Verghese, J., Makizako, H. et al. (2017). Effects of cognitive leisure activity on cognition in mild cognitive impairment: Results of a randomized controlled trial. *Journal of the American Medical Directors Association*, **18**(8), 686–691.

Dollinger, S. J. (2003). Need for uniqueness, need for cognition, and creativity. *Journal of Creative Behavior*, **37**(2), 99–116.

Dollinger, S. J. (2011). "Standardized minds" or individuality? Admissions tests and creativity revisited. *Psychology of Aesthetics, Creativity, and the Arts*, **5**, 329–341.

Dollinger, S. J., Burke, P., & Gump, N. (2007). Creativity and values. *Creativity Research Journal*, **19**, 91–103.

Dollinger, S. J., & Clancy, S. M. (1993). Identity, self, and personality: II. Glimpses through the autophotographic eye. *Journal of Personality and Social Psychology*, **64**, 1064–1071.

Dollinger, S. J., Skaggs, A. (2011). Does the act predict "inside the box" thinking or creativity? Creative characters in the personality imagination exercise. *Imagination, Cognition and Personality*, **31**, 199–216.

Dowlen, R., Keady, J., Milligan, C. et al. (2018). The personal benefits of musicking for people living with dementia: A thematic synthesis of the qualitative literature. *Arts & Health*, **10**(3), 197–212.

Drake, J. E. (2019). Examining the psychological and psychophysiological benefits of drawing over one month. *Psychology of Aesthetics, Creativity, and the Arts*, **13**(3), 338–347.

Drake, J. E. (2021). How drawing to distract improves mood in children. *Frontiers in Psychology*, **12**, 78.

Drake, J. E., Coleman, K., & Winner, E. (2011). Short-term mood repair through art: Effects of medium and strategy. *Art Therapy*, **28**(1), 26–30.

Drake, J. E., Hastedt, I., & James, C. (2016). Drawing to distract: Examining the psychological benefits of drawing over time. *Psychology of Aesthetics, Creativity, and the Arts*, **10**(3), 325–331.

Drake, J. E., & Hodge, A. (2015). Drawing versus writing: The role of preference in regulating short-term affect. *Art Therapy*, **32**(1), 27–33.

Drake, J. E., Papazian, K., & Grossman, E. (2022). Gravitating toward the arts during the COVID-19 pandemic. *Psychology of Aesthetics, Creativity, and the Arts*. Advance online publication. http://dx.doi.org/10.1037/aca0000471.

Drake, J. E., & Winner, E. (2012). Confronting sadness through art-making: Distraction is more beneficial than venting. *Psychology of Aesthetics, Creativity, and the Arts*, **6**, 251–266.

Drake, J. E., & Winner, E. (2013). How children use drawing to regulate their emotions. *Cognition and Emotion*, **27**, 512–520.

Drew, H. (2020, July 8). Art and mental health: We must leave behind the "tortured genius" trope once and for all. *The Boar*. Retrieved from http://theboar.org/2020/07/artistmentalhealth.

Duan, H., Yang, T., Wang, X., Kan, Y., Zhao, H., Li, Y., & Hu, W. (2020). Is the creativity of lovers better? A behavioral and functional near-infrared spectroscopy hyperscanning study. *Current Psychology*, **41**, 41–54.

Duffy, R. D., & Richard, G. V. (2006). Physician job satisfaction across six major specialties. *Journal of Vocational Behavior*, **68**(3), 548–559.

Dufouil, C., Pereira, E., Chêne, G. et al. (2014). Older age at retirement is associated with decreased risk of dementia. *European Journal of Epidemiology*, **29**(5), 353–361.

Dunning, D., Johnson, K., Ehrlinger, J., & Kruger, J. (2003). Why people fail to recognize their own incompetence. *Current Directions in Psychological Science*, **12**, 83–86.

Dweck, C. S. (2000). *Self-theories: Their role in motivation, personality and development*. Philadelphia, PA: Taylor & Francis.

Dziedziewicz, D., Gajda, A., & Karwowski, M. (2014). Developing children's intercultural competence and creativity. *Thinking Skills and Creativity*, **13**, 32–42.

Eaton, J., & Tieber, C. (2017). The effects of coloring on anxiety, mood, and perseverance. *Art Therapy*, **34**(1), 42–46.

Edmondson, A. C. (1999). Psychological safety and learning behavior in work teams. *Administrative Science Quarterly*, **44**, 350–383.

Eekelaar, C., Camic, P. M., & Springham, N. (2012). Art galleries, episodic memory and verbal fluency in dementia: An exploratory study. *Psychology of Aesthetics, Creativity, and the Arts*, **6** (3), 262–272.

Eisenberger, R., & Shanock, L. (2003). Rewards, intrinsic motivation, and creativity: A case study of conceptual and methodological isolation. *Creativity Research Journal*, **15**, 121–130.

Eliot, T. S. (1915). The love song of J. Alfred Prufrock. *Poetry*, **6**, 130–135.

Elisondo, R. C. (2021). Creative activities, emotions, and resilience during the COVID-19 pandemic: A longitudinal study from Argentina. *Public Health*, **195**, 118–122.

Erikson, E. H. (1974). *Dimensions of a new identity*. New York: W. W. Norton.

Erikson, E. H. (1982). *The life cycle completed*. New York: W. W. Norton.

Ericsson, K. A., Roring, R. W., & Nandagopal, K. (2007). Giftedness and evidence for reproducibly superior performance: An account based on the expert-performance framework. *High Ability Studies*, **18**, 3–56.

Eschleman, K. J., Madsen, J., Alarcon, G. M., & Barelka, A. (2014). Benefiting from creative activity: The positive relationships between creative activity, recovery experiences, and performance-related outcomes. *Journal Occupational and Organizational Psychology*, **87**, 579–598.

Eschleman, K. J., Mathieu, M., & Cooper, J. (2017). Creating a recovery filled weekend: The moderating effect of occupation type on the relationship between non-work creative activity and state of feeling recovered at work. *Creativity Research Journal*, **29**(2), 97–107.

Eubanks, P. (2016). Epilogue. In E. Semino & Z. Demjén (eds.), *The Routledge handbook of metaphor and language* (pp. 517–528). London: Routledge.

Everson, H. T., & Tobias, S. (1998). The ability to estimate knowledge and performance in college: A metacognitive analysis. *Instructional Science*, **26**, 65–79.

Fancourt, D., Garnett, C., & Müllensiefen, D. (2020). The relationship between demographics, behavioral and experiential engagement factors, and the use of artistic creative activities to regulate emotions. *Psychology of Aesthetics, Creativity, and the Arts*. Advance online publication. http://dx.doi.org/10.1037/aca0000296.

Fancourt, D., Garnett, C., Spiro, N., West, R., & Müllensiefen, D. (2019). How do artistic creative activities regulate our emotions? Validation of the Emotion Regulation Strategies for Artistic Creative Activities Scale (ERS-ACA). *PLoS One*, **14**(2), e0211362.

Fancourt, D., & Steptoe, A. (2019). Present in body or just in mind: Differences in social presence and emotion regulation in live vs. virtual singing experiences. *Frontiers in Psychology*, **10**, 778.

Fancourt, D., Williamon, A., Carvalho, L. A. et al. (2016). Singing modulates mood, stress, cortisol, cytokine and neuropeptide activity in cancer patients and carers. *ecancermedicalscience*, **10**, 631.

Farmer, S. M., & Tierney, P. (2017). Considering creative self-efficacy: Its current state and ideas for future inquiry. In M. Karwowski & J. C. Kaufman (eds.), *The creative self: Effect of beliefs, self-efficacy, mindset, and identity* (pp. 23–47). San Diego, CA: Academic Press.

Faucounau, V., Wu, Y. H., Boulay, M., De Rotrou, J., & Rigaud, A. S. (2010). Cognitive intervention programmes on patients affected by mild cognitive impairment: A promising intervention tool for MCI?. *Journal of Nutrition, Health & Aging*, **14**(1), 31–35.

Feist, G. J. (1998). A meta-analysis of personality in scientific and artistic creativity. *Personality and Social Psychology Review*, **2**, 290–309.

Feist, G. J., Reiter-Palmon, R., & Kaufman, J. C. (eds.). (2017). *Cambridge handbook of creativity and personality research*. New York: Cambridge University Press.

Fink, A., & Woschnjak, S. (2011). Creativity and personality in professional dancers. *Personality and Individual Differences*, **51**(6), 754–758.

Fink, A., Weiss, E. M., Schwarzl, U. et al. (2017). Creative ways to well-being: Reappraisal inventiveness in the context of anger-evoking situations. *Cognitive, Affective, & Behavioral Neuroscience*, **17**, 94–105.

Fink, L., & Drake, J. E. (2016). Mood and flow: Comparing the benefits of narrative versus poetry writing. *Empirical Studies of the Arts*, **34**(2), 177–192.

Finke, R. A., Ward, T. B., & Smith, S. M. (1992). *Creative cognition: Theory, research, and applications*. Cambridge, MA: MIT Press.

Fiorelli, J., & Russ, S. (2012). Pretend play, coping, and subjective wellbeing in children: A follow-up study. *American Journal of Play*, **5**, 81–103.

Fiori, M., Fischer, S., & Barabasch, A. (2022). Creativity is associated with higher well-being and more positive COVID-19 experience. *Personality and Individual Differences*, **194**, 111646.

FioRito, T. A., Geiger, A. R., & Routledge, C. (2021). Creative nostalgia: Social and psychological benefits of scrapbooking. *Art Therapy*, **38**(2), 98–103.

Fivush, R. (2011). The development of autobiographical memory. *Annual Review of Psychology*, **62**, 559–582.

Flavell, J. H. (1979). Metacognition and cognitive monitoring: A new area of cognitive developmental inquiry. *American Psychologist*, **34**, 906–911.

Florida, R. (2012). *The rise of the creative class revisited*. New York: Basic Books.

Florida, R. (2019). The creative city. In J. C. Kaufman & R. J. Sternberg (eds.), *Cambridge handbook of creativity* (pp. 623–639). New York: Cambridge University Press.

Ford, C., & Sullivan, D. M. (2004). A time for everything: How timing of novel contributions influences project team outcomes. *Journal of Organizational Behavior*, **21**, 163–183.

Ford, D. Y. (2003). Desegregating gifted education: Seeking equity for culturally diverse students. In J. H. Borland (ed.), *Rethinking gifted education* (pp. 143–158). New York: Teachers College Press.

Forgeard, M. J. C. (2013). Perceiving benefits after adversity: The relationship between self-reported posttraumatic growth and creativity. *Psychology of Aesthetics, Creativity, and the Arts*, **7**, 245–264.

Forgeard, M. J. C. (2019). Creativity and healing. In J. C. Kaufman & R. J. Sternberg (eds.), *Cambridge handbook of creativity* (pp. 319–331). New York: Cambridge University Press.

Forgeard, M. J. C. (2022). Prosocial motivation and creativity in the arts and sciences: Qualitative and quantitative evidence. *Psychology of Aesthetics, Creativity, and the Arts*. https://doi.org/10.1037/aca0000435.supp.

Forgeard, M. J. C., & Elstein, J. G. (2014). Advancing the clinical science of creativity. *Frontiers in Psychology*, **5**, 613.

Forgeard, M. J. C., & Kaufman, J. C. (2016). Who cares about imagination, creativity, and innovation, and why? A review. *Psychology of Aesthetics, Creativity, and the Arts*, **10**, 250–269.

Forgeard, M. J. C., & Mecklenburg, A. C. (2013). The two dimensions of motivation and a reciprocal model of the creative process. *Review of General Psychology*, **17**(3), 255–266.

Forgeard, M. J. C., Mecklenburg A. C., Lacasse J. J., & Jayawickreme E. (2014). Bringing the whole universe to order: Creativity, healing, and posttraumatic growth. In J. C. Kaufman (ed.), *Creativity and mental illness* (pp. 321–342). New York: Cambridge University Press.

Forkosh, J., & Drake, J. E. (2017). Coloring versus drawing: Effects of cognitive demand on mood repair, flow, and enjoyment. *Art Therapy*, **34**(2), 75–82.

Foster, T. L., Dietrich, M. S., Friedman, D. L., Gordon, J. E., & Gilmer, M. J. (2012). National survey of children's hospitals on legacy-making activities. *Journal of Palliative Medicine*, **15**(5), 573–578.

Frank, M., & Sacco, L. R. (2008). *The museum of bad art: Masterworks*. Berkeley, CA: Ten Speed Press.

Frankl, V. E. (2006). *Man's search for meaning*. Boston, MA: Beacon Press. (Original work published 1946.)

Franklin, F. C., & Cheung, M. (2017). Legacy interventions with patients with co-occurring disorders: Legacy definitions, life satisfaction, and self-efficacy. *Substance Use & Misuse*, **52**(14), 1840–1849.

Freud, S. (1959). Creative writers and day-dreaming. In J. Strachey (ed.), *The standard edition of the complete psychological works of Sigmund Freud* (vol. 9, pp. 141–154). London: The Hogarth Press. (Original work published 1908.)

Freund, P. A., & Holling, H. (2008). Creativity in the classroom: A multilevel analysis investigating the impact of creativity and reasoning ability on GPA. *Creativity Research Journal*, **20**, 309–318.

Frey, M. C., & Detterman, D. K. (2004). Scholastic assessment or g? The relationship between the SAT and general cognitive ability. *Psychological Science*, **15**, 373–378.

Fürst, G., & Grin, F. (2018). A comprehensive method for the measurement of everyday creativity. *Thinking Skills and Creativity*, **28**, 84–97.

Furnham, A., Hughes, D. J., & Marshall, E. (2013). Creativity, OCD, narcissism and the Big Five. *Thinking Skills and Creativity*, **10**, 91–98.

Gable, S. L., Hopper, E. A., & Schooler, J. W. (2019). When the muses strike: Creative ideas of physicists and writers routinely occur during mind wandering. *Psychological Science*, **30**, 396–404.

Gajda, A. (2016). The relationship between school achievement and creativity at different educational stages. *Thinking Skills and Creativity*, **19**, 246–259.

Gajda, A., Karwowski, M., & Beghetto, R. A. (2017). Creativity and academic achievement: A meta-analysis. *Journal of Educational Psychology*, **109**, 269–299.

Gangadharbatla, H. (2010). Technology component: A modified systems approach to creative thought. *Creativity Research Journal*, **22**, 219–227.

Gardner, H. (1993). *Creating minds*. New York: Basic Books.

Gardner, H. (1999). *Intelligence reframed: Multiple intelligences for the 21st century*. New York: Basic Books.

Gaut, B. (2010). The philosophy of creativity. *Philosophy Compass*, **5**(12), 1034–1046.

Geda, Y. E., Topazian, H. M., Lewis, R. A. et al. (2011). Engaging in cognitive activities, aging, and mild cognitive impairment: A population-based study. *Journal of Neuropsychiatry and Clinical Neurosciences*, **23**(2), 149–154.

Geisinger, K. F. (2016). 21st century skills: What are they and how do we assess them?. *Applied Measurement in Education*, **29**, 245–249.

Genuth, A., & Drake, J. E. (2021). The benefits of drawing to regulate sadness and anger: Distraction versus expression. *Psychology of Aesthetics, Creativity, and the Arts*, **15**(1), 91–99.

Germeten, S. (2013). Personal narratives in life history research. *Scandinavian Journal of Educational Research*, **57**, 612–624.

Gerwig, A., Miroshnik, K., Forthmann, B. et al. (2021). The relationship between intelligence and divergent thinking: A meta-analytic update. *Journal of Intelligence*, **9**, 23.

Getzels, J. W., & Jackson, P. W. (1962). *Creativity and intelligence: Explorations with gifted students*. New York: Wiley.

Ghanizadeh, A., & Jahedizadeh, S. (2016). EFL teachers' teaching style, creativity, and burnout: A path analysis approach. *Cogent Education*, **3**(1), 1151997.

Gil Arroyo, C., Knollenberg, W., & Barbieri, C. (2021). Inputs and outputs of craft beverage tourism: The Destination Resources Acceleration Framework. *Annals of Tourism Research*, **86**. http://doi.org/10.1016/j.annals.2020.103102.

Gilhooly, K. J., Georgiou, G., & Devery, U. (2013). Incubation and creativity: Do something different. *Thinking & Reasoning*, **19**, 137–149.

Glăveanu, V. P. (2010). Paradigms in the study of creativity: Introducing the perspective of cultural psychology. *New Ideas in Psychology*, **28**(1), 79–93.

Glăveanu, V. P. (2012). Habitual creativity: Revisiting habit, reconceptualising creativity. *Review of General Psychology*, **16**, 78–92.

Glăveanu, V. P. (2013). Rewriting the language of creativity: The five As framework. *Review of General Psychology*, **17**, 69–81.

Glăveanu, V. P. (2014). Revisiting the "art bias" in lay conceptions of creativity. *Creativity Research Journal*, **26**, 11–20.

Glăveanu, V. P. (2015). Creativity as a sociocultural act. *Journal of Creative Behavior*, **49**(3), 165–180.

Glăveanu, V. P., Hanchett Hanson, M., Baer, J. et al. (2020). Advancing creativity theory and research: A socio-cultural manifesto. *Journal of Creative Behavior*, **54**(3), 741–745.

Gocłowska, M. A., Baas, M., Crisp, R. J., & De Dreu, C. K. (2014). Whether social schema violations help or hurt creativity depends on need for structure. *Personality and Social Psychology Bulletin*, **40**(8), 959–971.

Gocłowska, M. A., Baas, M., Elliot, A. J., & De Dreu, C. K. W. (2017). Why schema-violations are sometimes preferable to schema-consistencies: The role of interest and openness to experience. *Journal of Research in Personality*, **66**, 54–69.

Gocłowska. M. A., & Crisp, R. J. (2013). On counter-stereotypes and creative cognition: When interventions for reducing prejudice can boost divergent thinking. *Thinking Skills and Creativity*, **8**, 72–79.

Gocłowska, M. A., Crisp, R. J., & Labuschagne, K. (2013). Can counter-stereotypes boost flexible thinking? *Group Processes & Intergroup Relations*, **16**, 217–231.

Gocłowska, M. A., Damian, R. I., & Mor, S. (2018). The diversifying experience model: Taking a broader conceptual view of the multiculturalism–creativity link. *Journal of Cross-Cultural Psychology*, **49**(2), 303–322.

Goetz, J. L., Keltner, D., & Simon-Thomas, E. (2010). Compassion: An evolutionary analysis and empirical review. *Psychological Bulletin*, **136**(3), 351–374.

Goldberg, L. R. (1992). The development of markers for the Big-Five factor structure. *Psychological Assessment*, **4**, 26–42.

Goncalo, J. A., Flynn, F. J., & Kim, S. H. (2010). Are two narcissists better than one? The link between narcissism, perceived creativity, and creative performance. *Personality and Social Psychology Bulletin*, **36**, 1484–1495.

Goncalo, J. A., Vincent, L. C., & Krause, V. (2015). The liberating consequences of creative work: How a creative outlet lifts the physical burden of secrecy. *Journal of Experimental Social Psychology*, **59**, 32–39.

Gonzalez-Mulé, E., Mount, M. K., & Oh, I.-S. (2014). A meta-analysis of the relationship between general mental ability and nontask performance. *Journal of Applied Psychology*, **99**, 1222–1243.

Gortner, E., Rude, S. S., & Pennebaker, J. W. (2006). Benefits of expressive writing in lowering rumination and depressive symptoms. *Behavior Therapy*, **37**, 292–303.

Gralewski, J., & Karwowski, M. (2012). Creativity and school grades: A case from Poland. *Thinking Skills and Creativity*, **7**, 198–208.

Grant, A. M., & Berry, J. W. (2011). The necessity of others is the mother of invention: Intrinsic and prosocial motivations, perspective taking, and creativity. *Academy of Management Journal*, **54**(1), 73–96.

Grant, A. M., & Wade-Benzoni, K. A. (2009). The hot and cool of death awareness at work: Mortality cues, aging, and self-protective and prosocial motivations. *Academy of Management Review*, **34**(4), 600–622.

Grantham, T. (2013). Creativity and equity: The legacy of E. Paul Torrance as an upstander for gifted black males. *Urban Review*, **45**, 518–538.

Greenberg, J., Solomon, S., & Pyszczynski, T. (1997). Terror management theory of self-esteem and cultural worldviews: Empirical assessments and conceptual refinements.

In M. P. Zanna (ed.), *Advances in experimental social psychology* (vol. **29**, pp. 61–139). San Diego, CA: Academic Press.

Greenberg, J., Pyszczynski, T., Solomon, S., Rosenblatt, A., Veeder, M., Kirkland, S., & Lyon, D. (1990). Evidence for terror management theory II: The effects of mortality salience on reactions to those who threaten or bolster the cultural worldview. *Journal of Personality and Social Psychology*, **58**, 308–318.

Greenberg, M. A., Wortman, C. B., & Stone, A. A. (1996). Emotional expression and physical health: Revising traumatic memories or fostering self-regulation? *Journal of Personality and Social Psychology*, **71**, 588–602.

Gregerson, M., Snyder, H., & Kaufman, J. C. (eds.). (2013). *Teaching creatively and teaching creativity*. Dordrecht: Springer Science & Business Media.

Grigorenko, E. L., Jarvin, L., Diffley, R. et al. (2009). Are SATs and GPA enough? A theory-based approach to predicting academic success in secondary school. *Journal of Educational Psychology*, **101**(4), 964–981.

Griskevicius, V., Cialdini, R. B., & Kenrick, D. T. (2006). Peacocks, Picasso, and parental investment: The effects of romantic motives on creativity. *Journal of Personality and Social Psychology*, **91**(1), 63–76.

Groeneveld, W., Martin, D., Poncelet, T., & Aerts, K. (2022). Are undergraduate creative coders clean coders? A correlation study. *Proceedings of the 53rd ACM Technical Symposium on Computer Science Education*, **1**, 314–320.

Grohman, M. G., Ivcevic, Z., Silvia, P., & Kaufman, S. B. (2017). The role of passion and persistence in creativity. *Psychology of Aesthetics, Creativity, and the Arts*, **11**(4), 376–385.

Gross, M. E., Zedelius, C. M., & Schooler, J. W. (2020). Cultivating an understanding of curiosity as a seed for creativity. *Current Opinion in Behavioral Sciences*, **35**, 77–82.

Grossman, E., & Drake, J. E. (2023). The affective benefits of creative activities. In Z. Ivcevic, J. D. Hoffmann, & J. C. Kaufman (eds.), *Cambridge handbook of creativity and emotions* (pp. 376–393). New York: Cambridge University Press.

Grosul, M., & Feist, G. J. (2014). The creative person in science. *Psychology of Aesthetics, Creativity, and the Arts*, **8**(1), 30–43.

Groyecka, A. (2018). Will becoming more creative make us more tolerant? *Creativity: Theories–Research–Applications*, **5**(2), 170–176.

Groyecka, A., Gajda, A., Jankowska, D. M., Sorokowski, P., & Karwowski, M. (2020). On the benefits of thinking creatively: Why does creativity training strengthen intercultural sensitivity among children. *Thinking Skills and Creativity*, **37**, 100693.

Groyecka-Bernard, A., Karwowski, M., & Sorokowski, P. (2021). Creative thinking components as tools for reducing prejudice: Evidence from experimental studies on adolescents. *Thinking Skills and Creativity*, **39**, 100779.

Güler, O., & Haseki, M. İ. (2021). Positive psychological impacts of cooking during the COVID-19 lockdown period: A qualitative study. *Frontiers in Psychology*, **12**, 635957.

Guilford, J. P. (1950). Creativity. *American Psychologist*, **5**, 444–454.

Guilford, J. P. (1956). The structure of intellect. *Psychological Bulletin*, **53**, 267–293.

Guillemot, S., & Urien, B. (2016). Legacy writing and the consumption of biographic services. *Psychology & Marketing*, **33**(11), 971–981.

Hall, C. (1991, November 1). Second death from Cristo's umbrellas. *Washington Post*. Retrieved from www.washingtonpost.com/archive/lifestyle/1991/11/01/second-death-from-christos-umbrellas/689ec69b-c8cb-4225-bc2b-c897a39738ed.

Hall, W. B., & MacKinnon, D. W. (1969). Personality inventory correlates of creativity among architects. *Journal of Applied Psychology*, **53**, 322–326.

Hamby, S., Taylor, E., Grych, J., & Banyard, V. (2016). A naturalistic study of narrative: Exploring the choice and impact of adversity versus other narrative topics. *Psychological Trauma: Theory, Research, Practice, and Policy*, **8**(4), 477–486.

Han, S. J., Lee, Y., & Beyerlein, M. (2019). Developing team creativity: The influence of psychological safety and relation-oriented shared leadership. *Performance Improvement Quarterly*, **32**(2), 159–182.

Hansdottir, H., Jonsdottir, M. K., Fisher, D. E. et al. (2022). Creativity, leisure activities, social engagement and cognitive impairment: The AGES-Reykjavík study. *Aging Clinical and Experimental Research*, **34**, 1027–1035.

Harms, M., Reiter-Palmon, R., & Derrick, D. C. (2020). The role of information search in creative problem solving. *Psychology of Aesthetics, Creativity, and the Arts*, **14**, 367–380.

Harris, J. A. (2004). Measured intelligence, achievement, openness to experience, and creativity. *Personality and Individual Differences*, **36**(4), 913–929.

Haselhuhn, M. P., Wong, E. M., & Ormiston, M. E. (2022). Investors respond negatively to executives' discussion of creativity. *Organizational Behavior and Human Decision Processes*, **171**, 104155.

Hattie, J., & Timperley, H. (2007). The power of feedback. *Review of Educational Research*, **77**, 81–112.

Heidenreich, S., & Spieth, P. (2013). Why innovations fail: The case of passive and active innovation resistance. *International Journal of Innovation Management*, **17**, 1–42.

Heintzelman, S. J., & King, L. A. (2014a). Life is pretty meaningful. *American Psychologist*, **69**, 561–574.

Heintzelman, S. J., & King, L. A. (2014b). (The feeling of) meaning-as-information. *Personality and Social Psychology Review*, **18**, 153–167.

Helson, R. (1990). Creativity in women: Outer and inner views over time. In M. A. Runco & R. S. Albert, *Theories of creativity* (pp. 46–58). Newbury Park, CA: Sage.

Hempel, A. (1986). *Reasons to live*. New York: Penguin.

Hennessey, B. A. (2015). Reward, task motivation, creativity and teaching: Towards a cross-cultural examination. *Teachers College Record*, **117**, 1–28.

Hennessey, B. A. (2019). Motivation and creativity. In J. C. Kaufman & R. J. Sternberg (eds.), *Cambridge Handbook of Creativity* (2nd ed., pp. 374–395). New York: Cambridge University Press.

Hennessey, B. A., & Amabile, T. M. (2010). Creativity. *Annual Review of Psychology*, **61**, 569–598.

Hennessey, B. A., Kim, G., Guomin, Z., & Weiwei, S. (2008). A multi-cultural application of the Consensual Assessment Technique. *International Journal of Creativity and Problem Solving*, **18**, 87–100.

Hernández-Ruiz, E. (2005). Effect of music therapy on the anxiety levels and sleep patterns of abused women in shelters. *Journal of Music Therapy*, **42**(2), 140–158.

Hocevar, D. (1976). Dimensionality of creativity. *Psychological Reports*, **39**(3), 869–870.

Hocevar, D. (1979, April). *The development of the Creative Behavior Inventory (CBI)*. Paper presented at the annual meeting of the Rocky Mountain Psychological Association (ERIC Document Reproduction Service No. ED 170 350).

Hoffmann, J. D., & Russ, S. W. (2012). Pretend play, creativity and emotion regulation. *Psychology of Aesthetics, Creativity, and the Arts*, **6**, 175–184.

Hoffmann, J. D., & Russ, S. W. (2016). Fostering pretend play skills and creativity in elementary school girls: A group play intervention. *Psychology of Aesthetics, Creativity, and the Arts*, **10**, 114–125.

Holinger, M., & Kaufman, J. C. (2018). The relationship between creativity and feedback. In A. Lipnevich & J. Smith (eds.), *Cambridge handbook of instructional feedback* (pp. 575–588). New York: Cambridge University Press.

Holinger, M., & Kaufman, J. C. (2023). Everyday creativity as a pathway to meaning and well-being. In Z. Ivcevic, J. D. Hoffmann, & J. C. Kaufman (eds.), *Cambridge Handbook of Creativity and Emotion* (pp. 394–410). New York: Cambridge University Press.

Holland, J. L. (1997). *Making vocational choices: A theory of vocational personalities and work environments* (3rd ed.). Odessa, FL: Psychological Assessment Resources.

Holt, N. J. (2018). Using the experience-sampling method to examine the psychological mechanisms by which participatory art improves wellbeing. *Perspectives in Public Health*, **138**(1), 55–65.

Holt, N. J. (2020). Tracking momentary experience in the evaluation of arts-on-prescription services: Using mood changes during art workshops to predict global wellbeing change. *Perspectives in Public Health*, **140**(5), 270–276.

Holub, C. (2016, June 29). Bo Burnham gives advice to young artists. Entertainment Weekly. Retrieved from http://ew.com/article/2016/06/29/bo-burnham-advice-young-artists-conan.

Hopp, M. D., Zhang, Z. S., Hinch, L., O'Reilly, C., & Ziegler, A. (2019). Creative, thus connected: The power of sociometric creativity on friendship formation in gifted adolescents: A longitudinal network analysis of gifted students. *New Directions for Child and Adolescent Development*, **168**, 47–73.

Horng, J.-S., & Lin, L. (2009). The development of a scale for evaluating creative culinary products. *Creativity Research Journal*, **21**, 54–63.

Hosoya, G., Schindler, I., Beermann, U. et al. (2017). Mapping the conceptual domain of aesthetic emotion terms: A pile-sort study. *Psychology of Aesthetics, Creativity, and the Arts*, **11** (4), 457–473.

Housman, A. E. (1932). *A Shropshire Lad*. New York: Illustrated Editions Company. (Original work published 1896.)

Howard, G. S. (1991). Culture tales: A narrative approach to thinking, cross-cultural psychology, and psychotherapy. *American Psychologist*, **46**, 187–197.

Howe, M. L., & Courage, M. L. (1997). The emergence and early development of autobiographical memory. *Psychological Review*, **104**, 499–523.

Hunt, J. McV. (1961). *Intelligence and experience*. New York: Ronald Press.

Hunt, N., & McHale, S. (2007). Memory and meaning: Individual and social aspects of memory narratives. *Journal of Loss and Trauma*, **1**, 42–58.

Hunter, E. G. (2008). Legacy: The occupational transmission of self through actions and artifacts. *Journal of Occupational Science*, **15**(1), 48–54.

Hunter, E. G., & Rowles, G. D. (2005). Leaving a legacy: Toward a typology. *Journal of Aging Studies*, **19**(3), 327–347.

Huta, V., & Zuroff, D. C. (2007). Examining mediators of the link between generativity and well-being. *Journal of Adult Development*, **14**(1), 47–52.

Hutton, E. L., & Bassett, M. (1948). The effect of leucotomy on creative personality. *Journal of Mental Science*, **94**, 332–350.

IBM. (2010). IBM 2010 Global CEO Study: Creativity selected as most crucial factor for future success [press release]. Retrieved from www-03.ibm.com/press/us/en/pressrelease/31670.wss.

Ilies, R., Wagner, D., Wilson, K. et al. (2017). Flow at work and basic psychological needs: Effects on well-being. *Applied Psychology*, **66**(1), 3–24.

Ivcevic, Z., & Brackett, M. A. (2015). Predicting creativity: Interactive effects of openness to experience and emotion regulation ability. *Psychology of Aesthetics, Creativity, and the Arts*, **9**(4), 480–487.

Ivcevic, Z., Brackett, M. A., & Mayer, J. D. (2007). Emotional intelligence and emotional creativity. *Journal of Personality*, **75**, 199–235.

Ivcevic, Z., & Mayer, J. D. (2009). Mapping dimensions of creativity in the life-space. *Creativity Research Journal*, **21**, 152–165

Iverach, L., Menzies, R. G., & Menzies, R. E. (2014). Death anxiety and its role in psychopathology: Reviewing the status of a transdiagnostic construct. *Clinical Psychology Review*, **34**, 580–593

Iyer, A., & Jetten, J. (2011). What's left behind: Identity continuity moderates the effect of nostalgia on well-being and life choices. *Journal of Personality and Social Psychology*, **101**(1), 94–108.

James, C., Drake, J. E., & Winner, E. (2018). Expression versus distraction: An investigation of contrasting emotion regulation strategies when drawing, writing, talking, and thinking. *Empirical Studies of the Arts*, **36**(2), 162–179.

Jamison, K. R. (1993). *Touched with fire: Manic-depressive illness and the artistic temperament*. New York: Free Press.

Janssen, S. J., Chessa, A. G., & Murre, J. M. J. (2006). Memory for time: How people date events. *Memory & Cognition*, **34**, 138–147.

Jeffries, K. K. (2017). A CAT with caveats: Is the Consensual Assessment Technique a reliable measure of graphic design creativity? *International Journal of Design Creativity and Innovation*, **5**, 16–28.

Jones, B. K., & Destin, M. (2021). Effects of positive versus negative expressive writing exercises on adolescent academic achievement. *Journal of Applied Social Psychology*, **51**, 549–559.

Joseph, S., & Linley, P. A. (2006). Growth following adversity: Theoretical perspectives and implications for clinical practice. *Clinical Psychology Review*, **26**, 1041–1053.

Joy, S. P., & Breed, K. (2012). Innovation motivation, divergent thinking, and creative story writing: Convergence and divergence across the Torrance Tests and TAT. *Imagination, Cognition and Personality*, **32**, 179–185.

Kahneman, D. (2011). *Thinking, fast and slow*. New York: Macmillan.

Kainer, R. G. (1984). Art and the canvas of the self: Otto Rank and creative transcendence. *American Imago*, **41**(4), 359–372.

Kandemir, M. A., & Kaufman, J. C. (2020). The Kaufman Domains of Creativity Scale (K-DOCS): Turkish validation and relationship to academic major. *Journal of Creative Behavior*, **54**, 1002–1012.

Kapoor, H., & Kaufman, J. C. (2020). Meaning-making through creativity during COVID-19. *Frontiers in Psychology*, **11**, 595990.

Kapoor, H., & Kaufman, J. C. (2022). The evil within: The AMORAL model of dark creativity. *Theory & Psychology*, **32**(3), 467–490.

Kapoor, H., & Khan, A. (2017). Deceptively yours: Valence-based creativity and deception. *Thinking Skills and Creativity*, **23**, 199–206.

Kappes, A., & Crockett, M. J. (2016). The benefits and costs of a rose-colored hindsight. *Trends in Cognitive Sciences*, **20**(9), 644–646.

Karwowski, M. (2016). The dynamics of creative self-concept: Changes and reciprocal relations between creative self-efficacy and creative personal identity. *Creativity Research Journal*, **28**, 99–104.

Karwowski, M., & Brzeski, A. (2017). Selfies and the (creative) self: A diary study. *Frontiers in Psychology*, **8**, 172.

Karwowski, M., Czerwonka, M., & Kaufman, J. C. (2020). Does intelligence strengthen creative metacognition? *Psychology of Aesthetics, Creativity, and the Arts*, **14**, 353–360.

Karwowski, M., Czerwonka, M., Wiśniewska, E., & Forthmann, B. (2021). How is intelligence test performance associated with creative achievement? A meta-analysis. *Journal of Intelligence*, **9**, 28.

Karwowski, M., & Lebuda, I. (2016). The big five, the huge two, and creative self-beliefs: A meta-analysis. *Psychology of Aesthetics, Creativity, and the Arts*, **10**(2), 214–232.

Karwowski, M., Lebuda, I., Szumski, G., & Firkowska-Mankiewicz, A. (2017). From moment-to-moment to day-to-day: Experience sampling and diary investigations in adults' everyday creativity. *Psychology of Aesthetics, Creativity, and the Arts*, **11**(3), 309–324.

Karwowski, M., Lebuda, I., Wiśniewska, E., & Gralewski, J. (2013). Big Five personality factors as the predictors of creative self-efficacy and creative personal identity: Does gender matter? *Journal of Creative Behavior*, **47**, 215–232.

Karwowski, M., Zielińska, A., Jankowska, D. M. et al. (2021). Creative lockdown? A daily diary study of creative activity during pandemics. *Frontiers in Psychology*, **12**, 23.

Kashdan, T. B., Disabato, D. J., Goodman, F. R., & McKnight, P. E. (2020). The Five-Dimensional Curiosity Scale Revised (5DCR): Briefer subscales while separating overt and covert social curiosity. *Personality and Individual Differences*, **157**, 109836.

Kashdan, T. B., Stiksma, M. C., Disabato, D. J. et al. (2018). The five-dimensional curiosity scale: Capturing the bandwidth of curiosity and identifying four unique subgroups of curious people. *Journal of Research in Personality*, **73**, 130–149.

Kasof, J., Chen, C., Himsel, A., & Greenberger, E. (2007). Values and creativity. *Creativity Research Journal*, **19**, 105–122.

Kaufman, A. B., Call, J., & Kaufman, J. C. (eds.). (2021). *Cambridge handbook of animal cognition*. New York: Cambridge University Press.

Kaufman, A. S. (2000). Seven questions about the WAIS-III regarding differences in abilities across the 16 to 89 year life span. *School Psychology Quarterly*, **15**, 3–29.

Kaufman, A. S. (2001). WAIS-III IQs, Horn's theory, and generational changes from young adulthood to old age. *Intelligence*, **29**, 131–167.

Kaufman, A. S. (2009). *IQ testing 101*. New York: Springer.

Kaufman, A. S., & Kaufman, N. L. (1983). *Kaufman Assessment Battery for Children, Second Edition*. Circle Pines, MN: American Guidance Service.

Kaufman, J. C. (2001a). Genius, lunatics, and poets: Mental illness in prize-winning authors. *Imagination, Cognition, and Personality*, **20**, 305–314.

Kaufman, J. C. (2001b). The Sylvia Plath effect: Mental illness in eminent creative writers. *Journal of Creative Behavior*, **35**, 37–50.

Kaufman, J. C. (2002a). Dissecting the golden goose: Components of studying creative writers. *Creativity Research Journal*, **14**, 27–40.

Kaufman, J. C. (2002b). Narrative and paradigmatic thinking styles in creative writing and journalism students. *Journal of Creative Behavior*, **36**, 201–220.

Kaufman, J. C. (2003). The cost of the muse: Poets die young. *Death Studies*, **27**, 813–822.

Kaufman, J. C. (2005). The door that leads into madness: Eastern European poets and mental illness. *Creativity Research Journal*, **17**, 99–103.

Kaufman, J. C. (2009). *Creativity 101*. New York: Springer.

Kaufman, J. C. (2012). Counting the muses: Development of the Kaufman-Domains of Creativity Scale (K-DOCS). *Psychology of Aesthetics, Creativity, and the Arts*, **6**, 298–308.

Kaufman, J. C. (ed.). (2014a). *Creativity and mental illness*. New York: Cambridge University Press.

Kaufman, J. C. (2014b). Creativity and mental illness: Reasons to care and beware. In J. C. Kaufman (ed.), *Creativity and mental illness* (pp. 403–407). New York: Cambridge University Press.

Kaufman, J. C. (2016a). *Creativity 101* (2nd ed.). New York: Springer.

Kaufman, J. C. (2016b). Creativity and mental illness: So many studies, so many wrong conclusions. In J. A. Plucker (ed.), *Creativity and innovation: Theory, research, and practice* (pp. 199–204). Waco, TX: Prufrock Press.

Kaufman, J. C. (2017a). From the Sylvia Plath effect to social justice: Moving forward with creativity. *Europe's Journal of Psychology*, **13**, 173–177.

Kaufman, J. C. (2017b). Tracing the roots of a career in creativity. *International Journal for Talent Development and Creativity*, **5**, 181–188.

Kaufman, J. C. (2018a). Creativity's need for relevance in research and real life: Let's set a new agenda for positive outcomes. *Creativity: Theories–Research–Applications*, **5**, 124–137.

Kaufman, J. C. (2018b). Finding meaning with creativity in the past, present, and future. *Perspectives on Psychological Science*, **13**, 734–749.

Kaufman, J. C. (2018c). Uniquely creative: Developing a new outline for positive outcomes. *Creativity: Theories–Research–Applications*, **5**, 188–196.

Kaufman, J. C. (2019a). Dr. Laura M. Chassell Toops: Forgotten pioneer of creativity assessment. In V. P. Glăveanu (ed.), *The creativity reader* (pp. 73–86). New York: Oxford University Press.

Kaufman, J. C. (2019b). Self-assessments of creativity: Not ideal, but better than you think. *Psychology of Aesthetics, Creativity, and the Arts*, **13**, 187–192.

Kaufman, J. C. (2020). The danger of superficial success. In R. J. Sternberg (ed.), *My biggest research mistake* (pp. 219–220). Thousand Oaks, CA: Sage.

Kaufman J. C., Arrington, K., Barnett, P. J. et al. (2022). Creativity is our gig: Focusing on the positive and practical. *Translational Issues in Psychological Science*, **8** (1), 137–152.

Kaufman, J. C., & Baer, J. (2002a). Could Steven Spielberg manage the Yankees? Creative thinking in different domains. *Korean Journal of Thinking & Problem Solving*, **12**, 5–15.

Kaufman, J. C., & Baer, J. (2002b). I bask in dreams of suicide: Mental illness and poetry. *Review of General Psychology*, **6**, 271–286.

Kaufman, J. C., & Baer, J. (2004a). The Amusement Park Theoretical (APT) Model of creativity. *Korean Journal of Thinking and Problem Solving*, **14**, 15–25.

Kaufman, J. C., & Baer, J. (2004b). Sure, I'm creative – but not in mathematics! Self-reported creativity in diverse domains. *Empirical Studies of the Arts*, **22**, 143–155.

Kaufman, J. C., & Baer, J. (eds.). (2005a). *Creativity across domains: Faces of the muse*. Mahwah, NJ: Lawrence Erlbaum.

Kaufman, J. C., & Baer, J. (2005b). The Amusement Park Theory of Creativity. In J. C. Kaufman & J. Baer (eds.), *Creativity across domains* (pp. 321–328). Mahwah, NJ: Erlbaum.

Kaufman, J. C., & Baer, J. (2006). A tribute to E. Paul Torrance. *Creativity Research Journal*, **18**, 1–3.

Kaufman, J. C., & Baer, J. (2012). Beyond new and appropriate: Who decides what is creative? *Creativity Research Journal*, **24**, 83–91.

Kaufman, J. C., Baer, J., & Cole, J. C. (2009). Expertise, domains, and the Consensual Assessment Technique. *Journal of Creative Behavior*, **43**, 223–233.

Kaufman, J. C., Baer, J., Cole, J. C., & Sexton, J. D. (2008). A comparison of expert and nonexpert raters using the Consensual Assessment Technique. *Creativity Research Journal*, **20**, 171–178.

Kaufman, J. C., Baer, J., Cropley, D. H., Reiter-Palmon, R., & Sinnett, S. (2013). Furious activity vs. understanding: How much expertise is needed to evaluate creative work? *Psychology of Aesthetics, Creativity, and the Arts*, **7**, 332–340.

Kaufman, J. C., & Beghetto, R. A. (2009). Beyond big and little: The Four C Model of Creativity. *Review of General Psychology*, **13**, 1–12.

Kaufman, J. C., & Beghetto, R. A. (2013). In praise of Clark Kent: Creative metacognition and the importance of teaching kids when (not) to be creative. *Roeper Review*, **35**, 155–165.

Kaufman, J. C., & Beghetto, R. A. (2022). Where is the when of creativity? Specifying the temporal dimension of the four Cs of creativity. *Review of General Psychology*, https://doi.org/10.1177/10892680221142803.

Kaufman, J. C., Beghetto, R. A., Baer, J., & Ivcevic, Z. (2010). Creativity polymathy: What Benjamin Franklin can teach your kindergartener. *Learning & Individual Differences*, **20**, 380–387.

Kaufman, J. C., Beghetto, R. A., & Watson, C. (2016). Creative metacognition and self-ratings of creative performance: A 4-C perspective. *Learning and Individual Differences*, **51**, 394–399.

Kaufman, J. C., Bromley, M. L., & Cole, J. C. (2006). Insane, poetic, lovable: Creativity and endorsement of the "mad genius" stereotype. *Imagination, Cognition, and Personality*, **26**, 149–161.

Kaufman, J. C., Cole, J. C., & Baer, J. (2009). The construct of creativity: A structural model for self-reported creativity ratings. *Journal of Creative Behavior*, **43**, 119–134.

Kaufman, J. C., Evans, M. L., & Baer, J. (2010). The American Idol effect: Are students good judges of their creativity across domains? *Empirical Studies of the Arts*, **28**, 3–17.

Kaufman, J. C., Gentile, C. A., & Baer, J. (2005). Do gifted student writers and creative writing experts rate creativity the same way? *Gifted Child Quarterly*, **49**, 260–265.

Kaufman, J. C., & Glăveanu, V. P. (2022a). Making the CASE for shadow creativity. *Psychology of Aesthetics, Creativity, and the Arts*, **16**(1), 44–57.

Kaufman, J. C., & Glăveanu, V. P. (2022b). Positive creativity in a negative world. *Education Sciences*, **12**, 193.

Kaufman, J. C., & Glăveanu, V. P. (in press). The creativity ethos: A palette of benevolent processes and outcomes. *Possibility Studies & Society*.

Kaufman, J. C., Kapoor, H., Patston, T., & Cropley, D. H. (2021). Explaining standardized educational test scores: The role of creativity above and beyond GPA and personality. *Psychology of Aesthetics, Creativity, and the Arts*. http://doi.org/10.1037/aca0000433.

Kaufman, J. C., Kaufman, S. B., & Lichtenberger, E. O. (2011). Finding creativity on intelligence tests via divergent production. *Canadian Journal of School Psychology*, **26**, 83–106.

Kaufman, J. C., Pumaccahua, T. T., & Holt, R. E. (2013). Personality and creativity in realistic, investigative, artistic, social, and enterprising college majors. *Personality and Individual Differences*, **54**, 913–917.

Kaufman, J. C., Waterstreet, M. A., Ailabouni, H. S. et al. (2009). Personality and self-perceptions of creativity across domains. *Imagination, Cognition, and Personality*, **29**, 193–209.

Kaufman, S. B. (2013). Opening up openness to experience: A four-factor model and relations to creative achievement in the arts and sciences. *Journal of Creative Behavior*, **47**(4), 233–255.

Kaufman, S. B., Kozbelt, A., Silvia, P. et al. (2016). Who finds Bill Gates sexy? Creative mate preferences as a function of cognitive ability, personality, and creative achievement. *Journal of Creative Behavior*, **50**, 294–307.

Kaufman, S. B., Quilty, L. C., Grazioplene, R. G. et al. (2016). Openness to experience and intellect differentially predict creative achievement in the arts and sciences. *Journal of Personality*, **84**(2), 248–258.

Kaufman, J. C., & Sexton, J. D. (2006). Why doesn't the writing cure help poets? *Review of General Psychology*, **10**(3), 268–282.

Keating, F., Cole, L., & Grant, R. (2020). An evaluation of group reminiscence arts sessions for people with dementia living in care homes. *Dementia: The International Journal of Social Research and Practice*, **19**(3), 805–821.

Keneally, T. (1982). *Schindler's list*. New York: Penguin Books.

Kenett, Y. N., Ungar, L., & Chatterjee, A. (2021). Beauty and wellness in the semantic memory of the beholder. *Frontiers in Psychology*, **12**, 696507.

Kéri, S. (2011). Solitary minds and social capital: Latent inhibition, general intellectual functions and social network size predict creative achievements. *Psychology of Aesthetics, Creativity, and the Arts*, **5**(3), 215–221.

Kerr, B., & McKay, R. (2013). Searching for tomorrow's innovators: Profiling creative adolescents. *Creativity Research Journal*, **25**, 21–32.

Kershaw, T. C., & Ohlsson, S. (2004). Multiple causes of difficulty in insight: The case of the nine-dot problem. *Journal of Experimental Psychology: Learning, Memory, and Cognition*, **30**, 3–13.

Kessel, M., Kratzer, J., & Schultz, C. (2012). Psychological safety, knowledge sharing, and creative performance in healthcare teams. *Creativity and Innovation Management*, **21**(2), 147–157.

Kharkhurin, A. V. (2014). Creativity.4in1: Four-criterion construct of creativity. *Creativity Research Journal*, **26**, 338–352.

Kharkhurin, A. V., & Yagolkovskiy, S. R. (2019). Preference for complexity and asymmetry contributes to elaboration in divergent thinking. *Creativity Research Journal*, **31**(3), 342–348.

Kiernan, F., Chmiel, A., Garrido, S., Hickey, M., & Davidson, J. W. (2021). The role of artistic creative activities in navigating the COVID-19 pandemic in Australia. *Frontiers in Psychology*, **12**. https://doi.org/10.3389/fpsyg.2021.696202.

Kim, K. H. (2005). Can only intelligent people be creative? A meta-analysis. *Journal of Secondary Gifted Education*, **16**, 57–66.

Kim, S. H., Vincent, L. C., & Goncalo, J. A. (2013). Outside advantage: Can social rejection fuel creative thought? *Journal of Experimental Psychology: General*, **142**, 605–611.

Kim, T.-Y., Hon, A. H. Y., & Crant, J. M. (2009). Proactive personality, employee creativity, and newcomer outcomes: A longitudinal study. *Journal of Business and Psychology*, **24**(1), 93–103.

King, L. A. (2001). The health benefits of writing about life goals. *Personality and Social Psychology Bulletin*, **27**(7), 798–807.

King, L. A. (2002). Gain without pain? Expressive writing and self-regulation. In S. J. Lepore & J. M. Smyth (eds.), *The writing cure: How expressive writing promotes health and emotional well-being* (pp. 119–134). Washington, DC: American Psychological Association.

King, L. A., & Gurland, S. T. (2007). Creativity and experience of a creative task: Person and environment effects. *Journal of Research in Personality*, **41**, 1252–1259.

King, L. A., Heintzelman, S. J., & Ward, S. J. (2016). Beyond the search for meaning: A contemporary science of the experience of meaning in life. *Current Directions in Psychological Science*, **25**, 211–216.

King, L. A., & Hicks, J. A. (2021). The science of meaning in life. *Annual Review of Psychology*, **72**, 561–584.

Kleiman, E. M., & Beaver, J. K. (2013). A meaningful life is worth living: Meaning in life as a suicide resiliency factor. *Psychiatry Research*, **210**(3), 934–939.

Klein, K., & Boals, A. (2001). Expressive writing can increase working memory capacity. *Journal of Experimental Psychology: General*, **130**, 520–533.

Kock, N., Moqbel, M., Jung, Y., & Syn, T. (2018). Do older programmers perform as well as young ones? Exploring the intermediate effects of stress and programming experience. *Cognition, Technology & Work*, **20**(3), 489–504.

Koenig, K. A., Frey, M. C., & Detterman, D. K. (2008). ACT and general cognitive ability. *Intelligence*, **36**, 153–160.

Kohn, A. (1993). *Punished by rewards*. Boston: Houghton Mifflin.

Kramer, S. J., & Amabile, T. M. (2011). The power of small wins. *Harvard Business Review*, **89**(5), 2–12.

Kruger, J., & Dunning, D. (1999). Unskilled and unaware of it: How difficulties in recognizing one's own incompetence lead to inflated self-assessments. *Journal of Personality and Social Psychology*, **77**, 1121–1134.

Kruglanski, A. W., Chen, X., Dechesne, M., Fishman, S., & Orehek, E. (2009). Fully committed: Suicide bombers' motivation and the quest for personal significance. *Political Psychology*, **30**(3), 331–357.

Kurtzberg, T. R., & Amabile, T. M. (2000). From Guilford to creative synergy: Opening the black box of team level creativity. *Creativity Research Journal*, **13**, 285–294.

Kwok, I., Keyssar, J. R., Spitzer, L. et al. (2022). Poetry as a healing modality in medicine: Current state and common structures for implementation and research. *Journal of Pain and Symptom Management*. http://doi.org/10.1016/j.jpainsymman.2022.04.170.

Kyriazos, T., Galanakis, M., Karakasidou, E., & Stalikas, A. (2021). Early COVID-19 quarantine: A machine learning approach to model what differentiated the top 25% well-being scorers. *Personality and Individual Differences*, **181**, 110980.

Lafrenière, M.-A. K., St-Louis, A. C., Vallerand, R. J., & Donahue, E. G. (2012). On the relation between performance and life satisfaction: The moderating role of passion. *Self and Identity*, **11**, 516–530.

Langer, E., Pirson, M., & Delizonna, L. (2010). The mindlessness of social comparisons. *Psychology of Aesthetics, Creativity, and the Arts*, **4**, 68–74.

Lau, S., & Li, W. L. (1996). Peer status and perceived creativity: Are popular children viewed by peers and teachers as creative? *Creativity Research Journal*, **9**(4), 347–352.

Laukkanen, T., Sinkkonen, S., Kivijärvi, M., & Laukkanen, P. (2007). Innovation resistance among mature consumers. *Journal of Consumer Marketing*, **24**, 419–427.

Lebedeva, N., Schwartz, S. H., van de Vijver, F. J. R., Plucker, J. A., & Bushina, E. (2019). Domains of everyday creativity and personal values. *Frontiers in Psychology*, **9**, 2681.

Leder, H., Belke, B., Oeberst, A., & Augustin, D. (2004). A model of aesthetic appreciation and aesthetic judgments. *British Journal of Psychology*, **95**(4), 489–508.

Leder, H., Gerger, G., Brieber, D., & Schwarz, N. (2014). What makes an art expert? Emotion and evaluation in art appreciation. *Cognition and Emotion*, **28**(6), 1137–1147.

Leder, H., Gerger, G., Dressler, S. G., Schabmann, A. (2012). How art is appreciated. *Psychology of Aesthetics, Creativity, and the Arts*, **6**, 1–10.

Lee, C. S., Huggins, A. C., & Therriault, D. J. (2014). Examining internal and external structure validity evidence of the Remote Associates Test. *Psychology of Aesthetics, Creativity, and the Arts*, **8**, 446–460.

Lee, C. S., & Therriault, D. J. (2013). The cognitive underpinnings of creative thought: A latent variable analysis exploring the roles of intelligence and working memory in three creative thinking processes. *Intelligence*, **41**, 306–320.

Lee, F. R. (2004, April 24). Going early into that good night. *New York Times*, Arts, pp. **1**, 4.

Lee, R., Wong, J., Shoon, W. L. et al. (2019). Art therapy for the prevention of cognitive decline. *Arts in Psychotherapy*, **64**, 20–25.

Leone, C., Wallace, H. M., & Modglin, K. (1999). The need for closure and the need for structure: Interrelationships, correlates, and outcomes. *Journal of Psychology*, **133**(5), 553–562.

Lepisto, D. A., & Pratt, M. G. (2017). Meaningful work as realization and justification: Toward a dual conceptualization. *Organizational Psychology Review*, **7**(2), 99–121.

Lepore, S. J., & Smyth, J. M. (2002). *The writing cure: How expressive writing promotes health and emotional well-being*. Washington, DC: American Psychological Association.

Lepper, M. R., & Greene, D. (1975). Turning play into work: Effects of adult surveillance and extrinsic rewards on children's intrinsic motivation. *Journal of Personality and Social Psychology*, **31**, 479–486.

Li, Y., Wu, Q., Li, Y., Chen, L., & Wang, X. (2019). Relationships among psychological capital, creative tendency, and job burnout among Chinese nurses. *Journal of Advanced Nursing*, **75**(12), 3495–3503.

Liang, Y., Zheng, H., Cheng, J., Zhou, Y., & Liu, Z. (2021). Associations between posttraumatic stress symptoms, creative thinking, and trait resilience among Chinese adolescents exposed to the Lushan earthquake. *Journal of Creative Behavior*, **55**(2), 362–373.

Lichtenberg, J., Woock, C., & Wright, M. (2008). Ready to innovate: Are educators and executives aligned on the creative readiness of the US (Conference Board Research Report No. R-1424-08-RR). New York: The Conference Board.

Lichtenthal, W. G., Currier, J. M., Neimeyer, R. A., & Keesee, N. J. (2010). Sense and significance: A mixed methods examination of meaning making after the loss of one's child. *Journal of Clinical Psychology*, **66**, 791–812.

Lifton, R. J. (1979). *The broken connection*. New York: Simon & Schuster.

Lifton, R. J. (2011). *Witness to an extreme century: A memoir*. New York: Free Press.

Lifton, R. J. (2012). *Death in life: Survivors of Hiroshima*. Chapel Hill, NC: University of North Carolina Press. (Original work published 1967.)

Lifton, R. J., & Olson, E. (2004). Symbolic immortality. In A. C. G. M. Robben (ed.), *Death, mourning, and burial: A cross-cultural reader* (pp. 32–39). Oxford: Blackwell. (Original work published 1974.)

Ligon, G. S., Graham, K. A., Edwards, A. Osburn, H. K., & Hunter, S. T. (2012). Performance management: Appraising performance, providing feedback. In M. D. Mumford (ed.), *The organizational handbook of creativity* (pp. 633–666). Amsterdam: Elsevier.

Lilienfeld, S. O. (2017). Psychology's replication crisis and the grant culture: Righting the ship. *Perspectives on Psychological Science*, **12**, 660–664.

Lim, W., & Plucker, J. (2001). Creativity through a lens of social responsibility: Implicit theories of creativity with Korean samples. *Journal of Creative Behavior*, **35**, 115–130.

Lin, S.-Y., Park, G., Zhou, Q., & Hirst, G. (2023). Two birds, one stone: How altruism can facilitate both individual creativity and prosocial behavior in two different team contexts. *Group Dynamics: Theory, Research, and Practice*, **27**, 65–79.

Liu, C. (2015). Relevant researches on tolerance of ambiguity. *Theory and Practice in Language Studies*, **5**, 1874–1882.

Liu, D., Chen, X. P., & Yao, X. (2011). From autonomy to creativity: A multilevel investigation of the mediating role of harmonious passion. *Journal of Applied Psychology*, **96**(2), 294–309.

López, J., Camilli, C., & Noriega, C. (2015). Posttraumatic growth in widowed and non-widowed older adults: Religiosity and sense of coherence. *Journal of Religion and Health*, **54**, 1612–1628.

Lubart, T. (2017). The 7 Cs of creativity. *Journal of Creative Behavior*, **51**(4), 293–296.

Ludwig, A. M. (1995). *The price of greatness*. New York: Guilford Press.

Luh, D. B., & Lu, C. C. (2012). From cognitive style to creativity achievement: The mediating role of passion. *Psychology of Aesthetics, Creativity, and the Arts*, **6**(3), 282–288.

Luria, S. R., & Kaufman, J. C. (2017a). Examining the relationship between creativity and equitable thinking in schools. *Psychology in the Schools*, **54**, 1279–1284.

Luria, S. R., & Kaufman, J. C. (2017b). The dynamic force before intrinsic motivation: Exploring creative needs. In M. Karwowski & J. C. Kaufman (eds.), *The creative self: How our beliefs, self-efficacy, mindset, and identity impact our creativity* (pp. 318–323). San Diego, CA: Academic Press.

Luria, S. R., Sriraman, B., & Kaufman, J. C. (2017). Enhancing equity in the classroom by teaching for mathematical creativity. *ZDM: The International Journal of Mathematics Education*, **49**, 1033–1039.

Lynch, J. (2016). *You could look it up*. London: Bloomsbury.

Lysova, E. I., Allan, B. A., Dik, B. J., Duffy, R. D., & Steger, M. F. (2019). Fostering meaningful work in organizations: A multi-level review and integration. *Journal of Vocational Behavior*, **110**, 374–389.

Ma-Kellams, C., & Blascovich, J. (2012). Enjoying life in the face of death: East–West differences in responses to mortality salience. *Journal of Personality and Social Psychology*, **103**(5), 773–786.

MacLeod, M. D., & Macrae, C. N. (2001). Gone but not forgotten: The transient nature of retrieval-induced forgetting. *Psychological Science*, **12**, 148–152.

Madjar, N., Greenberg, E., & Chen, Z. (2011). Factors for radical creativity, incremental creativity, and routine, noncreative performance. *Journal of Applied Psychology*, **96**, 730–743.

Madjar, N., Shalley, C. E., & Herndon, B. (2019). Taking time to incubate: The moderating role of “what you do” and “when you do it” on creative performance. *Journal of Creative Behavior*, **53**, 377–388.

Mahoney, M. J. (1995). *Cognitive and constructive psychotherapies: Theory, research, and practice*. New York: Springer.

Martela, F., & Ryan, R. M. (2016a). The benefits of benevolence: Basic psychological needs, beneficence, and the enhancement of well-being. *Journal of Personality*, **84**(6), 750–764.

Martela, F., & Ryan, R. M. (2016b). Prosocial behavior increases well-being and vitality even without contact with the beneficiary: Causal and behavioral evidence. *Motivation and Emotion*, **40**(3), 351–357.

Martela, F., & Steger, M. F. (2016). The three meanings of meaning in life: Distinguishing coherence, purpose, and significance. *Journal of Positive Psychology*, **11**(5), 531–545.

Martin-Rios, C., & Parga-Dans, E. (2016). The early bird gets the worm, but the second mouse gets the cheese: Non-technological innovation in creative industries. *Creativity and Innovation Management*, **25**, 6–17.

Martindale, C. (1989). Personality, situation, and creativity. In J. A. Glover, R. R. Ronning, & C. R. Reynolds (eds.), *Handbook of creativity* (pp. 211–232). New York: Plenum Press.

Maslej, M. M., Oatley, K., & Mar, R. A. (2017). Creating fictional characters: The role of experience, personality, and social processes. *Psychology of Aesthetics, Creativity, and the Arts*, **11**(4), 487–499.

Maslej, M. M., Rain, M., Fong, K., Oatley, K., & Mar, R. A. (2014). The hierarchical personality structure of aspiring creative writers. *Creativity Research Journal*, **26**, 192–202.

Maslow, A. H. (1943). A theory of human motivation. *Psychological Review*, **50**, 370–396.

Mastandrea, S., Fagioli, S., & Biasi, V. (2019). Art and psychological well-being: Linking the brain to the aesthetic emotion. *Frontiers in Psychology*, **10**, 739.

Mathews, R. C., & Mister, R. D. (1988). Measuring an individual's investment in the future: Symbolic immortality, sensation seeking, and psychic numbness. *Omega: Journal of Death and Dying*, **18**(3), 161–173.

Maujean, A., Pepping, C. A., & Kendall, E. (2014). A systematic review of randomized controlled studies of art therapy. *Art Therapy*, **31**(1), 37–44.

May, R. (1994). *The courage to create*. New York: W. W. Norton. (Original work published 1975.)

Mayfield, M., Mayfield, J., & Ma, K. Q. (2020). Innovation matters: Creative environment, absenteeism, and job satisfaction. *Journal of Organizational Change Management*, **33**(5), 715–735.

McAdams, D. P. (2006). *The redemptive self: Stories Americans live by*. New York: Oxford University Press.

McAdams, D. P. (2013). The psychological self as actor, agent, and author. *Perspectives on Psychological Science*, **8**, 272–295.

McAdams, D. P., de St. Aubin, E., & Logan, R. L. (1993). Generativity among young, midlife, and older adults. *Psychology and Aging*, **8**, 221–230.

McAdams, D. P., & Guo, J. (2015). Narrating the generative life. *Psychological Science*, **26**(4), 475–483.

McAdams, D. P., & Pals, J. L. (2006). A new big five: Fundamental principles for an integrative science of personality. *American Psychologist*, **61**, 204–217.

McAdams, D. P., Reynolds, J., Lewis, M., Patten, A., & Bowman, P. J. (2001). When bad things turn good and good things turn bad: Sequences of redemption and contamination in life narrative, and their relation to psychosocial adaptation in midlife adults and in students. *Personality and Social Psychology Bulletin*, **27**, 472–483.

McCabe, M. P. (1991). Influence of creativity and intelligence on academic performance. *Journal of Creative Behavior*, **25**, 116–122.

McCrary, J. M., Altenmüller, E., Kretschmer, C., & Scholz, D. S. (2022). Association of music interventions with health-related quality of life: A systematic review and meta-analysis. *JAMA Network Open*, **5**(3), e223236–e223236.

McKay, A. S., Grygiel, P., & Karwowski, M. (2017). Connected to create: A social network analysis of friendship ties and creativity. *Psychology of Aesthetics, Creativity, and the Arts*, **11**(3), 284–294.

McKay, A. S., Mohan, M., & Reina, C. S. (2022). Another day, another chance: Daily workplace experiences and their impact on creativity. *Journal of Product Innovation Management*, **39**(3), 292–311.

McLean, K. C., & Pratt, M. W. (2006). Life's little (and big) lessons: Identity statuses and meaning-making in the turning point narratives of emerging adults. *Developmental Psychology*, **42**, 714–722.

McRae, K., Ciesielski, B., & Gross, J. J. (2012). Unpacking cognitive reappraisal: Goals, tactics, and outcomes. *Emotion*, **12**, 250–255.

McRae, K., & Gross, J. J. (2020). Emotion regulation. *Emotion*, **20**, 1–9.

Measelle, J. R., John, O. P., Ablow, J. C., Cowan, P. A., & Cowan, C. P. (2005). Can children provide coherent, stable, and valid self-reports on the Big Five dimensions? A longitudinal study from ages 5 to 7. *Journal of Personality and Social Psychology*, **89**, 90–106.

Medeiros, K. E., Partlow, P. J., & Mumford, M. D. (2014). Not too much, not too little: The influence of constraints on creative problem solving. *Psychology of Aesthetics, Creativity, and the Arts*, **8**, 198–210.

Medeiros, K. E., Steele, L. M., Watts, L. L., & Mumford, M. D. (2018). Timing is everything: Examining the role of constraints throughout the creative process. *Psychology of Aesthetics, Creativity, and the Arts*, **12**, 471–488

Mednick, S. A. (1962). The associative basis of the creative process. *Psychological Review*, **69**, 220–232.

Mednick, S. A. (1968). The Remote Associates Test. *Journal of Creative Behavior*, **2**, 213–214.

Meier, M. A., Burgstaller, J. A., Benedek, M., Vogel, S. E., & Grabner, R. H. (2021). Mathematical creativity in adults: Its measurement and its relation to intelligence, mathematical competence and general creativity. *Journal of Intelligence*, **9**(1), 10.

Meier, M., Unternaehrer, E., Schorpp, S. M. et al. (2020). The opposite of stress: The relationship between vagal tone, creativity, and divergent thinking. *Experimental Psychology*, **67** (2), 150–159.

Metzl, E. S. (2009). The role of creative thinking in resilience after hurricane Katrina. *Psychology of Aesthetics, Creativity, and the Arts*, **3**, 112–123.

Michalos, A. C., & Kahlke, P. M. (2008). Impact of arts-related activities on the perceived quality of life. *Social Indicators Research*, **89**(2), 193–258.

Midgley, C. (ed.). (2014). *Goals, goal structures, and patterns of adaptive learning*. London: Routledge.

Mihelič, K. K., & Aleksić, D. (2017). "Dear employer, let me introduce myself": Flow, satisfaction with work–life balance and millennials' creativity. *Creativity Research Journal*, **29**(4), 397–408.

Mikkelson, D. P. (2011, May 31). Wgasa. *Snopes*. Retrieved from www.snopes.com/business/names/wgasa.asp.

Miller, E. M., & Cohen, L. M. (2012). Engendering talent in others: Expanding domains of giftedness and creativity. *Roeper Review*, **34**, 104–113.

Miranda, D. (2020). The emotional bond between neuroticism and music. *Psychomusicology: Music, Mind, and Brain*, **30**(2), 53–63.

Miranda, D. (2021). Neuroticism, musical emotion regulation, and mental health. *Psychomusicology: Music, Mind, and Brain*, **31**(2), 59–73.

Miranda, D. (2022). Neuroticism, musical emotion regulation, musical coping, mental health, and musicianship characteristics. *Psychology of Aesthetics, Creativity, and the Arts*. Advance online publication. http://dx.doi.org/10.1037/aca0000486.

Miranda, D., & Blais-Rochette, C. (2020). Neuroticism and emotion regulation through music listening: A meta-analysis. *Musicae Scientiae*, **24**(3), 342–355.

Miron, E., Erez, M., & Naveh, E. (2004). Do personal characteristics and cultural values that promote innovation, quality, and efficiency compete or complement each other? *Journal of Organizational Behavior*, **25**, 175–199.

Miron-Spektor, E., Erez, M., & Naveh, E. (2011). The effect of conformist and attentive-to-detail members on team innovation: Reconciling the innovation paradox. *Academy of Management Journal*, **54**, 740–760.

Mlčák, Z., & Záškodná, H. (2008). Analysis of relationships between prosocial tendencies, empathy, and the five-factor personality model in students of helping professions. *Studia Psychologica*, **50**, 201–216.

Moneta, G. B. (2012). Opportunity for creativity in the job as a moderator of the relation between trait intrinsic motivation and flow in work. *Motivation and Emotion*, **36**(4), 491–503.

Montuori, A., & Purser, R. E. (1995). Deconstructing the lone genius myth: Toward a contextual view of creativity. *Journal of Humanistic Psychology*, **35**(3), 69–112.

Moore, M., & Russ, S. (2008). Follow-up of a pretend play intervention: Effects on play, creativity, and emotional processes in children. *Creativity Research Journal*, **20**, 427–436.

Mosko, J. E., & Delach, M. J. (2021). Cooking, creativity, and well-being: An integration of quantitative and qualitative methods. *Journal of Creative Behavior*, **55**(2), 348–361.

Mueller, J. S., Goncalo, J. A., & Kamdar, D. (2011). Recognizing creative leadership: Can creative idea expression negatively relate to perceptions of leadership potential? *Journal of Experimental Social Psychology*, **47**, 494–498.

Mueller, J. S., Melwani, S., & Goncalo, J. A. (2012). The bias against creativity: Why people desire but reject creative ideas. *Psychological Science*, **23**, 13–17.

Mullenix, J. W., & Robinet, J. (2018). Art expertise and the processing of titled abstract art. *Perception*, **47**(4), 359–378.

Mumford, M. D., Mobley, M. I., Uhlman, C. E., Reiter-Palmon, R., & Doares, L. M. (1991). Process analytic models of creative capacities. *Creativity Research Journal*, **4**, 91–122.

Mumford, T. (2015, May). Literary mysteries: Books that have been permanently lost. *MPR News*. Retrieved from www.mprnews.org/story/2015/05/12/books-book-question-lost.

Murray, M. (2011, December 14). Review of *Lysistrata Jones*. *Talkin' Broadway*. Retrieved from www.talkinbroadway.com/page/world/LJones.html.

Neimeyer, R. A., Klass, D., & Dennis, M. R. (2014). A social constructionist account of grief: Loss and the narration of meaning. *Death Studies*, **38**, 485–498.

Nell, W. (2014). Sources of life meaning among South African university students. *Journal of Psychology in Africa*, **24**(1), 82–91.

Neuberg, S. L., & Newsom, J. T. (1993). Personal need for structure: Individual differences in the desire for simpler structure. *Journal of Personality and Social Psychology*, **65**, 113–131.

Newton, N. J., Chauhan, P. K., & Pates, J. L. (2020). Facing the future: Generativity, stagnation, intended legacies, and well-being in later life. *Journal of Adult Development*, **27**(1), 70–80.

Newton, N. J., Herr, J. M., Pollack, J. I., & McAdams, D. P. (2014). Selfless or selfish? Generativity and narcissism as components of legacy. *Journal of Adult Development*, **21**(1), 59–68.

Ng, D. X., Lin, P. K., Marsh, N. V., & Ramsay, J. (2021). Associations between Openness facets, prejudice, and tolerance: A scoping review with meta-analysis. *Frontiers in Psychology*, **12**, 4108.

Nijstad, B. A., De Dreu, C. K., Rietzschel, E. F., & Baas, M. (2010). The dual pathway to creativity model: Creative ideation as a function of flexibility and persistence. *European Review of Social Psychology*, **21**(1), 34–77.

Niu, W., & Kaufman, J. C. (2005). Creativity in troubled times: Individual differences in prominent Chinese writers. *Journal of Creative Behavior*, **39**, 57–68.

Nolen-Hoeksema, S., McBride, A., & Larson, J. (1997). Rumination and psychological distress among bereaved partners. *Journal of Personality and Social Psychology*, **72**, 855–862.

Nolen-Hoeksema, S., Larson, J., & Grayson, C. (1999). Explaining the gender difference in depressive symptoms. *Journal of Personality and Social Psychology*, **77**, 1061–1072.

Novak-Leonard, J. L., Skaggs, R., & Robinson, M. (2022). Innovative and artistic: Conceptions of creativity among the American public. *Poetics*, **90**, 101599.

Oatley, K., & Djikic, M. (2017). The creativity of literary writing. In J. C. Kaufman, V. P. Glăveanu, & J. Baer (eds.), *The Cambridge handbook of creativity across domains* (pp. 63–79). New York: Cambridge University Press.

Ochse, R. (1991). Why there were relatively few eminent women creators. *Journal of Creative Behavior*, **25**(4), 334–343.

Okuda, S. M., Runco, M. A., & Berger, D. E. (1991). Creativity and the finding and solving of real-world problems. *Journal of Psychoeducational Assessment*, **9**(1), 45–53.

Olteţeanu, A. M., & Zunjani, F. H. (2020). A visual remote associates test and its validation. *Frontiers in Psychology*, **11**, 26.

Onraet, E., Van Hiel, A., Roets, A., & Cornelis, I. (2011). The closed mind: "Experience" and "cognition" aspects of openness to experience and need for closure as psychological bases for right-wing attitudes. *European Journal of Personality*, **25**(3), 184–197.

Oral, G., Kaufman, J. C., & Sexton, J. D. (2004). From empire to democracy: Effects of social progress on Turkish writers. *Journal of Psychology*, **138**, 223–232.

Orkibi, H., & Ram-Vlasov, N. (2019). Linking trauma to posttraumatic growth and mental health through emotional and cognitive creativity. *Psychology of Aesthetics, Creativity, and the Arts*, **13**, 416–430.

Osborn, A. F. (1963). *Applied imagination* (3rd ed.). New York: Charles Scribner's Sons.

Ovington, L. A., Saliba, A. J., Moran, C. C., Goldring, J., & MacDonald, J. B. (2018). Do people really have insights in the shower? The when, where and who of the Aha! Moment. *Journal of Creative Behavior*, **52**, 21–34.

Paek, S. H., Abdulla, A. M., & Cramond, B. (2016). A meta-analysis of the relationship between three common psychopathologies—ADHD, anxiety, and depression—and indicators of little-c creativity. *Gifted Child Quarterly*, **60**, 117–133.

Pang, W., & Plucker, J. A. (2022). *Lofty aims, limited actors, fewer artifacts: A sociocultural analysis of Confucian conceptions of creativity and innovation*. Article under review.

Parker, P., & Kermode, F. (eds.). (1996). *A reader's guide to twentieth-century writers*. New York: Oxford University Press.

Parnes, S. J. (ed.). (1992). *Source book for creative problem-solving: A fifty-year digest of proven innovation processes*. Buffalo, NY: Creative Education Foundation Press.

Paulus, P., & Dzindolet, M. (2008). Social influence, creativity and innovation. *Social Influence*, **3**, 228–247.

Pelowski, M., Specker, E., Boddy, J. et al. (2022). Together in the dark? Investigating the understanding and feeling of intended emotions between viewers and professional artists at the Venice Biennale. *Psychology of Aesthetics, Creativity, and the Arts*. Advance online publication. http://dx.doi.org/10.1037/aca0000436.

Pelowski, M., Specker, E., Gerger, G., Leder, H., & Weingarden, L. S. (2020). Do you feel like I do? A study of spontaneous and deliberate emotion sharing and understanding between artists and perceivers of installation art. *Psychology of Aesthetics, Creativity, and the Arts*, **14**(3), 276–293.

Pennebaker, J. W. (1997). Writing about emotional experiences as a therapeutic process. *Psychological Science*, **8**, 162–166.

Pennebaker, J. W., & Beall, S. (1986). Confronting a traumatic event: Toward an understanding of inhibition and disease. *Journal of Abnormal Psychology*, **95**, 274–281.

Pennebaker, J. W., & Seagal, J. D. (1999). Forming a story: The health benefits of narrative. *Journal of Clinical Psychology*, **55**, 1243–1254.

Perach, R., & Wisman, A. (2019). Can creativity beat death? A review and evidence on the existential anxiety buffering functions of creative achievement. *Journal of Creative Behavior*, **53** (2), 193–210.

Perrine, N. E., & Brodersen, R. (2005). Artistic and scientific creative behavior: Openness and the mediating role of interests. *Journal of Creative Behavior*, **39**, 217–236.

Perryman, K., Blisard, P., & Moss, R. (2019). Using creative arts in trauma therapy: The neuroscience of healing. *Journal of Mental Health Counseling*, **41**, 80–94.

Peterson, B. E., & Stewart, A. J. (1996). Antecedents and contexts of generativity motivation at midlife. *Psychology and Aging*, **11**, 21–33.

Peterson, C., & Seligman, M. E. (2004). *Character strengths and virtues: A handbook and classification*. Oxford: Oxford University Press.

Piirto, J. (1991). Why are there so few? (Creative women: Visual artists, mathematicians, musicians). *Roeper Review*, **13**, 142–147.

Plucker, J. A. (1998). Beware of simple conclusions: The case for the content generality of creativity. *Creativity Research Journal*, **11**, 179–182.

Plucker, J. A. (1999a). Is the proof in the pudding? Reanalyses of Torrance's (1958 to present) longitudinal study data. *Creativity Research Journal*, **12**, 103–114.

Plucker, J. A. (1999b). Reanalyses of student responses to creativity checklists: Evidence of content generality. *Journal of Creative Behavior*, **33**, 126–137.

Plucker, J. A. (2004). Generalization of creativity across domains: Examination of the method effect hypothesis. *Journal of Creative Behavior*, **38**, 1–12.

Plucker, J. A. (2022). The patient is thriving! Current issues, recent advances, and future directions in creativity assessment. *Creativity Research Journal*. https://doi.org/10.1080/10400419.2022.2110415.

Plucker, J. A., & Beghetto, R. A. (2004). Why creativity is domain general, why it looks domain specific, and why the distinction does not matter. In R. J. Sternberg, E. L. Grigorenko, & J. L. Singer (eds.), *Creativity: From potential to realization*. Washington, DC: American Psychological Association.

Plucker, J. A., Beghetto, R. A., & Dow, G. (2004). Why isn't creativity more important to educational psychologists? Potential, pitfalls, and future directions in creativity research. *Educational Psychologist*, **39**, 83–96.

Plucker, J. A., Kaufman, J. C., Temple, J. S., & Qian, M. (2009). Do experts and novices evaluate movies the same way? *Psychology & Marketing*, **26**, 470–478.

Poropat, A. E. (2009). A meta-analysis of the five-factor model of personality and academic performance. *Psychological Bulletin*, **135**, 322–338.

Poropat, A. E. (2014a). A meta-analysis of adult-rated child personality and academic performance in primary education. *British Journal of Educational Psychology*, **84**, 239–252.

Poropat, A. E. (2014b). Other-rated personality and academic performance: Evidence and implications. *Learning and Individual Differences*, **34**, 24–32.

Posnanski, J. (2021). *The baseball 100*. New York: Avid Reader Press.

Powers, D. E., & Kaufman, J. C. (2004). Do standardized tests penalize deep-thinking, creative, or conscientious students? Some personality correlates of Graduate Record Examinations test scores. *Intelligence*, **32**, 145–153.

Prati, F., Vasiljevic, M., Crisp, R. J., & Rubini, M. (2015). Some extended psychological benefits of challenging social stereotypes: Decreased dehumanization and a reduced reliance on heuristic thinking. *Group Processes & Intergroup Relations*, **18**(6), 801–816.

Pratt, M. G., Pradies, C., & Lepisto, D. A. (2013). Doing well, doing good, and doing with: Organizational practices for effectively cultivating meaningful work. In B. J. Dik, Z. S.

Byrne, & M. F. Steger (eds.), *Purpose and meaning in the workplace* (pp. 173–196). Washington, DC: American Psychological Association.

Prebble, S. C., Addis, D. R., & Tippett, L. J. (2013). Autobiographical memory and sense of self. *Psychological Bulletin*, **139**, 815–840.

Pretz, J. E., & Kaufman, J. C. (2017). Do traditional admissions criteria reflect applicant creativity? *Journal of Creative Behavior*, **51**, 240–251.

Priest, T. (2006). Self-evaluation, creativity, and musical achievement. *Psychology of Music*, **34**, 47–61.

Pringle, A., & Sowden, P. T. (2017). The Mode Shifting Index (MSI): A new measure of the creative thinking skill of shifting between associative and analytic thinking. *Thinking Skills and Creativity*, **23**, 17–28.

Puccio, G. J. (2017). From the dawn of humanity to the 21st century: Creativity as an enduring survival skill. *Journal of Creative Behavior*, **51**, 330–334.

Puente-Díaz, R., & Cavazos-Arroyo, J. (2017). Creative self-efficacy: The influence of affective states and social persuasion as antecedents and imagination and divergent thinking as consequences. *Creativity Research Journal*, **29**(3), 304–312.

Pullum, G. K. (1991). *The great Eskimo vocabulary hoax and other irreverent essays on the study of language*. Chicago, IL: University of Chicago Press.

Puryear, J. S., Kettler, T., & Rinn, A. N. (2017). Relationships of personality to differential conceptions of creativity: A systematic review. *Psychology of Aesthetics, Creativity, and the Arts*, **11**(1), 59–68.

Puryear, J. S., & Lamb, K. N. (2020). Defining creativity: How far have we come since Plucker, Beghetto, and Dow? *Creativity Research Journal*, **32**(3), 206–214.

Qian, M., & Plucker, J. A. (2018). Looking for renaissance people: Examining domain specificity-generality of creativity using Item Response Theory Models. *Creativity Research Journal*, **30**, 241–248.

Qian, M., Plucker, J. A., & Yang, X. (2019). Is creativity domain specific or domain general? Evidence from multilevel explanatory item response theory models. *Thinking Skills and Creativity*, **33**, 100571.

Ram, S., & Sheth, J. N. (1989). Consumer resistance to innovations: The marketing problem and its solutions. *Journal of Consumer Marketing*, **6**, 5–14.

Ramirez, K. (2019). *Animal training: Successful animal management through positive reinforcement* (3rd ed.). Lydney: First Stone Publishing.

Rank, O. (1989). *Art and artist: Creative urge and personality development*, trans. C. F. Atkinson. New York: Knopf. (Original work published 1932.)

Rank, O. (1998). *Psychology and the soul*, trans. G. C. Richter and E. J. Lieberman. Baltimore, MD: Johns Hopkins Press. (Original work published 1930.)

Ree, M. J., & Earles, J. A. (1992). Intelligence is the best predictor of job performance. *Current Directions in Psychological Science*, **1**, 86–89.

Reis, S. M. (2002). Toward a theory of creativity in diverse creative women. *Creativity Research Journal*, **14**, 305–316.

Reis, S. M. (2020). Creative productive giftedness in women: Their paths to eminence. In R. J. Sternberg & D. Ambrose (eds.), *Conceptions of giftedness* (3rd ed., pp. 317–334). New York: Cambridge University Press.

Reis, S. M., & Holinger, M. (2021). Creative productive eminence in talented women: Beliefs, motivation, and drive to create. *Gifted and Talented International*. http://doi.org/10.1080/15332276.2021.1947161.

Reis, S. M., & Peters, P. M. (2021). Research on the schoolwide enrichment model: Four decades of insights, innovation, and evolution. *Gifted Education International*, **37**(2), 109–141.

Reis, S. M., & Renzulli, J. S. (2003). Research related to the schoolwide enrichment triad model. *Gifted Education International*, **18**, 15–39.

Reiter-Palmon, R., Forthmann, B., & Barbot, B. (2019). Scoring divergent thinking tests: A review and systematic framework. *Psychology of Aesthetics, Creativity, and the Arts*, **13**(2), 144–152.

Reiter-Palmon, R., & Illies, J. J. (2004). Leadership and creativity: Understanding leadership from a creative problem-solving perspective. *Leadership Quarterly*, **15**(1), 55–77.

Reiter-Palmon, R., Illies, J. J., & Kobe-Cross, L. M. (2009). Conscientiousness is not always a good predictor of performance: The case of creativity. *International Journal of Creativity & Problem Solving*, **19**, 27–45.

Reiter-Palmon, R., & Kaufman, J. C. (2018). Creative styles in the workplace: New and different. In R. Reiter-Palmon, V. Kennel, & J. C. Kaufman (eds.), *Individual creativity in the workplace* (pp. 191–202). San Diego, CA: Academic Press.

Reiter-Palmon, R., & Robinson, E. J. (2009). Problem identification and construction: What do we know, what is the future? *Psychology of Aesthetics, Creativity, and the Arts*, **3**, 43–47.

Reiter-Palmon, R., Robinson-Morral, E., Kaufman, J. C., & Santo, J. (2012). Evaluation of self-perceptions of creativity: Is it a useful criterion? *Creativity Research Journal*, **24**, 107–114.

Renzulli, J. S. (1977). *The enrichment triad model: A guide for developing defensible programs for the gifted and talented*. Mansfield Center, CT: Creative Learning Press.

Renzulli, J. S. (2012, March 6). The three Es of successful academic achievement and enrichment. *The Creativity Post*. Retrieved from www.creativitypost.com/education/the_three_es_of_successful_academic_achievement_and_enrichment_enjoyment_en.

Renzulli, J. S., & Reis, S. M. (1997). *The schoolwide enrichment model: A how-to guide for educational excellence*. Mansfield Center, CT: Creative Learning Press.

Renzulli, J. S., & Reis, S. M. (2021). *The schoolwide enrichment model: A how-to guide for talent development*. London: Routledge.

Rhodes, M. (1961). An analysis of creativity. *Phi Delta Kappan*, **42**, 305–311.

Riessman, C. K. (2003). Analysis of personal narratives. In J. A. Holstein & J. F. Gubrium (eds.), *Inside interviewing* (pp. 331–347). London: Sage.

Rietzschel, E. F., De Dreu, C. K. W., & Nijstad, B. A. (2007). Personal need for structure and creative performance: The moderating influence of fear of invalidity. *Personality and Social Psychology Bulletin*, **33**, 855–866.

Rietzschel, E. F., Slijkhuis, J. M., & Van Yperen, N. W. (2014). Task structure, need for structure, and creativity. *European Journal of Social Psychology*, **44**(4), 386–399.

Ritter, S. M., Damian, R. I., Simonton, D. K. et al. (2012). Diversifying experiences enhance cognitive flexibility. *Journal of Experimental Social Psychology*, **48**, 961–964.

Roberts, R. O., Cha, R. H., Mielke, M. M. et al. (2015). Risk and protective factors for cognitive impairment in persons aged 85 years and older. *Neurology*, **84**, 1854–1861.

Rodriguez, R. M., Silvia, P. J., Kaufman, J. C., Reiter-Palmon, R., & Puryear, J. S. (2023). Taking inventory of the Creative Behavior Inventory: An item response theory analysis of the CBI. *Creativity Research Journal*. https://doi.org/10.1080/10400419.2023.2183322.

Rogers, C. (1961). *On becoming a person*. Boston, MA: Houghton Mifflin.

Rominger, C., Papousek, I., Weiss, E. M. et al. (2018). Creative thinking in an emotional context: Specific relevance of executive control of emotion-laden representations in the inventiveness in generating alternative appraisals of negative events. *Creativity Research Journal*, **30**, 256–265.

Ross, H. C., & Wolfe, S. E. (2016). Life after death: Evidence of the Hoover Dam as a hero project that defends against mortality reminders. *Water History*, **8**(1), 3–21.

Ross, M. (1981). The ice layer in Uranus and Neptune: Diamonds in the sky? *Nature*, **292**, 435–436.

Ross, M., & Buehler, R. (1994). Creative remembering. In U. Neisser & R. Fivush (eds.), *The remembering self* (pp. 205–235). New York: Cambridge University Press.

Rothenberg, A., & Hausman, C. R. (eds.). (1976). *The creativity question*. Durham, NC: Duke University Press.

Routledge, C., & Arndt, J. (2009). Creative terror management: Creativity as a facilitator of cultural exploration after mortality salience. *Personality and Social Psychology Bulletin*, **35**(4), 493–505.

Routledge, C., Arndt, J., & Sheldon, K. M. (2004). Task engagement after mortality salience: The effects of creativity, conformity and connectedness on worldview defense. *European Journal of Social Psychology*, **34**(4), 477–487.

Routledge, C., Arndt, J., Vess, M., & Sheldon, K. M. (2008). The life and death of creativity: The effects of mortality salience on self versus social-directed creative expression. *Motivation and Emotion*, **32**, 331–338.

Routledge, C., & Juhl, J. (2012). The creative spark of death: The effects of mortality salience and personal need for structure on creativity. *Motivation and Emotion*, **36**, 478–482.

Routledge, C., & Vess, M. (eds.). (2018). *Handbook of terror management theory*. San Diego, CA: Academic Press.

Routledge, C., Wildschut, T., Sedikides, C., Juhl, J., & Arndt, J. (2012). The power of the past: Nostalgia as a meaning-making resource. *Memory*, **20**, 452–460.

Rubinstein, D., & Lahad, M. (2022). Fantastic reality: The role of imagination, playfulness, and creativity in healing trauma. *Traumatology*. http://doi.org/10.1037/trm0000376.

Ruini, C., Albieri, E., Ottolini, F., & Vescovelli, F. (2020). Once upon a time: A school positive narrative intervention for promoting well-being and creativity in elementary school children. *Psychology of Aesthetics, Creativity, and the Arts*, **16**(2), 259–272.

Runco, M. A. (1996). Personal creativity: Definition and developmental issues. *New Directions for Child and Adolescent Development*, **72**, 3–30.

Runco, M. A. (1998). Suicide and creativity: The case of Sylvia Plath. *Death Studies*, **22**(7), 637–654.

Runco, M. A. (2003). Creativity, cognition, and their education implications. In J. C. Houtz (ed.), *The educational psychology of creativity* (pp. 25–56). Cresskill, NJ: Hampton Press.

Runco, M. A. (2014). "Big C, little c" creativity as a false dichotomy: Reality is not categorical. *Creativity Research Journal*, **26**, 131–132.

Runco, M. A. (2018). Authentic creativity: Mechanisms, definitions, and empirical efforts. In R. J. Sternberg & J. C. Kaufman (eds.), *The nature of human creativity* (pp. 246–263). New York: Cambridge University Press.

Runco, M. A., & Abdulla, A. M. (2014). Why isn't creativity being supported? Distressing analyses of grants and awards for creativity research – or lack thereof. *Creativity Research Journal*, **26**, 248–250.

Runco, M. A., & Acar, S. (2019). Divergent thinking. In J. C. Kaufman & R. J. Sternberg (eds.), *Cambridge handbook of creativity* (2nd ed., pp. 224–254). New York: Cambridge University Press.

Runco, M. A., Illies, J. J., & Eisenman, R. (2005). Creativity, originality, and appropriateness: What do explicit instructions tell us about their relationships?. *Journal of Creative Behavior*, **39**(2), 137–148.

Runco, M. A., & Jaeger, G. J. (2012). The standard definition of creativity. *Creativity Research Journal*, **24**(1), 92–96.

Runco, M. A., Millar, G., Acar, S., & Cramond, B. (2010). Torrance tests of creative thinking as predictors of personal and public achievement: A fifty-year follow-up. *Creativity Research Journal*, **22**, 361–368.

Rutherford, L., & Murray, L. E. (2021). Personality and behavioral changes in Asian elephants (Elephas maximus) following the death of herd members. *Integrative Zoology*, **16**(2), 170–188.

Ryan, R. M., & Deci, E. L. (2000). Intrinsic and extrinsic motivations: Classic definitions and new directions. *Contemporary Educational Psychology*, **25**, 54–67.

Ryan, R. M., & Deci, E. L. (2017). *Self-determination theory: Basic psychological needs in motivation, development, and wellness*. New York: Guilford Press.

Saef, R. M., Porter, C. M., Woo, S. E., & Wiese, C. (2019). Getting off on the right foot: The role of openness to experience in fostering initial trust between culturally dissimilar partners. *Journal of Research in Personality*, **79**, 176–187.

Said-Metwaly, S., Taylor, C. L., Camarda, A., & Barbot, B. (2022). Divergent thinking and creative achievement: How strong is the link? An updated meta-analysis. *Psychology of Aesthetics, Creativity, and the Arts*. https://doi.org/10.1037/aca0000507.

Salomon-Gimmon, M., Orkibi, H., & Elefant, C. (2022). The contribution of a music and arts rehabilitation program to the creative identity, well-being, and community integration of people with mental health conditions. *Journal of Humanistic Psychology*. https://doi.org/10.1177/00221678221105719.

Särkämö, T. (2018). Music for the ageing brain: Cognitive, emotional, social, and neural benefits of musical leisure activities in stroke and dementia. *Dementia*, **17**(6), 670–685.

Särkämö, T., Laitinen, S., Numminen, A. et al. (2016). Clinical and demographic factors associated with the cognitive and emotional efficacy of regular musical activities in dementia. *Journal of Alzheimer's Disease*, **49**(3), 767–781.

Särkämö, T., Tervaniemi, M., Laitinen, S. et al. (2014). Cognitive, emotional, and social benefits of regular musical activities in early dementia: Randomized controlled study. *Gerontologist*, **54**(4), 634–650.

Särkämö, T., Tervaniemi, M., Soinila, S. et al. (2009). Amusia and cognitive deficits after stroke: Is there a relationship? *Annals of the New York Academy of Sciences*, **1169**, 441–445.

Sassenberg, K., & Moskowitz, G. B. (2005). Don't stereotype, think different! Overcoming automatic stereotype activation by mindset priming. *Journal of Experimental Social Psychology*, **41**(5), 506–514.

Saunders Wickes, K. N., & Ward, T. B. (2006). Measuring gifted adolescents' implicit theories of creativity. *Roeper Review*, **28**(3), 131–139.

Sawyer, R. K. (2012). *Explaining creativity: The science of human innovation* (2nd ed.). New York: Oxford University Press.

Sawyer, R. K., & DeZutter, S. (2009). Distributed creativity: How collective creations emerge from collaboration. *Psychology of Aesthetics, Creativity, and the Arts*, **3**, 81–92.

Sayago, S., & Bergantiños, Á. (2021). Exploring the first experiences of computer programming of older people with low levels of formal education: A participant observational case study. *International Journal of Human-Computer Studies*, **148**, 102577.

Schaefer, M. R., Wagoner, S. T., Young, M. E. et al. (2020). Healing the hearts of bereaved parents: Impact of legacy artwork on grief in pediatric oncology. *Journal of Pain and Symptom Management*, **60**(4), 790–800.

Schellenberg, B. J. I., & Gaudreau, P. (2020). Savoring and dampening with passion: How passionate people respond when good things happen. *Journal of Happiness Studies: An Interdisciplinary Forum on Subjective Well-Being*, **21**(3), 921–941.

Schlesinger, J. (2009). Creative mythconceptions: A closer look at the evidence for "mad genius" hypothesis. *Psychology of Aesthetics, Creativity, and the Arts*, **3**, 62–72.

Schlesinger, J. (2020). *The insanity hoax* (2nd ed.). Ardsley-on-Hudson, NY: ShrinkTunes Media.

Schmitt, R. L. (1983). Symbolic immortality in ordinary contexts: Impediments to the nuclear era. *OMEGA-Journal of Death and Dying*, **13**(2), 95–116.

Schutte, N. S., & Malouff, J. M. (2020). A meta-analysis of the relationship between curiosity and creativity. *Journal of Creative Behavior*, **54**(4), 940–947.

Sedikides, C., Leunissen, J., & Wildschut, T. (2022). The psychological benefits of music-evoked nostalgia. *Psychology of Music*, **50**, 2044–2062.

Sedikides, C., & Wildschut, T. (2018). Finding meaning in nostalgia. *Review of General Psychology*, **22**, 48–61.

Seibert, S. E., Kraimer, M. L., & Crant, J. M. (2001). What do proactive people do? A longitudinal model linking proactive personality and career success. *Personnel Psychology*, **54**, 845–874.

Seligman, M. E. P. (2012). *Flourish: A visionary new understanding of happiness and well-being*. New York: Simon & Schuster.

Seligman, M. E. P., & Csikszentmihalyi, M. (2000). Positive psychology: An introduction. *American Psychologist*, **55**, 5–14.

Sexton, J. D., & Pennebaker, J. W. (2004). Non-expression of emotion and self among members of socially stigmatized groups: Implications for physical and mental health. In I. Nyklicek, L. Temoshok, & A. Vingerhoets (eds.), *Emotional expression and health* (pp. 321–333). New York: Brunner-Routledge.

Shalley, C. (1995). Effects of coaction, expected evaluation, and goal setting on creativity and productivity. *Academy of Management Journal*, **38**, 483–503.

Shaw, A. (2022). Creative minecrafters: Cognitive and personality determinants of creativity, novelty, and usefulness in minecraft. *Psychology of Aesthetics, Creativity, and the Arts*. http://doi.org/10.1037/aca0000456.

Sherman, A., & Shavit, T. (2018). The thrill of creative effort at work: An empirical study on work, creative effort and well-being. *Journal of Happiness Studies*, **19**(7), 2049–2069.

Shin, J., & Grant, A. M. (2021). When putting work off pays off: The curvilinear relationship between procrastination and creativity. *Academy of Management Journal*, **64**(3), 772–798.

Shoshani, A., & Russo-Netzer, P. (2017). Exploring and assessing meaning in life in elementary school children: Development and validation of the meaning in life in children questionnaire (MIL-CQ). *Personality and Individual Differences*, **104**, 460–465.

Shute, V. J. (2011). Stealth assessment in computer-based games to support learning. In S. Tobias & J. D. Fletcher (eds.), *Computer games and instruction* (pp. 503–524). Charlotte, NC: Information Age Publishers.

Shute, V. J., Almond, R., & Rahimi, S. (2019). Physics Playground (Version 1.3). Tallahassee, FL. Retrieved from http://pluto.coe.fsu.edu/ppteam/pp-links.

Shute, V. J., & Rahimi, S. (2021). Stealth assessment of creativity in a physics video game. *Computers in Human Behavior*, **116**, 106647.

Shute, V. J., Wang, L., Greiff, S., Zhao, W., & Moore, G. (2016). Measuring problem solving skills via stealth assessment in an engaging video game. *Computers in Human Behavior*, **63**, 106–117.

Sibley, C. G., & Duckitt, J. (2008). Personality and prejudice: A meta-analysis and theoretical review. *Personality and Social Psychology Review*, **12**, 248–279.

Sica, L. S., Kapoor, H., & Ragozini, G. (2022). Grasping creative valences: A person-centered study on creativity as a resource for young people's optimal identity formation. *Identity: An International Journal of Theory and Research*. https://doi.org/10.1080/15283488.2022.2050727.

Silverman, M. A., & Will, N. P. (1986). Sylvia Plath and the failure of emotional self-repair through poetry. *The Psychoanalytic Quarterly*, **55**(1), 99–129.

Silverman, M. J. (2021). Music-based emotion regulation and healthy and unhealthy music use predict coping strategies in adults with substance use disorder: A cross-sectional study. *Psychology of Music*, **49**(3), 333–350.

Silvia, P. J. (2018). Creativity is undefinable, controllable, and everywhere. In R. J. Sternberg & J. C. Kaufman (eds.), *Nature of human creativity* (pp. 291–301). New York: Cambridge University Press.

Silvia, P. J., Martin, C., & Nusbaum, E. C. (2009). A snapshot of creativity: Evaluating a quick and simple method for assessing divergent thinking. *Thinking Skills and Creativity*, **4**(2), 79–85.

Silvia, P. J., & Kaufman, J. C. (2010). Creativity and mental illness. In J. C. Kaufman & R. J. Sternberg (eds.), *Cambridge handbook of creativity* (pp. 381–394). New York: Cambridge University Press.

Silvia, P. J., Winterstein, B. P., Willse, J. T. et al. (2008). Assessing creativity with divergent thinking tasks: Exploring the reliability and validity of new subjective scoring methods. *Psychology of Aesthetics, Creativity, and the Arts*, **2**, 68–85.

Simonton, D. K. (1977). Creative productivity, age, and stress: A biographical time-series analysis of 10 classical composers. *Journal of Personality and Social Psychology*, **35**, 791–804.

Simonton, D. K. (1985). Quality, quantity, and age: The careers of 10 distinguished psychologists. *International Journal of Aging and Human Development*, **21**, 241–254.

Simonton, D. K. (1990). *Psychology, science, and history: An introduction to historiometry*. New Haven, CT: Yale University Press.

Simonton, D. K. (1994). *Greatness: Who makes history and why*. New York: Guilford Press.

Simonton, D. K. (1997). Creative productivity: A predictive and explanatory model of career trajectories and landmarks. *Psychological Review*, **104**, 66–89.

Simonton, D. K. (1998). Fickle fashion versus immortal fame: Transhistorical assessments of creative products in the opera house. *Journal of Personality and Social Psychology*, **75**, 198–210.

Simonton, D. K. (1999). Creativity as blind variation and selective retention: Is the creative process Darwinian? *Psychological Inquiry*, **10**, 309–328.

Simonton, D. K. (2000). Creative development as acquired expertise: Theoretical issues and an empirical test. *Developmental Review*, **20**, 283–318.

Simonton, D. K. (2009). *Genius 101*. New York: Springer.

Simonton, D. K. (2010). Creativity as blind-variation and selective-retention: Combinatorial models of exceptional creativity. *Physics of Life Reviews*, **7**, 156–179.

Simonton, D. K. (2011). Creativity and discovery as blind variation and selective retention: Multiple-variant definitions and blind-sighted integration. *Psychology of Aesthetics, Creativity, and the Arts*, **5**, 222–228.

Simonton, D. K. (2012). Taking the US Patent Office creativity criteria seriously: A quantitative three-criterion definition and its implications. *Creativity Research Journal*, **24**, 97–106.

Simonton, D. K (2013). What is a creative idea? Little-c versus Big-C creativity. In K. Thomas & J. Chan (eds.), *Handbook of research on creativity* (pp. 69–83). Cheltenham: Edward Elgar Publishing.

Simonton, D. K. (2014a). Creative performance, expertise acquisition, individual differences, and developmental antecedents: An integrative research agenda. *Intelligence*, **45**, 66–73.

Simonton, D. K. (2014b). The mad-genius paradox: Can creative people be more mentally healthy but highly creative people more mentally ill? *Perspectives on Psychological Science*, **9**, 470–480.

Simonton, D. K. (2014c). More method in the mad-genius controversy: A historiometric study of 204 historic creators. *Psychology of Aesthetics, Creativity, and the Arts*, **8**, 53–61.

Simonton, D. K. (2016). Creativity, automaticity, irrationality, fortuity, fantasy, and other contingencies: An eightfold response typology. *Review of General Psychology*, **20**(2), 194–204.

Simonton, D. K. (2018a). Creative genius as inherently relevant and beneficial: The view from Mount Olympus. *Creativity: Theories–Research–Applications*, **5**, 138–141.

Simonton, D. K. (2018b). Defining creativity: Don't we also need to define what is not creative? *Journal of Creative Behavior*, **52**(1), 80–90.

Simonton, D. K. (2018c). Genius, creativity, and leadership: A 50-year journey through science, history, mathematics, and psychology. In R. J. Sternberg & J. C. Kaufman (eds.), *The nature of human creativity* (pp. 302–317). New York: Cambridge University Press.

Simonton, D. K. (2018d). *The genius checklist*. Cambridge, MA: MIT Press.

Simonton, D. K. (2019). Creativity's role in society. In J. C. Kaufman & R. J. Sternberg (eds.), *Cambridge Handbook of Creativity* (2nd ed., pp. 462–480). New York: Cambridge University Press.

Simonton, D. K. (2022). The blind-variation and selective-retention theory of creativity: Recent developments and current status of BVSR. *Creativity Research Journal*. https://doi .org/10.1080/10400419.2022.2059919.

Sio, U. N., & Ormerod, T. C. (2009). Does incubation enhance problem solving? A meta-analytic review. *Psychological Bulletin*, **135**(1), 94–120.

Skinner, S., Bonnet, K., Schlundt, D., & Karlekar, M. (2019). Life story themes: A qualitative analysis of recordings from patients approaching the end of life. *American Journal of Hospice and Palliative Medicine*, **36**(9), 753–759.

Sligte, D. J., Nijstad, B. A., & De Dreu, C. K. (2013). Leaving a legacy neutralizes negative effects of death anxiety on creativity. *Personality and Social Psychology Bulletin*, **39**(9), 1152–1163.

Slijkhuis, J. M., Rietzschel, E. F., & Van Yperen, N. W. (2013). How evaluation and need for structure affect motivation and creativity. *European Journal of Work and Organizational Psychology*, **22**, 15–25.

Sloan, D. M., Marx, B. P., Epstein, E. M., & Dobbs, J. L. (2008). Expressive writing buffers against maladaptive rumination. *Emotion*, **8**, 302–306.

Smith, A. F. (1996). *Pure ketchup: A history of America's favorite condiment*. Columbia: University of South Carolina Press.

Smith, J. K. (2014). *The museum effect: How museums, libraries, and cultural institutions educate and civilize society*. Lanham, MD: Rowman & Littlefield.

Smyth, J. M. (1998). Written emotional expression: Effect sizes, outcome types, and moderating variables. *Journal of Consulting and Clinical Psychology*, **66**, 174–184.

Smyth, J., True, N., & Souto, J. (2001). Effects of writing about traumatic experiences: The necessity for narrative structure. *Journal of Social & Clinical Psychology*, **20**, 161–172.

Snow, C. P. (1959). *The two cultures*. New York: Cambridge University Press.

Snyder, C. R., & Fromkin, H. L. (1977). Abnormality as a positive characteristic: The development and validation of a scale measuring need for uniqueness. *Journal of Abnormal Psychology*, **86**(5), 518–527.

Snyder, H. T., Hammond, J. A., Grohman, M. G., & Katz-Buonincontro, J. (2019). Creativity measurement in undergraduate students from 1984–2013: A systematic review. *Psychology of Aesthetics, Creativity, and the Arts*, **13**, 133–143.

Sparkman, D. J., & Blanchar, J. C. (2017). Examining relationships among epistemic motivation, perspective taking, and prejudice: A test of two explanatory models. *Personality and Individual Differences*, **114**, 48–56.

Sparkman, D. J., Eidelman, S., & Blanchar, J. C. (2016). Multicultural experiences reduce prejudice through personality shifts in openness to experience. *European Journal of Social Psychology*, **46**(7), 840–853.

Sparkman, D. J., Eidelman, S., Dueweke, A. R., Marin, M. S., & Dominguez, B. (2019). Open to diversity: Openness to experience predicts beliefs in multiculturalism and colorblindness through perspective taking. *Journal of Individual Differences*, **40**, 1–12.

St.-Louis, A. C., Carbonneau, N., & Vallerand, R. J. (2016). Passion for a cause: How it affects health and subjective well-being. *Journal of Personality*, **84**(3), 263–276.

St.-Louis, A. C., & Vallerand, R. J. (2015). A successful creative process: The role of passion and emotions. *Creativity Research Journal*, **27**(2), 175–187.

Steger, M. F., & Dik, B. J. (2010). Work as meaning: Individual and organizational benefits of engaging in meaningful work. In P. A. Linley, S. Harrington, N. Garcea, & N. Page (eds.), *Oxford handbook of positive psychology and work* (pp. 131–142). New York: Oxford University Press.

Steger, M. F., Frazier, P., Oishi, S., & Kaler, M. (2006). The Meaning in Life Questionnaire: Assessing the presence of and search for meaning in life. *Journal of Counseling Psychology*, **53**, 80–93.

Steger, M. F., Kashdan, T. B., Sullivan, B. A., & Lorentz, D. (2008). Understanding the search for meaning in life: Personality, cognitive style, and the dynamic between seeking and experiencing meaning. *Journal of Personality*, **76**, 199–228.

Stein, M. (1953). Creativity and culture. *Journal of Psychology*, **36**, 311–322.

Stephan, E., Sedikides, C., & Wildschut, T. (2012). Mental travel into the past: Differentiating recollections of nostalgic, ordinary, and positive events. *European Journal of Social Psychology*, **42**(3), 290–298.

Stephan, E., Sedikides, C., Wildschut, T. et al. (2015). Nostalgia-evoked inspiration: Mediating mechanisms and motivational implications. *Personality and Social Psychology Bulletin*, **41**, 1395–1410.

Stephenson, K., & Rosen, D. H. (2015). Haiku and healing: An empirical study of poetry writing as therapeutic and creative intervention. *Empirical Studies of the Arts*, **33**, 36–60.

Stern, C., & Munn, Z. (2009). Cognitive leisure activities and their role in preventing dementia: A systematic review. *JBI Evidence Synthesis*, **7**(29), 1292–1332.

Stern, Y. (2006). Cognitive reserve and Alzheimer disease. *Alzheimer Disease & Associated Disorders*, **20**, S69–S74.

Sternberg, R. J. (1985). Implicit theories of intelligence, creativity, and wisdom. *Journal of Personality and Social Psychology*, **49**, 607–627.

Sternberg, R. J. (1999). A propulsion model of types of creative contributions. *Review of General Psychology*, **3**, 83–100.

Sternberg, R. J. (2018). A triangular theory of creativity. *Psychology of Aesthetics, Creativity, and the Arts*, **12**, 50–67.

Sternberg, R. J. (2020). Transformational giftedness: Rethinking our paradigm for gifted education. *Roeper Review*, **42**(4), 230–240.

Sternberg, R. J. (2021a). Identification for utilization, not merely possession, of gifts: What matters is not gifts but rather deployment of gifts. *Gifted Education International*, **38**(3). https://doi.org/10.1177/02614294211013345.

Sternberg, R. J. (2021b). Positive creativity. In A. Kostic & D. Chadee (eds.), *Current Research in Positive Psychology* (pp. 33–42). Cham: Palgrave Macmillan.

Sternberg, R. J. (2021c). Transformational creativity: The link between creativity, wisdom, and the solution of global problems. *Philosophies*, **6**(3), 75. https://doi.org/10.3390/philosophies6030075.

Sternberg, R. J. (2021d). Transformational vs. transactional deployment of intelligence. *Journal of Intelligence*, **9**(1), 15.

Sternberg, R. J. (2022). Personal talent curation in the lifetime realization of gifted potential: The role of adaptive intelligence. *Gifted Education International*, **38**(2), 354–361.

Sternberg, R. J., & Chowkase, A. (2021). When we teach for positive creativity, what exactly do we teach for? *Education Sciences*, **11**(5), 237.

Sternberg, R. J., Glăveanu, V., & Kaufman, J. C. (2022). In quest of creativity: Three paths toward an elusive grail. *Creativity Research Journal*. http://doi.org/10.1080/10400419.2022.2107299.

Sternberg, R. J., & Karami, S. (2022). An 8P theoretical framework for understanding creativity and theories of creativity. *Journal of Creative Behavior*, **56**(1), 55–78.

Sternberg, R. J., Kaufman, J. C., & Pretz, J. E. (2001). The propulsion model of creative contributions applied to the arts and letters. *Journal of Creative Behavior*, **35**, 75–101.

Sternberg, R. J., Kaufman, J. C., & Pretz, J. E. (2002). *The creativity conundrum*. Philadelphia, PA: Psychology Press.

Sternberg, R. J., Kaufman, J. C., & Pretz J. E. (2019). A propulsion perspective on creative contributions. In V. P. Glăveanu (ed.), *The Palgrave encyclopedia of the possible* (pp. 75–101). Basingstoke: Palgrave Macmillan.

Sternberg, R. J., & Lubart, T. I. (1995). *Defying the crowd*. New York: Free Press.

Stewart, A. E., & Neimeyer, R. A. (2001). Emplotting the traumatic self: Narrative revision and the construction of coherence. *Humanistic Psychologist*, **29**, 8–39.

Stietz, J., Jauk, E., Krach, S., & Kanske, P. (2019). Dissociating empathy from perspective-taking: Evidence from intra- and inter-individual differences research. *Frontiers in Psychiatry*, **10**, 126.

Stone, P., & Edwards, S. (1976). *1776*. New York: Penguin Books.

Stoppard, T. (1993). *Arcadia*. New York: Farrar, Straus, and Giroux.

Stoppard, T. (1988). *Artist descending a staircase*. New York: Samuel French (Original work published 1973.)

Storm, B. C., & Patel, T. N. (2014). Forgetting as a consequence and enabler of creative thinking. *Journal of Experimental Psychology: Learning, Memory, and Cognition*, **40**, 1594–1609.

Story, K. M., Yang, Z., & Bravata, D. M. (2021). Active and receptive arts participation and their association with mortality among adults in the United States: A longitudinal cohort study. *Public Health*, **196**, 211–216.

Strasbaugh, K., & Connelly, S. (2022). The influence of anger and anxiety on idea generation: Taking a closer look at integral and incidental emotion effects. *Psychology of Aesthetics, Creativity, and the Arts*, **16**(3), 529–543.

Strobel, A., Behnke, A., Gärtner, A., & Strobel, A. (2019). The interplay of intelligence and need for cognition in predicting school grades: A retrospective study. *Personality and Individual Differences*, **144**, 147–152.

Suddeath, E. G., Kerwin, A. K., & Dugger, S. M. (2017). Narrative family therapy: Practical techniques for more effective work with couples and families. *Journal of Mental Health Counseling*, **39**, 116–131.

Sun, C., Fu, H., Zhou, Z., & Cropley, D. H. (2020). The effects of different types of social exclusion on creative thinking: The role of self-construal. *Personality and Individual Differences*, **166**, 110215.

Sunga, A. B., & Advincula, J. L. (2021). The "plantito/plantita" home gardening during the pandemic. *Community Psychology in Global Perspective*, **7**(1), 88–105.

Suskin, S. (1990). *Opening nights on Broadway*. New York: Schirmer Books.

Suskin, S. (1997). *More opening nights on Broadway*. New York: Schirmer Books.

Sutu, A., Phetmisy, C. N., & Damian, R. I. (2021). Open to laugh: The role of openness to experience in humor production ability. *Psychology of Aesthetics, Creativity, and the Arts*, **15**(3), 401–411.

Tadmor, C. T., Chao, M. M., Hong, Y. Y., & Polzer, J. T. (2013). Not just for stereotyping anymore: Racial essentialism reduces domain-general creativity. *Psychological Science*, **24**(1), 99–105.

Tak, S. H., Zhang, H., Patel, H., & Hong, S. H. (2015). Computer activities for persons with dementia. *Gerontologist*, **55**(Suppl_1), S40–S49.

Takeuchi, R., Guo, N., Teschner, R. S., & Kautz, J. (2021). Reflecting on death amidst COVID-19 and individual creativity: Cross-lagged panel data analysis using four-wave longitudinal data. *Journal of Applied Psychology*, **106**(8), 1156–1168.

Talarico, J. M., & Rubin, D. C. (2003). Confidence, not consistency, characterizes flashbulb memories. *Psychological Science*, **14**, 455–461.

Taubman–Ben-Ari, O. (2014). How are meaning in life and family aspects associated with teen driving behaviors? *Transportation Research Part F: Traffic Psychology and Behaviour*, **24**, 92–102.

Tavares, S. M. (2016). How does creativity at work influence employee's positive affect at work? *European Journal of Work and Organizational Psychology*, **25**(4), 525–539.

Taylor, C. L. (2017). Creativity and mood disorder: A systematic review and meta-analysis. *Perspectives on Psychological Science*, **12**, 1040–1076.

Taylor, C. L., & Kaufman, J. C. (2021). Values across creative domains. *Journal of Creative Behavior*, **55**(2), 501–516.

Tedeschi, R. G., & Calhoun, L. G. (2004). Posttraumatic growth: Conceptual foundations and empirical evidence. *Psychological Inquiry*, **15**, 1–18.

Tedeschi, R. G., Shakespeare-Finch, J., Taku, K., & Calhoun, L. G. (2018). *Post-traumatic growth: Theory, research, and applications*. London: Routledge.

Thakral, P. P., Devitt, A. L., Brashier, N. M., & Schacter, D. L. (2021). Linking creativity and false memory: Common consequences of a flexible memory system. *Cognition*, **217**, 104905.

Theorell, T., Kowalski, J., & Horwitz, E. B. (2019). Music listening as distraction from everyday worries. *Nordic Journal of Arts, Culture and Health*, **1**(1), 35–46.

Thomson, P., & Jaque, S. V. (2016). Visiting the muses: Creativity, coping, and PTSD in talented dancers and athletes. *American Journal of Play*, **8**(3), 363–378.

Thomson, P., & Jaque, S. V. (2019). *Creativity, trauma, and resilience*. Lanham, MD: Lexington Books.

Tinio, P. L. (2013). From artistic creation to aesthetic reception: The mirror model of art. *Psychology of Aesthetics, Creativity, and the Arts*, **7**, 265–275.

Toivainen, T., Olteteanu, A. M., Repeykova, V., Likhanov, M., & Kovas, Y. (2019). Visual and linguistic stimuli in the remote associates test: A cross-cultural investigation. *Frontiers in Psychology*, **10**, 926.

Tolleson, A., & Zeligman, M. (2019). Creativity and posttraumatic growth in those impacted by a chronic illness/disability. *Journal of Creativity in Mental Health*, **14**, 499–509.

Tongchaiprasit, P., & Ariyabuddhiphongs, V. (2016). Creativity and turnover intention among hotel chefs: The mediating effects of job satisfaction and job stress. *International Journal of Hospitality Management*, **55**, 33–40.

Torrance, E. P. (1974). *Torrance tests of creative thinking: Directions manual and scoring guide, verbal test booklet B*. Lexington, MA: Personnel Press.

Torrance, E. P. (2008). *The Torrance tests of creative thinking norms: Technical manual figural (streamlined) forms A and B*. Bensenville, IL: Scholastic Testing Service.

Totterdell, P., & Poerio, G. (2021). An investigation of the impact of encounters with artistic imagination on well-being. *Emotion*, **21**(6), 1340–1355.

Travagin, G., Margola, D., & Revenson, T. A. (2015). How effective are expressive writing interventions for adolescents? A meta-analytic review. *Clinical Psychology Review*, **36**, 42–55.

Turturro, N., & Drake, J. E. (2022). Does coloring reduce anxiety? Comparing the psychological and psychophysiological benefits of coloring versus drawing. *Empirical Studies of the Arts*, **40**(1), 3–20.

Tyagi, V., Hanoch, Y., Hall, S. D., Runco, M., & Denham, S. L. (2017). The risky side of creativity: Domain specific risk taking in creative individuals. *Frontiers in Psychology*, **8**, 145.

Urban, T. (2015, December 11). The tail end. *Wait but why?* Retrieved from http://waitbutwhy.com/2015/12/the-tail-end.html.

Usher, J. A., & Neisser, U. (1993). Childhood amnesia and the beginnings of memory for four early life events. *Journal of Experimental Psychology: General*, **122**, 155–165.

Vallerand, R. J., Blanchard, C., Mageau, G. A. et al. (2003). Les passions de l'âme: On obsessive and harmonious passion. *Journal of Personality and Social Psychology*, **85**(4), 756–767.

Van Broekhoven, K., Cropley, D., & Seegers, P. (2020). Differences in creativity across Art and STEM students: We are more alike than unalike. *Thinking Skills and Creativity*, **38**, 100707.

Van Paasschen, J., Bacci, F., & Melcher, D. P. (2015). The influence of art expertise and training on emotion and preference ratings for representational and abstract artworks. *PLoS One*, **10**(8), e0134241.

Van Tilburg, W. A. P., & Igou, E. R. (2014). From Van Gogh to Lady Gaga: Artist eccentricity increases perceived artistic skill and art appreciation. *European Journal of Social Psychology*, **44**, 93–103.

Van Tilburg, W. A. P., Sedikides, C., & Wildschut, T. (2015). The mnemonic muse: Nostalgia fosters creativity through openness to experience. *Journal of Experimental Social Psychology*, **59**, 1–7.

Van Westrhenen, N., & Fritz, E. (2014). Creative arts therapy as treatment for child trauma: An overview. *The Arts in Psychotherapy*, **41**, 527–534.

Vartanian, O. (2009). Variable attention facilitates creative problem solving. *Psychology of Aesthetics, Creativity, and the Arts*, **3**, 57–59.

Vartanian, O., Vartanian, A., Beaty, R. E. et al. (2017). Revered today, loved tomorrow: Expert creativity ratings predict popularity of architects' works 50 years later. *Psychology of Aesthetics, Creativity, and the Arts*, **11**, 386–391.

Verghese, J., Lipton, R. B., Katz, M. J. et al. (2003). Leisure activities and the risk of dementia in the elderly. *New England Journal of Medicine*, **348**(25), 2508–2516.

Vernon, D., Hocking, I., & Tyler, T. C. (2016). An evidence-based review of creative problem solving tools: A practitioner's resource. *Human Resource Development Review*, **15**, 230–259.

Vock, M., Preckel, F., & Holling, H. (2011). Mental abilities and school achievement: A test of a mediation hypothesis. *Intelligence*, **39**, 357–369.

Vonnegut, K. (1991). *Slaughterhouse Five*. New York: Dell. (Original work published 1969.)

Wade-Benzoni, K. A. (2019). Legacy motivations and the psychology of intergenerational decisions. *Current Opinion in Psychology*, **26**, 19–22.

Wade-Benzoni, K. A., Tost, L. P., Hernandez, M., & Larrick, R. P. (2012). It's only a matter of time: Death, legacies, and intergenerational decisions. *Psychological Science*, **23**(7), 704–709.

Wallace, C. E., & Russ, S. W. (2015). Pretend play, divergent thinking, and math achievement in girls: A longitudinal study. *Psychology of Aesthetics, Creativity, and the Arts*, **9**, 296–305.

Wallach, M. A., & Kogan, N. (1965). *Modes of thinking in young children: A study of the creativity-intelligence distinction*. New York: Holt, Rinehart & Winston.

Wallas, G. (1926). *The art of thought*. New York: Harcourt, Brace, & World.

Walpole, M. B., Burton, N. W., Kanyi, K., & Jackenthal, A. (2002). *Selecting successful graduate students: In-depth interviews with GRE users* (Graduate Record Examination [GRE] Board Research Rep. No. 99-11R; Educational Testing Service [ETS] Research Rep. 02-08). Princeton, NJ: Educational Testing Service.

Wang, Q., Peterson, C., Khuu, A. et al. (2019). Looking at the past through a telescope: Adults postdated their earliest childhood memories. *Memory*, **27**, 19–27.

Wang, R., Qiu, C., Dintica, C. S. et al. (2021). Shared risk and protective factors between Alzheimer's disease and ischemic stroke: A population-based longitudinal study. *Alzheimer's & Dementia*, **17**(2), 191–204.

Ward, M. C., Milligan, C., Rose, E., Elliott, M., & Wainwright, B. R. (2020). The benefits of community-based participatory arts activities for people living with dementia: A thematic scoping review. *Arts & Health*, **13**(4), 1–27.

Ward, T. B. (1994). Structured imagination: The role of category structure in exemplar generation. *Cognitive Psychology*, **27**, 1–40.

Ward, T. B. (1995). What's old about new ideas? In S. M. Smith, T. B. Ward, & R. A. Finke (eds.), *The creative cognition approach* (pp. 157–178). Cambridge, MA: MIT Press.

Ward, T. B. (2008). The role of domain knowledge in creative generation. *Learning and Individual Differences*, **18**, 363–366.

Ward, T. B., Dodds, R. A., Saunders, K. N., & Sifonis, C. M. (2000). Attribute centrality and imaginative thought. *Memory & Cognition*, **28**, 1387–1397.

Ward, T. B., & Kolomyts, Y. (2010). Cognition and creativity. In J. C. Kaufman & R. J. Sternberg (eds.), *Cambridge handbook of creativity* (pp. 93–112). New York: Cambridge University Press.

Ward, T. B., Patterson, M. J., Sifonis, C. M., Dodds, R. A., & Saunders, K. N. (2002). The role of graded category structure in imaginative thought. *Memory & Cognition*, **30**, 199–216.

Ward, T. B., & Sifonis, C. M. (1997). Task demands and generative thinking: What changes and what remains the same? *Journal of Creative Behavior*, **31**, 245–259.

Waterman, A. S. (2013). The humanistic psychology–positive psychology divide: Contrasts in philosophical foundations. *American Psychologist*, **68**, 124–133.

Waters, T. E., & Fivush, R. (2015). Relations between narrative coherence, identity, and psychological well-being in emerging adulthood. *Journal of Personality*, **83**, 441–451.

Watkins, C. E. (2011). Does psychotherapy supervision contribute to patient outcomes? Considering thirty years of research. *Clinical Supervisor*, **30**(2), 235–256.

Watts, L. L., Steele, L. M., & Song, H. (2017). Re-examining the relationship between need for cognition and creativity: Predicting creative problem solving across multiple domains. *Creativity Research Journal*, **29**(1), 21–28.

Weber, H., Loureiro de Assunção, V., Martin, C., Westmeyer, H., & Geisler, F. C. (2014). Reappraisal inventiveness: The ability to create different reappraisals of critical situations. *Cognition & Emotion*, **28**, 345–360.

Webster's dictionary of American authors. (1996). New York: Smithmark Publishers.

Webster's dictionary of American women. (1996). New York: Smithmark Publishers.

Weisberg, R. W. (2021). *Rethinking creativity*. New York: Cambridge University Press.

Wen, F., Zuo, B., Xie, Z., & Gao, J. (2019). Boosting creativity, but only for low creative connectivity: The moderating effect of priming stereotypically inconsistent information on creativity. *Frontiers in Psychology*, **10**, 273.

West, M. A. (2002). Sparkling fountains or stagnant ponds: An integrative model of creativity and innovation implementation in work groups. *Applied Psychology*, **51**, 355–387.

West, M. A., Hirst, G., Richter, A., & Shipton, H. (2004). Twelve steps to heaven: Successfully managing change through developing innovative teams. *European Journal of Work and Organizational Psychology*, **13**, 269–299.

Westby, E. L., & Dawson, V. L. (1995). Creativity: Asset or burden in the classroom? *Creativity Research Journal*, **8**, 1–10.

Westie, F. R. (1972). Academic expectations for professional immortality: A study of legitimation. *Sociological Focus*, **5**(4), 1–25.

Westie, F. R., & Kick, E. L. (1980). Retired sociologists' expectations for professional immortality: Further demonstrations of the constructed nature of reality. *American Sociologist*, **13**(2), 93–99.

Wildschut, T., Sedikides, C., Routledge, C., Arndt, J., & Cordaro, F. (2010). Nostalgia as a repository of social connectedness: The role of attachment-related avoidance. *Journal of Personality and Social Psychology*, **98**(4), 573–586.

Williamson, C., & Wright, J. K. (2018). How creative does writing have to be in order to be therapeutic? A dialogue on the practice and research of writing to recover and survive. *Journal of Poetry Therapy*, **31**(2), 113–123.

Wilson, R. S., De Leon, C. F. M., Barnes, L. L. et al. (2002). Participation in cognitively stimulating activities and risk of incident Alzheimer disease. *Journal of the American Medical Association*, **287**(6), 742–748.

Winger, J. G., Adams, R. N., & Mosher, C. E. (2016). Relations of meaning in life and sense of coherence to distress in cancer patients: A meta-analysis. *Psycho-Oncology*, **25**, 2–10.

Wolfe, S. E., & Brooks, D. B. (2017). Mortality awareness and water decisions: A social psychological analysis of supply-management, demand-management and soft-path paradigms. *Water International*, **42**(1), 1–17.

Wu, C. L., Huang, S. Y., Chen, P. Z., & Chen, H. C. (2020). A systematic review of creativity-related studies applying the Remote Associates Test from 2000 to 2019. *Frontiers in Psychology*, **11**, 573432.

Wu, X., Guo, T., Tan, T., Shi, B., & Luo, J. (2017). Role of creativity in the effectiveness of cognitive reappraisal. *Frontiers in Psychology*, **8**, 1598.

Wu, X., Guo, T., Tan, T. et al. (2019). Superior emotional regulating effects of creative cognitive reappraisal. *Neuroimage*, **200**, 540–551.

Xu, H., & Brucks, M. L. (2011). Are neurotics really more creative? Neuroticism's interaction with mortality salience in determining creative interest. *Basic and Applied Social Psychology*, **33**(1), 88–99.

Yalom, I. (1980). *Existential psychotherapy*. New York: Basic Books.

Yan, W., Zhang, M., & Liu, Y. (2021). Regulatory effect of drawing on negative emotion: A functional near-infrared spectroscopy study. *The Arts in Psychotherapy*, **74**, 101780.

Yang, J. S., & Hung, H. V. (2015). Emotions as constraining and facilitating factors for creativity: Companionate love and anger. *Creativity and Innovation Management*, **24**(2), 217–230.

Yang, W., Green, A. E., Chen, Q. et al. (2022). Creative problem solving in knowledge-rich contexts. *Trends in Cognitive Sciences*, **26**, 849–859.

Ye, S., Ngan, R. L., & Hui, A. N. (2013). The state, not the trait, of nostalgia increases creativity. *Creativity Research Journal*, **25**, 317–323.

Yi, X., Plucker, J. A., & Guo, J. (2015). Modeling influences on divergent thinking and artistic creativity. *Thinking Skills and Creativity*, **16**, 62–68.

Young, R., Camic, P. M., & Tischler, V. (2016). The impact of community-based arts and health interventions on cognition in people with dementia: A systematic literature review. *Aging & Mental Health*, **20**(4), 337–351.

Young, R., Tischler, V., Hulbert, S., & Camic, P. M. (2015). The impact of viewing and making art on verbal fluency and memory in people with dementia in an art gallery setting. *Psychology of Aesthetics, Creativity, and the Arts*, **9**(4), 368–375.

Zanjani, F., Downer, B. G., Hosier, A. F., & Watkins, J. D. (2015). Memory banking: A life story intervention for aging preparation and mental health promotion. *Journal of Aging and Health*, **27**(2), 355–376.

Zeilig, H., Killick, J., & Fox, C. (2014). The participative arts for people living with a dementia: A critical review. *International Journal of Ageing and Later Life*, **9**(1), 7–34.

Zenasni, F., Besançon, M., & Lubart, T. (2008). Creativity and tolerance of ambiguity: An empirical study. *Journal of Creative Behavior*, **42**, 61–73.

Zhai, H. K., Li, Q., Hu, Y. X. et al. (2021). Emotional creativity improves posttraumatic growth and mental health during the COVID-19 pandemic. *Frontiers in Psychology*, **12**, 600798.

Zhang, Z., Meng, J., Li, Z. et al. (2022). The role of creative cognitive reappraisals in positively transforming negative emotions. *PsyCh Journal*. http://doi.org/10.1002/pchj.589.

Zielińska, A. (2020). Mapping adolescents' everyday creativity. *Creativity. Theories–Research–Applications*, **7**(1), 208–229.

Zielińska, A., Lebuda, I., & Karwowski, M. (2022). Simple yet wise? Students' creative engagement benefits from a daily intervention. *Translational Issues in Psychological Science*, **8**(1), 6–23.

Zimmermann, N., & Mangelsdorf, H. H. (2020). Emotional benefits of brief creative movement and art interventions. *Arts in Psychotherapy*, **70**, 101686.

Zuo, B., Wen, F., Wang, M., & Wang, Y. (2019). The mediating role of cognitive flexibility in the influence of counter-stereotypes on creativity. *Frontiers in Psychology*, **10**, 105.

INDEX

For EU product safety concerns, contact us at Calle de José Abascal, 56–1°, 28003 Madrid, Spain or eugpsr@cambridge.org.

www.ingramcontent.com/pod-product-compliance
Ingram Content Group UK Ltd.
Pitfield, Milton Keynes, MK11 3LW, UK
UKHW020352140625
459647UK00020B/2417

* 9 7 8 1 0 0 9 2 4 4 5 5 8 *